Best wishes
Eugene R. Hart
3/7/2024

Salt & Snow: Lansford W. Hastings, The Donner Party, and the Haste to Blame

"Persons attempting to find a motive in this narrative will be prosecuted; persons attempting to find a moral in it will be banished; persons attempting to find a plot in it will be shot."
Mark Twain

"I'm the first to admit that I'm an amateur on many of the subjects that I've written about, and so I'll be the first again to admit that I'm probably going to get some stuff wrong. This is no reason not to write the book you want to write. If you wait until you're absolutely sure you've got everything right, you will never publish a word. So, you do the best you can, acknowledge that, okay, I'm going to get some stuff wrong here, and I just hope it's not crucial to the argument, or crucial to the story, for that matter."
H. W. Brands

"History is not to be liked or disliked; it is a measure of progress."
E. Hart

All Rights Reserved
Including the right to reproduction
in whole or part in any form without special written permission.
Manufactured in the United States of America.
Copyright 2021

Library of Congress Cataloging-in-Publication Data
Eugene R. Hart
Salt & Snow: Lansford W. Hastings, The Donner Party, and the Haste to Blame
Pictorial Hardbound Binding. 80# Gloss Paper
Includes bibliographical references, index, and fold-out map
ISBN 978-0-578-95592-6
1. United States—History—Western Expansion—19th century

This first edition of *Salt & Snow* is limited to 500 privately published copies.

Front cover photograph courtesy of Ray Boren. Back cover photo by Eugene Hart.

Special thanks to Rocco Bowman whose cartographic expertise produced the outstanding map included in this book. Also thanks to Christopher Caskey whose editing skills and suggestions greatly contributed to the readability of this book for which I take full responsibility. And my son, Rylan, whereby my examples will offer guidance in his future endeavors.

Table of Contents

INTRODUCTION: *SALT AND SNOW* III

1. MANIFEST DESTINY: ABSTRACT FORCE TO REALITY 1

2. ENTERPRISE, ADVICE, EQUIPAGE 14

3. TRAILS AND EXPECTATIONS 21

4. DEATH AND A CHANGE OF PLANS 29

5. CUTOFFS AND CALAMITIES 33

6. THE MOST DIRECT ROUTE AND A SAVINGS OF 350 TO 400 MILES 37

7. CLYMAN'S 40 51

8. TIME LOST AND GAMBLES 56

9. MISUNDERSTOOD MAN OF MANIFEST DESTINY 75

10. EVERYONE FOR THEMSELVES 91

11. BATTLING WINTER WHILE WINNING A WAR 99

12. A COLD HELL OF TRUTH AND TALES 110

13. THE CALIFORNIA CONVENTION AND BEYOND 118

14. THE MAKING OF A SCAPEGOAT 126

15. AN UNSETTLED MAN AND THE HASTE TO BLAME 135

APPENDIX: DONNER PARTY ENCAMPMENTS 139

INDEX 141

Introduction: *Salt and Snow*

    A midafternoon August sun cast down parching rays as James Reed and two companions of the Donner Party slowly rode their hard-worn horses toward a reassuring caravan of humanity. Resting their animals among an expanse of grasses and spring water near the southern end of the Great Salt Lake, this was the vanguard of nearly 300 emigrants and seventy wagons who were attempting Lansford Hastings' new cutoff— a route claiming to shave hundreds of miles off the well-known California Trail. Made up of the substantial Harlan and Young companies, along with several smaller groups, they had been led down the Wasatch Mountains from Fort Bridger by Hastings' co-partner, James Hudspeth, by way of the demanding Weber River canyons into the Great Basin. Without consulting Hastings, he selfishly led a spaced-out jumble of wagons through a difficult exploratory route instead of taking the way they had previously examined last spring. And as it turned out, it was not the best way to go.[1]

    Only two days earlier, Reed's own party had found a trailside note left by Hastings for anyone behind stating that "if we would send a messenger after him he would return and pilot us through a route much shorter and better than the [Weber] canyon."[2] Unfortunately, the trailside missive only served to confuse the belated Donner Party since it was clear that Hastings had descended the Weber canyons. Unsure of how to proceed, and having more questions than answers, members of the Donner Party thought it prudent to seek out the man himself which resulted in James Reed, Charles Stanton, and William Pike heading out on horseback to find him.

    Having caught up with Hastings' wagon train two days later, Reed inquired to the whereabouts of their guide. Word spread quickly that three strangers had just arrived, and in a few minutes, a small group of men approached Reed while he was caring for his horse. Reaching out his hand, Lansford Hastings introduced himself and offered any assistance he might provide. A cordial exchange led to lengthy conversation and Hastings' first positive confirmation that the Donner Party was indeed following behind.

    During their discussion, there would be no practical reason for Hastings to personally return to the waiting Donner Party and lead them, although Reed certainly made an appeal to allow his company to catch up. If Hastings considered the plea at all, it was in vain. He could not

---

[1] Morgan, Dale L. *Overland in 1846: Diaries and Letters of the California-Oregon Trail. Vol. 1.* Lincoln, Neb.: University of Nebraska Press, 1993.

* James Hudspeth was looking for a better connection into the Great Basin via the Weber River canyons. Taking advantage of the large number of able-bodied men he was leading, they supplied the manpower to clear the road for future use if it turned out to be practicable—which it was not. Hudspeth was not one to play it safe, nor were the participants who decided to take the developing cutoff. Everyone knew there would be geographic challenges and unforeseen difficulties in the effort to bring the first wagons through.

[2] Johnson, Kristin. Unfortunate Emigrants Narratives of the Donner Party. First ed. Logan, Utah: Utah State UP, 1996. Page 186.

* Reed recalled this much later.

neglect the emigrants he had already committed to lead. Especially after a week of unnecessarily difficult travel caused by Hudspeth's debacle. An extended halt at this point would only result in additional loss of time that would be better spent moving ahead in anticipation of unforeseen complications.[3] He did, however, agree to ride with Reed to a mountain top where he could point out the original trace he and Hudspeth scouted through the Wasatch two months earlier with pack animals. His initial path would be shorter and less arduous for wagons than the Weber canyons, but not without its own challenges.

Because of limited remaining daylight, the men were unable to reach the crest of the mountain they hoped to summit, and they spent the night in a canyon below. Leaving early the next morning, the men rode to a spectacular vantage point that would later be known as Big Mountain. Looking east, a sweeping view of the rugged Wasatch peaks and forested canyons were in sharp contrast the opposite way by the almost surreal blue sheet of the Great Salt Lake stretching out for miles across the Great Basin. There, Hastings was able clarify critical details about the path Reed should follow. By taking his previously explored track through the Wasatch, there was no reason to believe that Reed's trailing group could not reach the Sierra by early fall which was Hastings' prescribed margin of safety as stated in his recently published *Emigrants' Guide to Oregon and California*. By midmorning the men said their farewells, Hastings returning to captain his emigrants, and Reed (his partners to catch up later) making his way up the designated route marking trees with his hatchet as he returned to his company.

It can be concluded then, that Hastings did, in fact, essentially fulfill his commitment to pilot anyone farther behind who had made the decision to take his new cutoff. He was very active among the emigrants he was leading and supported the straggling Donner Party with equal attentiveness. More importantly, his behavior was not by any means "recklessly ambitious" as historian Bernard DeVoto has suggested.[4] Hastings did not deceive Reed nor provide him with

---

[3] One of those complications was the issue of finding an adequate water source that would narrow an extensive gap across the Salt Desert. Another would be encountered while traveling along the base of the Ruby mountain range (the only section of the cutoff Hastings had never personally traveled) where a potential wagon pass could be accessed while circumnavigating it.

* After Hastings' encountered Fremont while in California in early 1846, he quickly set out to examine the potential wagon cutoff Fremont had just explored (neither Fremont or Hastings used wagons). When he arrived at a point named Secret Pass at the head of the Ruby Mountain Range, he knew that Fremont had divided his men there and ordered one group to find a route to the Humboldt River which they did (naming it Secret Pass). As Hastings contemplated the situation, it was obvious that pack animals were the only way to take advantage of the pass; wagons could not penetrate it without significant roadwork. But Hastings also knew that Fremont presented another possible option for wagons. With the remainder of his men, Fremont explored south along the eastern base of the Rubies. Somewhere along the way he traversed the mountains and headed toward California. In kind, Hastings would lead emigrants in the same way by flanking the range as Fremont had done while scouting for a useable wagon pass (which would be found near its southern terminus; today's Overland Pass). Unfortunately, the circumnavigation of the Rubies was necessary for wagon travel in order to reconnect with the California Trail. This resulted in lost time and added distance that would negate part of the cutoff's advantage. Because of a combination of various obstacles and extended rests, it would never be a practical route for wagon-based travel without improvements made through government intervention.

[4] DeVoto, Bernard. *The Year of Decision*. Boston, MA: Little, Brown and Company, 1943.

inaccurate information. It was Reed who chose to act upon the advice he received. Besides, when Reed learned how to forge ahead, he was able to successfully work his way back to the awaiting Donner Party having been gone four days. During his reconnaissance, he saw first-hand the obvious difficulties of breaking trail for wagons. Yet, speculation suggests that Reed was confident that it could be accomplished in perhaps a week. Any doubts he may have privately harbored were overshadowed by his unwavering determination and ability to influence others.

Late that evening, having reunited with his party, Reed sold his fellow emigrants on the rugged path he had just traced as the expedient choice over backtracking to Fort Bridger and taking the traditional California Trail. He voiced his notion by reporting that the new way was "fair but would take considerable labor in clearing and digging." Still, no one seemed to be overly concerned about the effort it would take to open a gap through the Wasatch, or they just simply failed to understand the difficulties they were taking on. Reed who "reported in favor" of the new route "induced the Company to proceed." After all, it was reasonable to conclude that if they turned around, it would be six days back to Fort Bridger, and from there, another fourteen days to reach Fort Hall on the regular California Trail. With that in mind, they could reckon to use fewer days pushing on from their present situation by taking advantage of the cutoff.[5] A vote was taken and a "unanimous" decision secured the new route's approval. At sunup the next day, August 11, 1846, 24 wagons supporting 87 emigrants, half of whom were children, set off down the defiles of the Wasatch toward an unforgiving stretch of formidable geography that was crowned by the vast Salt Desert. Confident, and with resolute boldness, they bound themselves to the crossroad of no return on a cutoff that would become associated with misery and loss, blurring real-time prudence with historical interpretation.[6]

---

[5] To provide some insight as to the mileage estimates of the regular California Trail and Hastings Cutoff, here are some general distances. From Fort Bridger to Fort Hall and then to the Humboldt River's headwaters, the distance was about 478 miles; that translates into some thirty-two days travel. A group leaving Fort Bridger by pack-train on the Hastings Cutoff via Secret Pass could expect to cover about 300 miles. Traveling at about twenty-five miles per day, it took twelve days to reach the Humboldt and the traditional California Trail. After the Donner Party descended the Wasatch from Fort Bridger on Hastings Cutoff, they followed the same general route as any other group, but could not utilize Secret Pass with wagons. Having to detour around the Ruby Mountains added at least 127 miles in order to rejoin the California Trail and the Humboldt; total: about 449 miles from Fort Bridger which would be about thirty days travel not including any rests or delays that would add more time. Pack trains via Secret Pass could expect about a 65-mile advantage from Warm Springs—wagons going around the Rubies—much less. In the end, Hastings Cutoff would be shorter in distance than the California Trail, but difficult geography, the addition of more rest time, and limited water and pasture resources would negate part of the original optimistic advantages.

[6] The Donner Party arrived at Fort Bridger 8 days after Hastings had left. They were far enough behind the main emigration as to be unable to catch up, but close enough to optimistically follow. At this point they were still within the window of crossing the Sierra before snow blocked the pass (it would be passible until about October 25). Unfortunately, the route down the Wasatch's Echo and Emigration Canyons would require many days to cut a wagon trail through 35 miles of rugged terrain. This was completed with a workforce of roughly 28 able-bodied males from a group of 87 members—a huge offset of the necessary manpower needed to complete such a task in a reasonable amount of time. When they reached the Great Basin on August 22, there was still well over 600 miles to go. Even then, it was still possible to make it to the Sierra as they still had about 47 days to meet the early October deadline at

****

The families and individuals who became the Donner Party started their collective quest in the simplest of terms: They were following Hastings because they sought a better life in California. But as their wagons ambled west, the choices they made culminated into a complex drama that led to their entrapment high in the Sierra Nevada mountains just a few miles from the final snow-sealed pass. Losing a gamble with alpine weather, they became isolated in an intense physical and emotional ordeal unique in American history. Today, as we interpret their affair, we have empathy for a perceived innocence, and an obsessive interest over the details regarding their experience concerning a brutal last resort—cannibalism. Yet the chain of events that led to their misfortune in 1846-47 are often overlooked apart from one man—trail guide, expansionist, promoter, attorney, and author Lansford Warren Hastings who is almost universally denounced as the cause of their tragedy.

But something is amiss in the Hastings-Donner Party story. Most surprisingly is that there have been only limited attempts to start a conversation about Hastings' role from his perspective. He has not fared well under the caustic pens of his critics, and his biased treatment has changed little over the culmination of years that is approaching two centuries. Surprisingly, there have been few successful calls for reassessment notwithstanding the prominent appeals of historians Dale Morgan, Thomas Andrews and more recently a growing number of others. Ignoring the positive contributions of his endeavors, writers have given wings to the negative character of Hastings while engaging in the full advantage of hindsight with little consideration regarding the fluid conditions, complexities, and major events taking place at the time. Because of this, an obstinate and hostile mindset toward Hastings has all but become an accepted, yet convoluted, truth. The historical veracity of his challengers requires additional scope that expands upon a one-sided portrayal of an elusive man in the context of *his* time. This book considers the evidence and interpretations that facilitates the redemption of Lansford Hastings' supposed adverse character, actions, and long overdue misconnection with the Donner Party disaster.

Hastings' contagious enthusiasm for western lands and getting there with immediacy is apparent in his promotional 1845 booklet *The Emigrants' Guide to Oregon and California*. He made no excuses about the failure of the Mexican Government to control Upper California and was certain that it would fall into the hands of the United States; thus, his desire to populate the region with Americans. And by pure coincidence that same year, explorer John Charles Fremont's Third Expedition had just tracked a new route south of the Great Salt Lake that was wildly purported to shave off hundreds of miles to California. After a chance encounter with Fremont at Sutter's Fort a short time later, Hastings acted by retracing Fremont's trail in reverse determined to open a new wagon road. This was followed by a written invitation that encouraged emigrants who were actively on the trail to take his recently traveled route. He insured confidence by stating that he would personally lead their wagons from Fort Bridger.

In the eyes of many, Hastings and his association with the Donner Party has nearly

---

an average of 15 miles per day. But a continuation of geographic obstacles and approach of changing weather still loomed. The cutoff's advantage would be further reduced by having to circumnavigate the Ruby Mountains.

patented a condemning evaluation of him to the present date. The risk the Donner Party took on Hastings' new wagon road was only an acceleration of their troubles that began even as they prepared for their journey west. Future hardships, although unrealized at first, were being shaped from their starting point in Illinois. The sheer idea that ordinary nineteenth century people who were about to traverse the country, essentially into the unknown, is something that can only be imagined today. Nevertheless, we connect with them, as they are very much like modern-day Americans who meet today's challenges with the same spirit. Emigrants heading toward the Pacific in 1846 were looking forward to the exciting economic possibilities of the future while confronting a host of difficulties along the way. They were American risk-takers who reached out for opportunities that the cautious were not as quick to grasp. And the temptation to realize a promising land grant in Mexican California drew many enterprising self-starters to prepare for their venture west.

Long before the Donner and Reed families set out for California, they informed themselves through a variety of available sources about the benefits of Oregon Country and especially Mexico's loosely governed and sparsely populated Alta, or Upper California. There was an enthusiastic United States congressional publication compiled from the famed travels of "pathfinder" John C. Fremont's western explorations that was devoured by a fascinated public. There were also lively newspaper accounts based on letters from an American merchant named Thomas Larkin who resided in California's Mexican capital Monterey. He was specifically appointed by President James Knox Polk as his Special Confidential Agent to keep him informed of events there.[7] And certainly the most enticing and enthusiastic issuance of all available information was set forth in the flurry of words within a practicable guidebook published by Lansford Hastings. Each of these declarations described California in the best terms while alluding to an American takeover and was paramount at the time in propelling American influence toward this remarkably robust country abounding in untapped potential. Any of these resources, including friends, or travelers who made their accounts public, would inescapably affect the Donner brothers and Reed families' preparations boosting their optimism well before they set out proper.

The core of the Donner-Reed wagon trains, originally departing from Springfield, Illinois consisted of nine wagons and at least thirty-one well-equipped members including hired hands.[8] The roster would eventually grow to include 87 individuals. Their overland journey encompassed spectacular open spaces and the everyday routine and physical endurance required for trail life, but no one could imagine the unforeseen hardships that lay ahead on a scale almost impossible to

---

[7] Hague, Langum and Harlan, David J. *Thomas O. Larkin: A Life of Patriotism and Profit in Old California.* Oklahoma: University of Oklahoma Press, 1990.

[8] Kristen Johnson, author of *Unfortunate Emigrants*, suggests the possibility that there may have been more than the oft-quoted thirty-one members who left Springfield.

* Donner-Reed will be used as they loosely traveled independently while joined with the Russell-Boggs Company. At the "parting of the ways," after George Donner was elected captain, they will be referred to as the Donner Party.

contemplate. Unlike Hastings, who successfully guided nearly 300 emigrants to California in 1846, the Donner Party would eventually languish more than a month behind the main emigration. Approaching the final rocky crest of the Sierra luminous with snow, they missed crossing the daunting pass into the safety of the Sacramento Valley by about two weeks. Regardless of circumstances, Lansford Hastings and emigrants like the Donner Party exemplify the psyche of America's historic westward expansion by solidifying the maxim that risk is the price of progress.

But as the party moved beyond the massive grasslands west of Missouri, an accumulation of poor decisions slowly took shape. Starting with the insidious impact of overloaded wagons, and the escalation of overworked animals and lost time, their struggles would soon become magnified as geographic obstacles further west became more pronounced. There is no debate that emigrants taking any trail to the Pacific Coast anticipated innumerable hardships and the potentially lethal consequences of moving one's entire family west. To believe there would be little or no risk would be naive and unrealistic. Still, the Donner Party's critical decisions that they freely made en route, gave no cause to curse Hastings for their troubles, and if they did, it was only in retrospect, if at all.

****

The mythos of Hastings and defamation of the man has been entrenched over decades. Many authors, historians, and movie producers alike have exuded a singular point of view wrongfully assailing and vilifying him as the Donner Party's chief antagonist. They have second guessed his motives and cynically scrutinized his guidebook's occasional hyperbolic rants while disregarding the valuable advice it contained. He has been adversely portrayed without full regard to the cultural, economic, and political whirlwinds of westward migration spurred on by America's belief in Manifest Destiny. Detractors overwhelmingly cherry-pick or parrot a one-sided point of view that reviles the man, belittles his significance, and ultimately packages him as the chief cause of the Donner Party's misfortune as if there were no other considerations.

This book offers a different interpretation of Hastings as someone who personifies something we have lost. He represents an unbridled initiative and American spirit that seems to be increasingly washed out today. Hastings lived in a time when personal safety was set aside in order to accomplish what others thought improbable. This is in complete opposition of our society today where one is not only sheltered physically and legally from potential danger in an endless multitude of ways, but also overly protects us from moving forward without fear of disappointment or failure. Therefore, the real antagonist in this story is not Lansford Hastings, but Manifest Destiny itself. He simply tried to harness the spirit that propelled his aspirations like countless others of the period. He brought to the forefront American ideals that reached across the country with a "we can do better" attitude and the idea that risk leads to reward. Hastings was no different than any of the emigrants he led on his new cutoff as all believed in Manifest Destiny on some level. He simply embraced a leadership role filling in the gap for those who stood face to face with the unknown, and he met the life and death challenges of the day with ambitions that would lead to greater compensation for those who followed.

The unfavorable perception of Hastings began with his contemporaries who had never traveled his new wagon route but wrote of the emigrants who did—allegedly in their own uncomplimentary words or in far-removed reminisces. Others have blamed him for deceiving emigrants into taking his toilsome and demanding cutoff, and his alleged broken "promise" to lead the Donner Party.[9] These assumptions have literally extended into modern times focusing on his supposed selfish goals, and dubious cold-eyed lack of compassion. This is in contrast of the fact that every emigrant he guided or instructed did so successfully. Those who subsequently took his cutoff during the California Gold Rush years of 1849-50 have left us varied accounts. They range from an almost complete disaster to a seemingly uneventful crossing depending on preparation and mode of travel. This judgment of Hastings and those who "fell under his spell" has been extended far beyond his generation.[10] In reality, the trail-blazing cutoff he personally bolstered was thought to be a legitimate mile-shaving route reconnecting with the traditional California Trail at the head of the Humboldt River (then called the Mary's River) in modern-day Nevada. His reasoning was not built upon fantasy by any stretch of the imagination.

Historical interpretations from the nineteenth century and beyond have critically focused on Hastings' seemingly self-centered intentions and have relentlessly echoed bias. His manufactured reputation, much of it precipitated upon circumstantial evidence, elusive hearsay, limited or questionable historical sources, and after-the-fact reminisces, have solidified the man into an archetype of ambition gone awry. He has been pushed to the forefront of treachery and villainously fortified by writers of fiction and nonfiction alike with great success. In the process of this crowning judgment, other opinions have been muted. Hastings must be chronicled in the context, mindset, and realities he and others faced during their period of history.

Examining the sources that have been employed to berate Hastings, there is little doubt that his role as an influential expansionist, encompassing the constructs of Manifest Destiny, illustrate that he was an optimistic and forward-thinking leader of America's western frontier who challenged the apathetic and timid with convincing fervor. He was a man who viewed opportunity with an eye for success even though it relentlessly eluded him. Was he overzealous? There is little doubt. Self-serving and ambitious? Put in perspective, no more than any other active expansionist of the time. His association with the Donner Party reveals a common connection in what many emigrants chose to pursue—ambitious triumph. His promotional guidebook of Oregon and especially California, includes how to prepare for the journey and is overwhelmingly commendable; his accomplishments must be rightfully recognized. Thus, this book will offer a more comprehensive and realistic view of an impassioned man living in the ubiquitous transformations of his day, adding an important and long-awaited facet to the historiography.
****

Hastings, as well as every participant who followed his cutoff, knowingly migrated

---

[9] Stewart, George R. *Ordeal by Hunger*. New Edition ed. Boston, MA: Houghton Mifflin, 1960. p 32.
  * The word "promise" is an invention of Stewart. Hastings made no promise regarding the Donner Party.

[10] Houghton, Eliza Poor Donner. *The Expedition of the Donner Party and Its Tragic Fate*. Chicago: A.C. McClurg, 1911.

through a variety of obstacles and were willing to face the dangers. If Hastings is guilty of anything, it is promoting what he thought to be a challenging but worthy wagon road south of the Great Salt Lake. Author Irene Paden points out in her book *Prairie Schooner Detours* that a choice to take an unknown trail was not uncommon, "as every captain of every emigrant train had to do so since the first adventurous wagon wandered from the accepted trail to leave wheel tracks on an alternate route."[11] Hastings Cutoff was no exception.

During the geographical uncertainty of the day, new routes worthy of examination were frequently branching out from the established Emigrants' Trail. Hastings himself had theorized that a road below the Great Salt Lake was an enigmatic possibility before it was explored. He was simply engaging the time-honored search for a viable mile-reducing cutoff that appeared to have logical merit. He tantalized readers in his newly published guidebook with an enticing yet vague forty-word description of a *potential* distance-shaving route that would redefine the trail to California.

Although his hunch was certainly not a realistic option in 1845, the southern alternative would emerge as a reality the following year. Events moved quickly in the mid-1840s, and almost as if to justify Hastings' brief mention in his guide of this supposed "most direct" route, the first preliminary exploration was underway by one of the greatest government explorers of the era— John Charles Fremont. So, as Hastings was returning to California via the regular route by Fort Hall, Fremont's third mapping expedition was simultaneously navigating a new southern departure below the Great Salt Lake that would connect with the California Trail.[12] This plausible mile-clipping option held promise to challenge the northerly arcing Emigrants' Trail that went far above the Salt Lake where the traditional route to California branched off from Fort Hall. In the coming months, Hastings would take it upon himself to be the first to open this new barren stretch across the Great Basin for wagon travel.

Lansford Hastings is discernibly woven into the Donner Party's spectrum of events as he sought to accelerate emigration to the Pacific Coast and encourage a growing population of Americans who would bring California into the political forefront of conquest almost by default. Cutting-edge trail information acquired from John C. Fremont and his men while at Sutter's Fort fueled Hastings' ambition to make this happen. Armed with illuminating intelligence, Hastings with a small group of fellow travelers headed east over the Sierra in the early spring of 1846 with a pack-train just as the westbound Donner-Reed wagon trains rolled out from Illinois. By June, Hastings had succeeded in working out the new wagon trail. Negotiating most of Fremont's desert route in reverse, he extended it up the Wasatch Range to Fort Bridger—the planned rendezvous point where he would personally lead emigrants.

Hastings' initial accomplishment was in real-time to actively moving emigrants. The news came fresh from the lips of the promoter himself or through a hand-written open letter he sent

---

[11] Paden, Irene Dakin. *Prairie Schooner Detours*. New York, NY: MacMillian, 1949.

[12] Although quasi military in nature, they were officially known as the Corps of Topographical Engineers whose purpose was to map the west. Fremont's several scientific expeditions were in large part to map the west and search out possible routes for a future transcontinental railroad.

forth with a lone eastbound horseman, Wales Bonney. Its content hinted of probable opposition to American immigration in California, since war had recently broken out with Mexico, and suggested they concentrate their numbers. Mexico had previously closed Texas to American immigration in 1830 so there was a precedent. It also announced that a new cutoff had been explored and was to be piloted by Hastings himself in which the distance to California would be "materially shortened" according to Edwin Bryant.[13] As hundreds of emigrants congregated at Fort Bridger, he would keep his word to lead emigrant wagons down his cutoff into the Salt Lake basin. Arriving at the fort more than a week later, the Donner Party only had a spectral presence with Hastings until sought out by Reed and two others on horseback. This is what the late historian J. S. Holliday described as a "hinge moment" which in this case means to either reject or take Hastings Cutoff. And when they chose to take it, many unfavorable versions of Lansford Hastings took on lives of their own.

Many place Hastings' new trail and his promotion of it as the crux of the Donner Party's cumulative setbacks. Because of their suffering, there has been perhaps a desire to justify or excuse their poor decisions while conveniently placing blame on the shoulders of Hastings. Few have considered the actual efforts and the conditions that he as well as the Donner Party themselves faced. In short, we begin to understand that those involved were fallible human beings, and who, like anyone willing to hazard such commitment, often find there are unintended outcomes. Americans genuinely thought of themselves as exceptional in the nineteenth century, and their expectations reflected that exceptionalism no matter what lay ahead.

For many, the Donner Party's undeniable resolve leads us to be mindful of our own perceptive nature. It brings us to question almost everything they did as if we could take charge of their reasoning and actions. By failing to consider the complexity of the larger picture, it becomes easy to simplify, mislabel, blame, or judge in an amended scheme of revisionist tinkering. History discerns that someone had to be responsible for their mishap, and Hastings has been the convenient scapegoat to fill that void. But the undeniable truth is that cards laid are played, and all should marvel at the Donner Party's self-reliance and optimism to persevere through demanding extremities. It should also embrace a refreshing reassessment of Lansford Hastings and his contributions to help, not harm them. It was the members of the Donner Party who determined to beat the odds within an unforgiving state of affairs that eventually closed in on them. Yet there would be no immediate consensus nor hardly a murmur among those snowbound individuals in denouncing Hastings as a major or singular cause of their disaster.

The sobering outcome of the Donner Party's demise was the result of a unique alchemy of options and developments that had taken shape over months which positioned them onto a course of tragic consequences. Their story incorporates the risk-taking American spirit; yet, it is also matched with reckless decision-making. Familiar dramatics aside, their adventure still fascinates us because of the various episodes of eating human flesh during their struggle within the snowy grip of the Sierra. We still seek clarity in the details of what culminated into the subtle calculus of

---

[13] Bryant, Edwin. *What I Saw in California*. Palo Alto, California: L. Osborne, 1967.

their irreversible course. In the end, it all conspired to humble them in the form of two stopgap layovers: One group at an isolated meadow by Alder Creek; the other, six miles farther up near the eastern edge of Truckee (now Donner) Lake.

The Donner Party narratives are neither on par with a life-altering discovery, nor as consequential as the larger picture of continental conquest. But their *minor* incident surpasses all trans-Sierra crossings in time and place because we are curious as to what we would have done during their experience that added up to the impossibility of recourse. Unknown at the time, their calamity would be the by-product of incautious deliberations made over months on the trail that slowly closed in on them. Their grim endpoint was the culmination of problematic geography over a long trek, lost time, and the oft unpredictable dynamic forces of Mother Nature.

Pulled by events of fast-moving change, we find that members of the Donner Party were not fools nor did Hastings mislead them. They simply followed through with an almost blind, optimistic hope, not grasping the insidious cost of time and the increasing, ever-demanding challenges of western geography. Strung together in an irrevocable web of impending catastrophe, they embraced their situation as the gravity of their on-the-fly decisions eventually brought down the fell hand of crushing adversity and the impossibility to alter their chess-like undertaking. Moreover, they did not place responsibility or blame on Hastings for their tragedy. That in itself is a somewhat novel concept to grasp in our present age of entitlements.

Lansford Hastings by contrast is more difficult to pinpoint in the historical record. As a result, he has been an easy target; branded almost exclusively as the shadowy figure of a man who brought doom to others long after his promotion of Oregon, California, and his cutoff had faded away. There is simply not an abundance of available information about him. But we can place ourselves into the nineteenth century mindset within the context of Manifest Destiny to help us better understand Hastings' initiative to lead others to the Pacific Coast. By definition the words Manifest Destiny (obvious future) conveys the idea that Americans, as a matter of course, were to audaciously spread their culture and values from the Atlantic to Pacific. By questioning what we have been led to believe, there is a man who is not only daring but much more compassionate and public-spirited than what has been advocated.

Narratives about Hastings, well into the first half of the twentieth century, are not kind to him, and their connotations essentially label him as unprincipled with grandiose plans for his political ambitions in California. They are not of a man who published a helpful guidebook for emigrants explaining how to prepare, when to travel, and what to expect. They are not of a man who took a newly explored route to the next level of development facing numerous obstacles head-on. But rather, he is presented as a calculating oily-tongued charlatan who led lemmings over the cliff through misrepresentation. Few consider Hastings as a decisive leader pushing the limits of change who successfully navigated scores of emigrants over his cutoff—and no one died as a direct cause of it—ever.

The ultimate calamity of the Donner Party belongs to themselves. Hastings would have insured their successful arrival into California's Sacramento Valley had they applied the sage advice laid out in his guide which was possessed by the Donner-Reed party from the very start.

Had they done so, they may have been remembered only as marginal participants in the halls of western migration after arriving at Fort Bridger and staying on the regular trail due to their lateness. Circumstantial evidence, while short of irrefutable proof, can support conclusions that entertain the firm as well as less concrete aspects of both Lansford Hastings' promotion of his new cutoff and the Donner Party's unfolding plight. Their story renders a timeless lesson of human experience—not an insignificant footnote of western lore hanging on the desires of one man.

Lansford Hastings set out to lead what he thought would promote American progress (himself included) and speed up events in California that were already taking shape. Hastings was not arrogant; he was a seasoned guide whose fervor challenged the bittersweet reality his cutoff demanded. At the very least he opened a door for determined emigrants who wanted to expediently reach California to reap its benefits. His intensity to move forward would give rise as to how others viewed him, but in reality, he was unapologetically promoting his country and helping to benefit those who would follow in the light of Manifest Destiny.

There will always be those who seek victimization or fault in others. Arguably, we need to be reminded that it is our own intuition that allows us to form what we believe will be our own destinies. This strikes a mindful contrast with the Donner Party and Lansford Hastings. To some extent, there is little difference as we strive to consider the duality of their separate journeys and unwavering adaptability. This in turn offers us an opportunity to examine not only Lansford Hastings and the Donner Party, but ourselves. It provokes comparative insight that makes each of these nineteenth century participants comprehensible within a valuable window of reality that perhaps we all share.

1. Manifest Destiny: Abstract Force to Reality

Americans were very active throughout the tumble of decades during the 1800s. It was an exhaustive period of amazing changes and events that would include treaties with former enemies and a war with a weak neighbor that established new borders bringing the American expansionist sphere of influence to the western shores for good—not to mention shortly thereafter the incredible news of California gold in such shocking quantities that it seemed ludicrous to entertain the possibility. Our maturing nation at this time consisted of just thirty states. It was a world powered by beasts of burden, wind-borne sails, water-driven wheels, and the emergence of steam power. Daylight often determined hours of operation for most businesses, and homes were lit with animal-fat candles or whale-oil lamps. Cooking was done on wood burning iron stoves. Children learned the alphabet and arithmetic using soft graphite pencils on thin, wood-rimmed, laptop-sized writing slates. Communications were overwhelmingly conducted by post, and it was the receiver of the letter, not the sender, who paid postage. It was a time when medical knowledge was primitive at best but on the edge of great change with the unfolding awareness that disease was caused by invisible microorganisms. A typical American surviving the first ten years of childhood could expect to live at least forty or more years.

During this first era of the Industrial Revolution, the United States was accelerating and transforming itself into a mechanized market economy North America had never seen before. In sharp contrast to the agricultural South, its northern counterpart with its thriving factories established the groundwork of manufacturing and transportation strength with engines of steam belching smoke from wood and coal fuels. Miles of railroad tracks and canals connected commerce, people, ideas, and opportunities. Spans of copper telegraph wires, forged by American workers, crisscrossed state boundaries with instant information by the hour. Before long, there would be the emergence of cast-iron frames providing the structural skeletons for multiple-storied buildings thus altering the chaotic sprawl of our cities toward the sky.[14] All were technological advances of greater things to come. And there was always the ever-present issue of territorial expansion pressing upon the controversies of states' rights and slavery that would ultimately lead to a brutal civil war. Boundless excitement stirred the air; progress and politics were intertwined in the encompassing term Manifest Destiny—pregnant in the minds of many Americans who unceasingly looked west.

California, on the other hand, was a world away. It was inhabited by thousands of Native Americans long before they were *reformed* by the sparse colonizing efforts of the Spanish and the establishment of their first mission and presidio in 1769. The mission system,

---

[14] Gayle, Carol and Margot. *Cast-Iron Architecture in America: The Significance of James Bogardus*. New York: W. W. Norton & Company, 1998.

largely spanning California's coast, failed miserably on the most part and was followed by Mexican rule from 1821-1846 after their independence from Spain. Thus, seventy-seven years of occupation had led to less than 7,600 non-Indians who inhabited the region.[15] By the 1840s native Indian populations had been decimated from 300,000 to perhaps 14,000 individuals due to the contagious diseases Europeans inadvertently brought with them during exploration, trade, or conquest.[16] The new, fragile Mexican Government in Mexico City dismantled the Spanish crown's tool of power in Upper California—the Catholic church—but ultimately created a unique, far-removed, land-rich, cash-poor, cattle-based society loosely controlled by a series of appointed frontier governors sent from Mexico City. By the end of the 1840s, Mexico, as well as European powers and Native Americans, would be brought to terms by the United States' determination to possess the West all the way to the Pacific Coast.

In the early decades of nineteenth century California, there were no steam engines, no saw mills; most houses were made of mud bricks that had dirt floors, and none were two-stories in the Mexican capital of Monterey until an American, Thomas Larkin, built one in 1835. There was not a solitary bridge, not a section of paved highway nor a mile of railroad, and no four-wheeled vehicles until Americans brought them over the Sierra in 1845. There was not one hospital, library, regular newspaper, or monument of any kind.[17] Education was limited to private institutions which were irregular at best, and only a few isolated trade schools such as carpentry and ship building were available. Things that were commonplace on the East Coast of the United States simply did not exist on the shores of its western counterpart. Given this set of circumstances, California was ripe for the taking in the minds of expansionist America, anxious to secure its borders from threat, open new trade routes, and consciously or not, spread the ideals of Manifest Destiny among the surge of countless changes taking place.

It is important to discern the origin of the term that motivated Americans to head west in the nineteenth century, and it is best exemplified in the phrase that would eventually become known as Manifest Destiny. In the context of its ill-defined beginning, the idea embraced an overall simplicity, yet there is much complexity within the folds of the concept. Difficult to characterize at first, it was always on the move defining Americans who embraced it. This included democratic government, religion, education, technological innovations, commerce, and the economic rewards risk and hard work can bring. Although open to interpretation, this was not an imaginary episode of history made up after the fact; it was a real movement that had been emerging essentially undefined for decades. Nonetheless, the ideals of Manifest Destiny were carried west and in due time became the phrase that would drive those ideals into an

---

[15] Holliday, J. S. *Rush for Riches*. Oakland: Oakland Museum of California & University of California, 1999.

[16] Derby, George Horatio, Gary Clayton Anderson, and Laura L. Anderson. *The Army Surveys of Gold Rush California: Reports of the Topographical Engineers, 1849-1851.*

[17] Lawrence, Deborah and Jon. "An Interview with J. S. Holliday." *The California Territorial Quarterly*. Spring 2007, 22-34.

offering to humanity and a force of action across North America. Recognized or not, it became a reality reaching beyond the Mississippi Valley all the way to the Pacific Coast for the first-time during Thomas Jefferson's presidency by way of the Lewis and Clark Expedition (1804-1806).

But long before that famous outfit of exploration set their sights west, Spanish and British oceanic mapping expeditions along the North American western coast were taking place. This was viewed with great interest by the United States and accelerated by the investigations of an American seafaring trader, Robert Gray, who happened upon what he named the Columbia River in 1792 while pioneering the region's fur trade. His reconnaissance was significant as that body of water would later be used by the American Government to lay claim to Oregon Country. That same year, British explorer Captain George Vancouver acquired Gray's charts of the lower Columbia from the Spanish while anchored at Nootka Sound on the island that would one day adopt his name. Realizing the importance of verifying Gray's information, in October 1792 he sent Lieutenant William Broughton in several smaller craft up the Columbia River. He examined the waterway for over a hundred miles up to the Columbia River Gorge thus justifying England's claim to the territory as well. Thirteen years later, Lewis and Clark's Corps of Discovery would carry a copy of Broughton's map as they canoed their way down the Columbia to its Pacific exit.[18]

Furthermore, it wasn't just foreign sea-faring expeditions that signaled concern to American interests, it was also the transcontinental explorations of Englishman Alexander Mackenzie and his successful 1792-93 overland trek across British Canada to the Pacific. This would not be lost on Thomas Jefferson's worldly radar when he became president in 1800. With the purchase of Louisiana Territory from France in 1803, and his second election to the presidency in 1804, he directed his aide Meriwether Lewis to embark on a comprehensive scientific and diplomatic journey. Choosing his long-time friend William Clark to be co-captain, the goal of the 45-man paramilitary expedition was to map the Missouri River to its source in order to confirm a portion of the Louisiana Territory's western border. It also included collecting specimens, recording observations, and informing native inhabitants that the United States now possessed the province. Jefferson further charged the expedition to go beyond the waters of the Missouri all the way to the Pacific Coast. The purpose, to find a practical water and land trade route thereby establishing an American display in a territory contested by foreign nations.[19]

The motivation for the Lewis and Clark Expedition was in large part a reaction to

---

[18] Jackson, Donald. *Letters of the Lewis and Clark Expedition: With Related Documents. 1783-1854.* Second ed. Vol. 1. 2 Vols. Urbana: University of Illinois Press, 1978.

[19] Spain, France, England, and Russia had all sent "scientific" expeditions on the Pacific side of North America with California in mind between 1792 and 1816. It wasn't until 1841 that American Charles Wilkes convinced the United States Government to make a similar expedition in order to further "survey" American interests in commerce and navigation. His explorations on the Pacific Coast included the Columbia River down to San Francisco Bay where Wilkes personally traveled inland up the Sacramento River to collect information about the land and native inhabitants. In 1845 Wilkes published *A Narrative of the United States Exploring Expedition.*

British activities in the Pacific Northwest. Two objectives were on Jefferson's mind that surpassed the western boundary of Louisiana. One was to let the British in particular, or any other nation for that matter, know there would be a United States presence in the far west. Secondly, there was the long-term desire to establish a Pacific economic connection that would eventually link trade with China. Jefferson had the forethought to anticipate the needs of our growing nation and the sagacity to take action that would help secure American interests along the Pacific Coast. Thus, upon the explorers' return, it was his intention to have Lewis publish the expedition's enticing observations in book form to stimulate American settlement in the West.

Jefferson recognized that a long history of distrust and rivalry between American and European interests contributed to the suspicious and competitive mind-set that continued to incubate over the next half century. Territory controlled by the United States meant capital for funding the government, and new western holdings would feed the insatiable demands of a growing American population who would inhabit it. Land meant security, new trade, and room to expand. Foreign intrigue also helped drive the United States into a frenzy that focused on one irreversible historic direction—west. The issues of securing our borders from the potential designs of Europeans, as well as the future prosperity of the country were on the table. Even though the ideals of Manifest Destiny were not yet conspicuously laid out, the actions and progress of America's push to the west physically and politically were essentially defining it on the fly.

Unlike presidents after him, Jefferson intended to include Native Americans as part of the extensive trade link he wished to establish. This far-reaching idea was simple: The United States would provide manufactured goods Native Americans desired in return for the valuable furs they could supply—everyone would be happy. The Enlightenment philosophy that the public good would benefit through common commercial, political and scientific interests would insure the success of American endeavors. Indians would be active partners in his plan—so long as they became farmers.

Jefferson thought that the overall problem Native Americans had was simply too much land. This allowed them to wander for resources which would inevitably lead to conflict with other tribes as well as its determined new possessor—the United States. Unification and inclusiveness through trade were the goals. The speeches of Lewis and Clark given formally in full military dress to major tribes signaled American intentions and that great changes were about to take place. How much the natives understood is debatable, but America's quasi militaristic political stance, and display of technology (an air rifle for example), along with items that were given away or traded, made the seriousness of the expedition's purpose unmistakable.

Jefferson understood the difficulties that foreign countries could impose upon the United States. While secretary of state under George Washington, he learned first-hand how easily the Spanish had cut off the port of New Orleans at the mouth of the Mississippi River. This crippled the commerce of Americans who sent their commodities to this all-important city.

He also saw how England interfered with American free trade on the open seas and agitated Indian tribes on the North American mainland, all of which inhibited American progress.

Grievances with England came to a climax under the presidency of James Madison who declared the United States at war in 1812. During this conflict, groups of Native Americans allied themselves with the British seeing it as an opportunity to save their homelands by banking on a European victory—which did not materialize. After the conflict's end, negative long-term relations with Indians ensued as American merchants and emigrants were in no mood to establish amicable relations with former foes. The emerging idea of the individual over the common good was becoming the norm, not the exception. The issues of Indian relocation, which was part of Jefferson's plan as well as succeeding presidents, began to differ in method. Jefferson wanted Indians to be transplanted west in small family groups and set up with farms with the idea to encourage peace among the tribes, thus opening an extensive trade network. But after the War of 1812, the prevailing standpoint was to contain or eliminate Indians and make new territories safe for American settlement— an attitude that would persist for the remaining decades of the century.

The inconspicuous vapor of Manifest Destiny was advanced by the international respect the United States gained due to the conflict of 1812 as the concept continued to evolve into a politically centered philosophy. By the 1830s it was propelling America's expansionist character of what would later be termed "rugged individualism." Highly appealing, it was popularized by 1812 war hero Andrew Jackson. It stressed that success of the individual was determined by the strong belief in self-reliance and hard work. The West was also becoming an influential political power that threatened East Coast political domination. Winning the election of 1832, President Andrew Jackson, a Westerner from Tennessee, made no apologies about expansion or love of country. He not only challenged the political status quo, he put an end to any kind of cooperative Native American relations envisioned by Jefferson. By the 1840s Americans were on a path of western migration and cultural influence that would soon become welded into the idealistic term Manifest Destiny.

Politics and American culture were driving Manifest Destiny into a definable term in the contest of westward expansion. Spain realized early on that United States settlers could not be stopped, as it was impossible to "put doors on open country." And then, after nearly 300 years of conquest and exploitation, they saw their massive overextended empire rapidly crumble before their eyes. In 1821 Mexican independence became part of the fallout that ended Spanish domination in North America. But as the wobbly republic struck out on its own, its rightful perception that the United States was a threat to its northwestern provinces was becoming clear.

The massive territory the new Republic of Mexico inherited after gaining independence created an increasingly distinct problem. To populate its thinly peopled upper provinces, the policy of awarding massive land grants to foreign immigrants continued while the evolution of the undefined notion of Manifest Destiny was being seeded by Americans who migrated into

Mexican holdings. The turbulent government welcomed settlers at first in hope of winning over their allegiance, but too much American influence led Mexico to forestall the ballooning expansion of Americans. This also included resisting pressure by the American Government to sell parts of their sparsely populated upper territory. Mexico's friendship with potential European enemies of the United States such as France, and especially England, stirred even more mistrust. Adding to the turmoil was Mexico's persistently unstable government, essentially spanning four decades, that would eventually assist in its loss of lands through war beginning with Texas and ending with the Mexican Cession. The 525,000 square miles given up included parts of today's Wyoming, Colorado, Texas, and New Mexico, most of Arizona, and all of Utah, Nevada, and California.

There was also a genuine interest that European adversaries neither introduce new footholds, nor expand existing settlements along North America's oceanic coasts on some future date. This threatening uncertainty gave cause for the United States to oppose any European desires to recolonize former holdings or establish new colonies anywhere in the Americas. This was addressed through the Monroe Doctrine in 1823, a policy that would grant the United States power to exert its own domination of the Western Hemisphere undisturbed by additional foreign interference. Thus, American warships patrolled the Pacific to insure United States protocol was recognized.

Washington statesmen continued to push negotiated treaties and policies that complimented American interests and the acquisition of new territories. They also condoned

emigrants who were jointly occupying Oregon Country with England and quietly overlooked Americans who challenged Mexican holdings from Texas to Upper California. There was also a series of United States presidents throughout the 1840s, in particular James Knox Polk, who vigorously promoted the western expansion of the country. His leadership would eventually result in a peaceful agreement that divided the Oregon Country with England in 1846. During that same year, when negotiations failed with Mexico, he declared war over a border dispute in Texas that resulted in the cession of land ceded to the United States at its conclusion in 1848.
****

Before the Mexican War of 1846-48, England was cautious not to become too strongly allied with Mexico and certainly did not want to antagonize the United States into war. If England did become overly entangled on the Mexican political front, English creditors feared the crushing debt owed by Mexico ($50 million) would result in a total loss. They did, however, keep politicians in Washington, D. C. guessing as to what their intentions really were. And they, like the United States, were very good at the game.

Mexico failed to create a hoped-for alliance with England as a buffer to keep the United States' western expansion in check and maintain control of its acquired lands. England was not about to fall into the trap of colonizing a territory with little to gain. Still, newspapers in the United States and England fueled the fire of pretense regarding England's perceived interest in Mexican territory west of Texas to the Pacific. The truth was that England had no need nor desire for any lands beyond Texas including the Bay of San Francisco which was known as Yerba Buena at the time. They had already established highly lucrative ports on the South American Pacific Coast linking trade routes to China and the world. There was little justification for commerce with Upper California for the limited cowhide and tallow trade Californios offered, (American traders would fill that gap). From a business point of view, there was no necessity for another port so far north. It just wasn't feasible where high tariffs were the norm for cash-strapped Mexican officials in Monterey. American and English fur trading outposts scattered throughout Oregon Country did not require major colonization to profit immensely. On the other hand, the Oregon Trail was not a practical American trade route to the Pacific Coast, but it was the migration path where settlers entered—especially American farmers—whose permanence would soon overwhelm the British at a rate of more than 5-to-1.[20]

England was also cognizant of the fact that during Spanish rule they had only established a crude string of twenty-one mission outposts in the fifty-two years they controlled Upper California; Mexico struggled to populate it as well during their twenty-five-year reign. Again, it was simply too far off and created too little interest to stimulate a major colonization effort. Therefore, England had no practical interest in promoting colonies they could not prosperously develop or manage. Conversely, the United States' strong presence invited expansion for

---

[20] Jones, Howard, and Donald A. Rakestraw. *Prologue to Manifest Destiny: Anglo-American Relations in the 1840s*. Wilmington, DE: SR Books, 1997.

Americans who saw opportunity in the west as Washington, D. C. leaders maneuvered politically to gain western lands through purchase, treaty, or annexation. There also remained the military option if all else failed.

Texas is a case-in-point example of the complexity that Manifest Destiny embodied. Mexico encouraged Americans to populate and stimulate trade in this southwestern province in the early half of the nineteenth century. Mexico also wanted a frontier buffer zone to stem the loss of territory claimed by Native Americans, specifically, the Comanches, who were in deadly competition for control of that land.[21] In order to achieve those objectives, generous frontier land grants were offered to American settlers to create an early warning system. The drawback was that this greatly increased the American population that soon outnumbered Mexicans 4-to-1 by the time Mexico attempted to ban them.

American culture and ideals were supported by Tejanos (Mexican Texans) who would soon challenge the quagmire of erratic rule from Mexico City's far-reaching but weak authority. The situation was complicated even more so when Santa Anna, the Mexican president-dictator, suspended his country's constitution in 1833 to gain order—It was a move viewed with contempt by Texans as an unforgivable affront to democracy. This would ultimately lead to revolt in 1836 against the Mexican regime, ending with the independent Lone Star Republic of Texas. Shortly thereafter, England once again dabbled in actions that were interpreted as meddling with American expansion. Post-rebellion, debt-ridden Texas struggled as an independent country desperately in need of trade and currency both of which England was ready to provide. Helping Texas become a strong republic would effectively inhibit United States expansion further west. And since Texas was an alternative source of cotton for English textile mills, it would create an economic wedge the American Government would strongly denounce. At the same time, Texas' potential annexation by the United States was complicated due to its acceptance of slavery.

Similarly, in 1836 the Californios of Alta California were also feeling neglected by Mexico City. They in turn issued a proclamation declaring the northern province a "free and sovereign state" until the Mexican Government restored the Federalist Constitution of 1824. This threat of secession forced Mexican-appointed governors to deal with the increasingly militant demands of Californios for autonomy in their internal affairs. Small-scale political confrontations and armed skirmishes occurred repeatedly between California provincial factions. This dissension did not go unnoticed by foreigners, especially Americans, who saw insubstantial military action, unpreparedness, and the tenuous grip of the distant Republic of Mexico hundreds of miles to the south.[22]

It is equally interesting to consider that the distillation of Manifest Destiny may well have influenced the American presidential election of 1844. Former Senator Henry Clay "the silver-

---

[21] Gwynne, S. C. *Empire of the Summer Moon.* New York: Scribner, 2010.

[22] "Mexican Diplomacy on the Eve of War with the United States." *The American Historical Review* XVIII (1913). https://doi.org/10.1086/ahr/18.2.275.

tongued orator from Kentucky," and his wishy-washy stance on Texas annexation, essentially cost him the presidency to former Governor of Tennessee James K. Polk. Even though President John Tyler had provided a path for Texas statehood just before the next president took office, Clay was against the "Texas question" as it was a slave state, and the country was in a growing mood to stem its expansion further west. Polk on the other hand, vehemently supported adding Texas to the Union and sweetened his expansionist position by reaching out to the anti-slavery Free Soil Party who aggressively backed Oregon Country's inclusion as a U. S. territory banning slavery. He never wavered—Clay did. Unfortunately for Clay, although he reversed position on Texas, it came much too late. A majority of Americans placed their votes on the Polk ticket; therefore, it can be argued that Americans fundamentally supported the idea of westward movement wrapped within the ideals of Manifest Destiny while setting aside controversial issues that would limit expansion. The atmosphere of the country was contentious at best with the specter of civil war looming, but Americans were still looking west.

During the 1840s, American expansion was at its height, and as a country, the United States was not holding back its ambitions. Beyond the Mississippi, overland explorers and trappers whetted the appetites of the curious. Americans who once feared the western horizon were now stimulated by adventurous trade opportunities. It seemed the farther west Americans went, the greater the resources that had never been capably utilized by the earliest controlling powers.

Alexis de Tocqueville, a well-to-do Frenchman, came to America in 1831 to study our prison system. However, he was such an astute observer of culture that he became more curious about the optimism of the average American during the flourishing of Manifest Destiny:

"In the United States a man builds a house in which to spend his old age, and he sells it before the roof is on; Men will then be seen continually to change their track for fear of missing the shortest cut to happiness."[23]

Tocqueville adeptly picked up on the essence of the energy: Keep moving or miss out. He must have found it equally interesting that an American who was on the lower end of the social ladder felt that he could become prominently successful himself within a generation. This was a highly notable observation; he thought of us as "exceptional." American society was forward-looking, growing, and its mixture of people on the verge of creating something even greater—a world power—one constantly in motion politically, economically, and militarily— very much in that order. Although not without problems and controversies, American restlessness would shake the Western World in a variety of ways. In short, potential economic opportunity agitated unparalleled excitement within a movement of people who would drive the unique future of our country unlike any other place in the world.

From a nationalistic point of view, the United States rallied around the idea that the country would expand from coast to coast and spread all things American. Believing they had

---

[23] Tocqueville, Alexis de. *Democracy in America.* New York: Knopf, 1994.

the most to offer, it was a viewpoint now coming together into a definable term. New York journalist John O'Sullivan finally labeled and clarified the elusive idea for the first time in his *United States Magazine and Democratic Review*. Manifest Destiny, as the phrase optimistically suggests, implies an obvious or undeniable fate. This led both shrewd and unoffending advocates alike to grasp its literal meaning in word and action.

In 1845, the same year that Texas was brought into American statehood, O'Sullivan wrote of "our manifest destiny to overspread the continent allotted by Providence [God] for the free development of our yearly multiplying millions." He did not conceive Manifest Destiny as a call for territorial expansion by force; he was against the War with Mexico for example. He viewed its ideals as peaceful and simply believed that the United States' form of democracy and the host of positive contributions it represented would inevitably be beneficial for all in the long run. He was not alone in this thinking as the phrase became the embodiment of a nation.

The nineteenth century was a time of fantastic change, fast-moving events, and opportunities for Americans. Trailing the purchase of Louisiana four decades earlier, the Annexation of Texas was followed by a major territorial agreement with Britain in 1846 leaving Americans with a large portion of the Oregon Country. This innocuous agreement set the United States and British North American border on the 49th parallel to the Pacific Ocean relieving tensions between the two nations. Even more spectacularly during that same year, the confrontational War with Mexico lasting just two years yielded to the United States a vast section of Mexican territory. Beset by a willing population to fill this void, it gave the United States uninterrupted commanding geographical and political control spanning across the entire North American continent. This resulted in two massive oceans protecting the East and West Coasts of American possessions, a weak and volatile Republic of Mexico to the south, and on the northern border, a stretched-out collection of colonies comprising British Canada. Manifest Destiny had been achieved physically for the time being, but the psychological pride it evoked was still on the move.

Contemporaries of the 1840s who supported Manifest Destiny may have felt justified and motivated by the constructs of the phrase, but opponents were quick to ridicule it. One such voice was congressional Representative Robert Winthrop, from Massachusetts, who stated "I suppose the right of a manifest destiny to spread will not be admitted to exist in any nation except the universal Yankee nation." The biting sarcasm of his appraisal did not stop with him, and it is important to point out that the northeastern industrial states could afford to criticize and take the high road as their section of the country had long rid themselves of Native American issues and foreign influence. This, of course, meant that their version of "Yankees" would continue as a powerful sphere of political and economic sway that was now being challenged.

This superiority would not be easily conceded. What better way to stake a claim against the advancing ascendency of "Westerners" than to suggest that they were intolerant, land-grabbing hypocrites. Perhaps they were, and perhaps there was a hypocritical bend from the Northeast as well to maintain the current and future power structure while conveniently fogging over their own checkered past. Despite abundant criticism, expansionists from all parts of the country would embrace the term.

Opportunities in the West were not going to slip by unnoticed; if one missed that chance, the push and rush would become someone else's gain. The desire to initiate a perceived advantage was open to any individual who grasped it first and got there before everyone else did. This was not lost on those who organized wagon trains and were prepared to risk new cutoffs on developing trails. This "destiny" carried across the continent a quiet boil that whispered of a better future and encompassed the wholesale movement of a people determined to make it happen.

In 1846 the fact remained that planning for a wagon journey across the North American interior over prairies, mountains, and deserts to the Pacific Slope was a huge undertaking. Established trails such as the Emigrants' or Oregon Trail, and the California Trail were still being improved upon by ceaseless explorations and new modifications. These trails crossed over territory that began on United States soil and continued through foreign land beyond the Rockies. All within the limited geographic knowledge that was still being understood, tied to the development of mile-shortening cutoffs, and led by those who would follow in the context of life-threatening risks. It was a critical period of fast-moving events during the turbulent expansion of the United States that influenced Americans like Lansford Hastings and typical emigrants such as the Donner and Reed families. Sparked by the emotional combustion of potential opportunity, book-ended by the Oregon Country treaty with England, and start of the Mexican War, there was no turning back.

Following the emigration of the previous year was another group of Americans who embraced the umbrella of Manifest Destiny. Known as the Great Mormon Migration, the Latter-day Saints created a uniquely American-borne form of Judeo-Christianity becoming the only utopian society in America that worked. Failing to find acceptance in a variety of states, chiefly because of their practice of polygamy, in 1847 they spearheaded the largest westward migration movement that the United States had ever experienced. It resulted in the establishment of a new territorial settlement centered in a lush valley near the southeastern shore of Utah's Great Salt Lake. Here they could freely practice their faith and independent theocratic governance in relative isolation.

With the conclusion of the Mexican War in 1848, the United States completed its transformation into a continental nation. Even more amazing, as the treaty was being finalized, California's hidden gold was awash in James Marshall's full-scale discovery of the metal. Unknown to anyone except for a handful of settlers in the Sacramento Valley, which didn't last long, a massive rush for gold began in 1849, and to everyone's incredulity, gave cause for Americans to feel as though the country had been, in fact, truly touched by the hand of God. In a short timeframe, and largely because of California's newfound wealth, the primitive Pacific settlement of Yerba Buena gave rise to San Francisco thrusting it headlong into a blossoming entrepot, or zone of free exchange.[24] It was the world's first truly cosmopolitan city. There was nothing like it.

By the tail end of the boisterous 1840s, sailing ships from around the world plied the Pacific carrying gold seekers and competing for increasing trade opportunities to and from California. Because of this rapid transformation, faster routes to the Golden State were being sought. Anyone who once traveled the overland journey by wagon in four to six months was amazed that a return trip to America's East Coast by steamship took just three weeks via Panama with relative ease. This was the quintessential era of the United States' unstoppable growing pains. And it did not stop there.

Equally amazing, within twenty years after the short-lived Pony Express and stagecoaches served their purposes, the Transcontinental Telegraph and Railroad advanced communication, commerce, and travel with lightning speed. These technological aspects of Manifest Destiny determined just how the nation would bind the Atlantic and Pacific Coasts together for good. Thus by 1869, travel time across the entire continent took merely a week and sealed San Francisco's importance as a world commerce center. Pulled by belching train engines, the physical and intellectual progress spanning the entire country was bound by the tracks of democratic ideals, speed of travel, economic advancement, and a cultural revolution of ideas. Manifest Destiny was now reality.

John R. McBride an emigrant heading west in 1846 reflected many years later the inspiration of Manifest Destiny:

> "…in looking back to that long journey and striving to find what could have been the motive which influenced people at that date to brave such perils, dangers, and hardships, I can find immigrants from across the continent none that seems adequate to account for it. The emigration and settlement of Oregon by American pioneers will ever remain to human reason the most mysterious, unreasonable and reckless movement that has occurred in our national history. Behind it must have been a blind instinct or impulse, not realized by those who were affected by it; or a providence which uses all men for its purposes and sends them to do its will, as it sends the stars in their circuits and causes the rivers to run to the sea."[25]

It is not surprising then, that the terms freedom, commerce, industry, democracy, education, technology, and the decree of the almighty were used repeatedly by newspapers and politicians of the day creating an emotional and physical appeal of the American spirit that evolved into a two-word phrase that encompassed so much.[26]

---

[24] Delgado, James. *Gold Rush Port: The Maritime Archaeology of San Francisco's Waterfront.* Berkeley: University of California Press, 2009.

[25] McBride, John R., reminiscent account, *Capital Journal* (Salem, Oregon, February 4 to March 23, 1926).

[26] Clark, Dan E. "Manifest Destiny and the Pacific." *Pacific Historical Review* 1, no. 1 (1932): 1-17. Accessed September 21, 2020. doi:10.2307/3633743.

Given the outlook of the American landscape at the time, entitlements of the day were comprised of a confident, bulletproof conviction in providence, country, and self. Rugged individualism prevailed.[27] It is a concept nearly unfathomable to comprehend today in an age where government bureaucracy has become so intrusive that something as simple as a carry-out drink includes a printed warning revealing the impending danger of a hot liquid within.

Manifest Destiny is perfectly illustrated in John Gast's 1872 painting entitled *American Progress*.

---

[27] A term first presented at a meeting of the World Congress of Historians held in Chicago in the summer of 1893 but certainly existed long before it was defined.

2. Enterprise, Advice, Equipage

It was James Reed who became intrigued with the possibilities the Mexican province of Upper California presented: The powerful attraction of untapped resources and large tracts of free land, literally square miles of it, just for the asking, was available for anyone willing to make the journey. In addition, the appeal of a healthful year-round climate would benefit his wife's frail constitution; a companion he dearly loved as their marriage ceremony took place while she was bed-ridden during one of her bouts with illness. By 1845, a year before setting out, he spearheaded his family's move from Springfield, Illinois. Like any potential emigrant considering such a major life-changing decision, Reed was no different as he gathered a variety of information for his enterprising plan.

Knowledge of how to outfit and what to anticipate were paramount for such an undertaking, and no one understood this better than Reed. A mercurial businessman, his ventures over the years included a general store, a starch factory, sawmill, and furniture manufacturing. He also speculated in railroad contracts, real estate, and served as the United States pension agent for Springfield.[28] His wide variety of pursuits lacked any notable accomplishments, but he was never shy about taking risks nor was he ever short of optimism or money. He did, however, see California as an opportunity to better his family's future, and he set out to make it happen using a variety of sources to prepare for such a journey.

Captivated by the same excitement, two prominent Springfield farming families, the Donner brothers George and Jacob, joined Reed with like-minded prospects. Pouring over the advantages of California, they decided to sell their farms and sought out advice from a range of available sources. Their research included newspaper accounts of those who had made the trip, the hugely popular government publication of explorer John C. Fremont's *Report*, and the slim newly published *Emigrants' Guide to Oregon and California* by Lansford W. Hastings—a first of its kind. His 152-page guide was in part hyperbolic advertisement and promotion, but it was also full of excellent recommendations based on Hastings' own western experiences. It was not intended as a day by day instructive mapping out the availability of campsites, water, wood, grass, or daily point-to-point distances covered in Fremont's publication, but rather practical advice on how to prepare, equip, and what to expect on such a journey—all for fifty cents.

Neither George nor his brother Jacob needed to make this move as they had achieved relative financial comfort—particularly George who allegedly stashed away $10,000 in gold coins for use in California which added thirty-nine pounds of dead weight in one of his wagons. George also planned to carry a significant collection of valuable goods to give his family an economic edge upon arrival. This included school materials at the behest of his wife Tamsen.

---

[28] Johnson, Kristin. *New Light on the Donner Party*. Accessed May 14, 2008. http://www.utahcrossroads.org/DonnerParty/Reed.htm

With their own special interests in mind, the Donners prepared for a worthwhile opportunity and exciting new beginning. All adventurous speculation aside, the lure of something better in the West rang out as prominently as a siren call, and they were going to have their share.

As part of Reed's information gathering, he wrote to a friend, James Maxey, who owned a dry goods store in Independence, Missouri one of the "jumping-off" places bordering the western frontier. The reference implied that such towns were the last visages of civilization until reaching a destination. Even though Maxey had never been to California himself, he was a good source for advice and familiar with the needs of westbound emigrants and traders. When he wrote back, he explained that by choosing the Oregon Trail taking too many trade goods will be hard on the cattle and "cannot stand to go to California[.] you had better get you a good family ox waggon[.]"[29] He told Reed to take his flour and meal in sacks—Using barrels would only add unwanted weight. He advised Reed to arrive in Independence early in April to prepare before setting out. He also informed him that there was a large party leaving about the fifteenth of May which may have influenced Reed to consider departing at that time, and he certainly shared that information with the Donners. Pooling Maxey's advice with a variety of other sources all contributed toward the success of their journey as they readied themselves to set out for California in the spring of 1846.

One of the many suggestions Hastings made in his guide was that "good and substantial wagons should always be selected" to minimize defects that will become apparent only after a few hundred miles of travel. To power the vehicles, they were to be pulled by slower but more powerful oxen over mules. Both Donner brothers and Reed all embraced this advice as they outfitted their rigs. Each of the families ordered three wagons constructed from durable local hardwoods built to take on the increasingly difficult obstacles that lay ahead. James Reed, however, took comfort to a new level by ordering a substantially larger wagon in his lineup. His "family wagon" later referred to as the "pioneer palace car" integrated an upper sleeping deck especially for his aged and infirm mother-in-law, Sarah Keyes, who he must have had in mind since she refused to stay behind. Other build qualities incorporated into this unique wagon were an extended bed over the wheels which added more floorspace, and the convenience of a stagecoach-like side door. There was also a small stove with a chimney extending through a tin plate sewn into the wagon's canvas top shielding it from sparks.

There has been much debate as to just how sizeable this wagon was compared to a standard version, but there is no question that this custom vehicle was larger all the way around. Common wagons of the day had a wheelbase of 58 to 60 inches that supported a wagon bed five feet wide. Reed's family wagon was 86 inches, and his daughter Virginia recalled that "A board about a foot wide extended over the wheels on either side the full length of the wagon, thus forming the foundation for a large and roomy second story in which were placed our beds." This means that the wagon was nine feet across. Wheels five feet in diameter and ten

---

[29] Morgan, Dale L. *Overland in 1846: Diaries and Letters of the California-Oregon Trail*. Lincoln, NE: University of Nebraska Press, 1993.

inches wide suggest it was unmistakably distinct when compared to a standard wagon.[30] It is also reasonable to conclude that it was somewhat longer, too, than a commonplace wagon that was ten to twelve feet in length. Noticeably bigger than a typical vehicle of the day, this well-appointed home on wheels had one other glaring distinction—it was significantly heavier requiring four yokes (eight animals) to pull it; a typical wagon in comparison was powered by two yokes. Since the Donner and Reed families all used oxen—the diesel engines of the nineteenth century so to speak—they were following the advice in Hastings' guide that stated oxen would be the best choice since they can "endure the fatigue and heat, much better…."

Virginia, James Reed's stepdaughter, described the family wagon many years later calling it the "pioneer palace car" and provided details as to how it was equipped. Stepping inside, one entered a small room in the center of the wagon where a "tiny sheet-iron stove was placed. On each end were comfortable spring seats with compartments under them which held a full assortment of medicines and other necessities." She points out that clothing was "not stored in Saratoga trunks" which are essentially fancy reinforced wooden boxes. Instead, weight saving "strong canvas bags plainly marked" were used. She goes on to recall that "a good library of standard works was carried, and a cooking stove which never had a fire in it." Looking back, she stated that "no family ever started across the plains with more provisions or a better outfit for the journey…."

In addition to the family wagon, two other well-equipped vehicles were outfitted for Reed's six family members and five hired hands who were employed to drive and care for the oxen, assist with trail duties, and engage in domestic chores. These individuals were Milt Elliott, Reed's former factory employee, Walter Herron, James Smith, and two servants, Baylis Williams and his sister Eliza.[31] He also purchased a few powerful Durham steers, and a small herd of milk and beef cattle for good measure. Virginia's saddle pony Billy, and her stepfather's prized horse Glaucus were included along with the family's five dogs: Tyler, Barney, Trailor, Tracker, and Cash.

Like Reed, the Donners required ox drivers to help tend to their livestock and wagons as well. George made an appeal to enlist hired hands in his optimistic advertisement that he ran twice in the Springfield, Illinois *Sangamo Journal* just two months before heading out for Independence, Missouri.

WESTWARD HO!

> "For Oregon and California. Who wants to go to California without costing them anything? As many as eight young men, of good character, who can drive an ox team, will be accommodated by gentlemen who will leave this vicinity about the middle of April. Come on Boys. You can have as much land as you want

---

[30] Hawkins, Bruce R., and David B. Madsen. *Excavation of the Donner-Reed Wagons: Historic Archaeology along the Hastings Cutoff.* Salt Lake City: University of Utah Press, 1990.

[31] Johnson, Kristin. *New Light on the Donner Party.* Accessed May 14, 2008. http://www.utahcrossroads.org/DonnerParty/Reed.htm

without costing you anything. The Government of California gives large tracts of land to persons who move there. The first suitable persons who apply will be engaged."

George Donner and Others.

The notices resulted in the hiring of six young men: two German immigrants, Joseph Reinhardt and Augustus Spitzer, three locals, Noah James, Sam Shoemaker, Hiram Miller, and an Englishman named John Denton.

Referring to Hastings' guide, it was full of practical instruction. He advocated starting with a good gun, lead, and powder. He goes on to assert that a quality wagon cover, tent, blankets, bedding, assortment of common tools, ropes, extra wagon axletrees, chains, and variety of medicines should be included—the list went on. He advised that emigrants bring goods to trade with Indians. These might include beads, tobacco, handkerchiefs, cheap types of clothing, knives, and fish hooks. He also admonished emigrants to use tin cups and plates and to carry only the most essential cooking utensils "as they very much increase the load which, is always a consideration of paramount importance."[32] Basic food staples included flour, bacon, cornmeal, beans, rice, dried fruits, salt, sugar, tea, and coffee.

According to one newspaper account, a fully loaded wagon should weigh no more than 2,000 pounds. Wagon space for items of practical use came first and foremost. As for food, Hastings' book suggested that each emigrant should be provided with at least, two hundred pounds of flour or meal, one hundred and fifty pounds of bacon, 20 pounds of sugar, 10 pounds of coffee, and 10 pounds of salt. This translates into about 390 pounds for each of the Donner's ten adults including hired hands which totals 3,900 pounds. However, a letter appearing in the *Springfield* (Illinois) *Journal* sent by Tamsen Donner written on the Platte River on June 16, 1846 states that "Bread has been the principal article of food in our camp. We laid in 150 pounds of flour and 75 pounds of meat for each individual, and I fear bread will be scarce." If her calculation is correct, and there is no reason why it wouldn't be, that is a difference of 1,250 pounds less in flour and bacon for the ten adults in her group than the 3,500 pounds Hastings recommended. Carrying less food meant more room for non-food goods to bring into California, and one wonders if that was a consideration before they left Illinois.

Hastings also furnished guidelines for the quantities of food required for children. Rations for the Donner families twelve children (excluding coffee) would range in the area of 190 pounds each. Assuming this is an appropriate measure, the four older children's sum would amount to 760 pounds. The remaining eight Donner children, nine years of age and younger, could perhaps have their allowance reduced by half: 95 pounds each, totaling 760 pounds. The aggregate for all children would be 1,520 pounds (and very likely less). Adding that to the

---

[32] This advice was at least, in part, ignored as revealed by the 2004 archaeological excavation of the Donner brothers' Alder Creek camp. The site yielded a number of ceramic fragments that could be dated to the 1840s. Salvagers at the time reported recovering "kitchen ware," and there is little doubt that anonymous souvenir hunters picked up a number of pieces over the years.

entire adult's figure of 2,650 pounds, a grand total of 4,170 pounds was to be distributed among their transports. Reed undoubtedly calculated his own figures based on his three wagons, family members, plus hires. The Donner brothers had six wagons, so foodstuffs alone for their twenty-two members, excluding extra items that might have been stored in barrels or trunks, would weigh in at about 800 pounds per wagon. This approached the halfway mark for a vehicle's practicable capacity based on a 120-day trip that consumed about forty-five pounds of edibles per day. Hastings guide stated that emigrants should not encumber themselves with food luxuries, nor depend on buffalo as a food source en route. He did, however, offer a way to increase their overall food stores by driving a small herd of cattle, which the Reed and Donner families did. Thus, the weight of cured meat carried in wagons could be lessened somewhat with a reliable source of living protein on the trail.

To contrast the sensible proposals related by Hastings, we have the record of George Donner's youngest daughter, Eliza, who was a three-year-old in 1846. She, like Virginia Reed, recalled many years later how her father's wagons were equipped just before they set out for California. In 1911 she published a book titled *The Expedition of the Donner Party*. It was in part a biography but also included some of her experiences before setting out for California. Eliza undoubtedly relied heavily on the memories of others since she was so young, and as one might suspect, the text is unreliable at times. Nevertheless, there is valuable information that can be corroborated.

Eliza recalled starting out from Illinois: "The preparations made for the journey by my parents were practical. Strong, commodious emigrant wagons were constructed especially for the purpose. The oxen to draw them were hardy, well trained, and rapid walkers. Three extra yokes were provided for emergencies. Cows were selected to furnish milk on the way. A few young beef cattle, five saddle-horses, and a good watch-dog completed the list of livestock." She continues by stating that "After calculating the requisite amount of provisions, father stored in his wagons a quantity that was deemed more than sufficient to last until we should reach California." This would be in direct opposition to what Tamsen later wrote while on the Platte River. In addition to food stores, there were a number of articles brought for trade or economic gain.[33] She lists goods for peace offerings to Indians such as inexpensive bolts of cloth, and glass beads and also "Seed and implements for use on the prospective farms in the new country [which] constituted an important part of our outfit." She completes her family's inventory by listing the "rich stores of laces, muslins, silks, satins, velvets and like cherished fabrics." Eliza states that a number of these items were deemed important by her mother Tamsen as she "was energetic in all these preparations, but her special province was to make and otherwise get in

---

[33] Archaeologically, the 1986 excavation of the Donner-Reed wagon sites on the Salt Desert in Utah revealed that some goods were discarded at that point—but not all that could be. Many unnecessary items were recovered from the Donners' Alder Creek camp by salvagers in 1847. This confirms that non-essential merchandise was still hauled up the Sierra by their jaded animals to their final snowbound site. The 2004 excavation of the Donners' Alder Creek campsite revealed ceramic dishware fragments and many other items that the Donners were determined to bring into California.

readiness a bountiful supply of clothing. She also superintended the purchase of materials for women's handiwork, apparatus for preserving botanical specimens, water colors and oil paints, books, and school supplies; the latter being selected for a young ladies' seminary which she hoped to establish in California."[34]

Eliza includes in her book how her family's three wagons were loaded: "In the first were stored the merchandise and articles "not to be handled until they should reach their destination; in the second, [there were] provisions, clothing, camp tools, and other necessaries of camp life. The third was our family home on wheels, with feed boxes attached to the back of the wagon-bed for Fanny and Margaret, the favorite saddle-horses, which were to be kept ever close at hand for emergencies."

Thus, what she describes suggests a degree of circumstantial evidence that some of the Donner wagons were suspiciously, if not decidedly, overloaded creating an insidious complication from the start that would erode their oxen's stamina over time even before a single wheel rolled west. It is also important to point out that one of George Donner's wagons carried exclusive merchandise and articles not to be touched until reaching California. This meant that the 800 pounds of foodstuffs assigned to that wagon now had to be redistributed in the two remaining.

It may not be surprising then that the gray area of essential verses non-essential items posed a very real dichotomy to emigrants: Leaving behind possessions was difficult; hanging on to them often justifiable since they would be difficult if not impossible to replace. In addition to practical provisions, many non-essential goods were taken ignoring what was in strict contrast to Hastings' recommendations. It was a potential time-bomb just waiting to go off down the trail. But as Eliza describes, with help from her supporters' memories, she clearly lays out choices that were made as they prepared for their extensive undertaking. She contributes insight as to the chief purpose of those goods and supplies which was to provide a comfortable start with a degree of economic advantage for their new life in a far-off land. As the Donner-Reed families finished preparations for their long trek, Hastings' guide left emigrants with some parting advice that bespoke of an urgency for what lay ahead:

> "Nothing now remains to be done, but to notice the method of traveling, which I will proceed to do…Emigrants should, invariably, arrive at Independence, Mo., on, or before, the fifteenth of April, so as to be in readiness, to enter upon their journey, on, or before, the first day of May; after which time, they should never start, if it can, possibly, be avoided." He goes on to state, "The advantages to be derived, from setting out, at as early a day as that above suggested, are those of having an abundance of good pasturage, in passing over those desolate and thirsty plains; and being able to cross the mountains, before the falling mountains of snow, or floods of rain, which usually occurs, in that region, early in October."

The Donner-Reed wagons departed Independence, Missouri on May 12, 1846.

---

[34] Houghton, Eliza Poor Donner. *The Expedition of the Donner Party and Its Tragic Fate*. Chicago: A.C. McClurg, 1911.

The excitement of their initial start-up, fueled by the fervor of Manifest Destiny, looked bright for the Reed and Donner families. For now, the matter of overloaded wagons was overshadowed by the fresh vigor of their powerful oxen as they traveled through the undulating western plains. But far into their journey, having decided to take Hastings' new cutoff, the last rest stop for animals and emigrants alike would be Fort Bridger, in modern Wyoming. When they departed the fort, a number of seemingly marginal factors would become frightfully apparent on the new trail when they realized that it was not as clear-cut as they had imagined. Contributing to their errors, information provided by the fort's proprietors was either misleadingly given, held back, or ignored which would soon magnify the Donner Party's dilemma, profoundly affecting their perilous undertaking.[35]

---

[35] After weeks on the trail, food stores would naturally be consumed reducing overall weight. However, if a vehicle started with 300-500 pounds in material goods over the recommended maximum capacity of 2,000 pounds, by mid journey, the animals were essentially still pulling a full load when a weight reduction would have been welcomed. Animals weakened by months on the trail were now faced with increasingly difficult geography. So instead of reaping the much-needed benefit of a substantially lighter wagon, the animals continued to be stressed as they struggled with loads that impaired their well-being and progress.

3. Trails and Expectations

    Meriwether Lewis and William Clark quickly realized during their preliminary expedition that there was no practical wagon route to the Pacific, but they did open the way for further exploration along the Missouri River and its tributaries. For beaver trappers and traders this meant profitable operations using the natural waterways as "roads" to transport goods. An American fur trader named William Ashley and his partner were especially adept at making money using those liquid highways which expanded American influence. But things were about to take a different course in 1823 due to a deadly confrontation with Native Americans who were not happy with Ashley for undercutting their profits. This led to wider land-based explorations that ventured from the main waterways into the mountains that soon ushered in the rendezvous system where trappers and traders alike met at an arranged location to do business on a yearly basis, thus making it easier to bring furs to market.

    One big piece of the jigsaw puzzle to create a wagon road through the Rocky Mountains was still being sought. That is until 1824 when a trapper by the name of Jedediah Smith linked the previously used but unestablished keystone that made a wagon road possible. This was South Pass, a natural thirty-five-mile-wide corridor that provided easy access into the heart of the Rockies over the Continental Divide. This essential breach in the mountains would soon be incorporated into the main overland route of what would become known as the Oregon or Emigrants' Trail.

    There was still no wagon route that went completely through the Rocky Mountains, but that would change with the establishment of Fort William, later John, and finally renamed Laramie in modern Wyoming.[36] This led to further exploration and greater knowledge of the Rockies. The fort quickly became the central depot for beaver pelts and buffalo hides that the fort would virtually monopolize. As a result, the establishment helped promote the development of a wagon road following the shallow Platte River which was all but useless for boat navigation. More importantly, it connected Missouri's frontier towns that would sell and ship furs to markets around the world. Fort Laramie was also a welcomed destination for emigrants heading toward Oregon and California before penetrating the interior Rocky Mountains. It also benefitted trappers whose experience throughout the Rockies put them in demand as hired guides by anxious westbound emigrants.

    It wasn't long until wheeled vehicles made it all the way to Fort Hall (a British trading outpost in southern Idaho), but none had passed the iconic fur trading post until 1836 when missionaries Marcus and Narcissa Whitman decided to make the attempt. The first wagon

---

[36] The crude cottonwood log Fort William was renamed Fort John when it was rebuilt with adobe bricks. Fort John, however, was used interchangeably with Fort Laramie in honor of a trapper by that name. It was officially changed to Fort Laramie in 1849 when the United States military purchased the trading post.

beyond Fort Hall rolled out with a small group of emigrants guided by mountain men. Well away from the fort, the rugged trail exacted its toll on their wagon when an axle broke. Determined not to give up the effort, the disabled vehicle was modified into a two-wheeled cart and continued on to Fort Boise situated near the modern Idaho-Oregon border where it was finally abandoned. However, this was the first time a wagon (or at least half of one) had been brought that far.[37] This small breakthrough would be extended over the next decade by others who improved the trail with better variations and contributing road work until wagons on all four wheels finally reached the rich soil of Oregon's Willamette Valley.

Eighteen forty-two marked the first large scale migration to Oregon which began in part because of the economic depression in what we call the Midwest today. The lure of better farming prospects in Oregon, touted by fur traders, missionaries, and talk of free land through government interaction tempted the ambitious. Senator Thomas Hart Benton (explorer John Fremont's father-in-law) repeatedly introduced legislation that would provide grants up to 1,000 acres of land for anyone who would settle in Oregon Country. A version of it passed years later but in the interim speculation ran wild, and many were willing to take the risk in hopes that the government would catch up to them. Oregon was the destination of choice for now, but Mexican California's reputation for giving away huge land grants would inspire the emigrants' first feeble attempts to open a wagon road branching from Fort Hall all the way to California.

Like any new route, development of a trail to California was a messy proposition that would take years and not at all a guaranteed success. The Great Salt Lake had been circumnavigated by mountain men in 1826, but there was no formal wagon road that had been attempted or even partially developed in any direction from there. The Salt Lake had been approached *from* California with great difficulty by Jedediah Smith's group of trappers in 1827 who carefully veered away from the Salt Desert directly west of the lake. They would eventually connect with the slightly more hospitable southern edge of the Salt Lake and its varied springs.

Mountain men had explored the north side of the lake in a westerly direction, but there was no wagon road to California until the Bartleson-Bidwell party of 1841 attempted to establish one through this geographically unforgiving terrain. John Bidwell, a Missouri school teacher caught up in the promising advantages of California, may have described the undertaking best when he later recalled that "Our ignorance was complete. We knew that California lay west, and that was the extent of our knowledge."

The first long section of their journey started from Missouri where they were guided by missionary Father De Smet and trapper Thomas "Broken Hand" Fitzpatrick, who both knew the road to Oregon but little of a way to California. Their travel began with the relatively easy rolling plains along the Platte River, but as the party entered the Rockies and approached the

---

[37] After an unsuccessful attempt to bring a wagon all the way into Oregon, the "Whitman-Spalding Missionary Party arrived at Fort Vancouver on September 12, 1836." Accessed March 25, 2019. https://www.historylink.org/File/9700.

British fur trading center Fort Hall, about half of the sixty-nine emigrants continued on to Oregon via the fort, De Smet and Fitzpatrick included, but not before setting Bidwell's group on their way down to the Bear River toward the northern end of the Great Salt Lake. The remaining members, including wagon leader John Bartleson, timidly headed in a southwesterly direction that only mountain men had pushed through before. However, to err on the side of caution, four members were selected to cut over to Fort Hall in order to glean as much information as they could on how to best advance through this country. When they returned ten days later, the only vague advice they got from the fort's trappers according to Bidwell was to "strike out west of Salt Lake—being careful not to go too far south, lest we should get into a waterless country without grass."[38] They were also advised not to go too far north as there were steep canyons to aimlessly wander into and perish. After days of blundering, and at times backtracking, they finally managed to wander west of the Salt Lake flats into the Pequop Range in eastern Nevada where they wisely decided to abandon their wagons that hindered progress. The remains of these wagons would be found and used for fire wood by the advance emigrants ahead of the Donner Party who followed Hastings Cutoff in 1846.

Now traveling with pack animals, they continued their difficult trek to the Humboldt River and vigilantly followed it for 300 miles to its "sink" or end. The hardships continued as they still had to span a testy forty-mile-long desert that led to the base of the Sierra. Reaching that goal, they then traveled south to the Walker River following it until they were able to crest the Sierra. Working their way across as best they could, they finally descended down the western slope of the Sierra by struggling along the rugged Stanislaus River Canyon that eventually spilled into California's San Joaquin Valley. It was an arduous, demoralizing trip that constantly bordered on starvation and disaster, but they made it. And even though this route was not the most practical for wagons, part of it, particularly the Humboldt River section pointing to the Sierra, would be an essential part of a wagon road in the successful development of an overland route to California.

****

No attempt to traverse into California took place in 1842, but Joseph Chiles, a former member of the Bartleson-Bidwell Party, returned to Missouri that year and prepared to try it again with another wagon train in 1843 under the leadership of mountain man Joseph Reddeford Walker. This time they would stay farther north of the Salt Lake which was a big improvement working west to connect with the Humboldt River to its terminus. Upon crossing the thick sand of what became known as Forty Mile Desert, they followed the base of the Sierra south to Walker Pass that was previously discovered by the man leading them. Unfortunately, they were forced to leave their wagons behind when difficult terrain made it impractical to continue with them. Finding the elusive gap that would make wagon travel possible into California's Great Central Valley remained unresolved, but was essential in order to sustain the

---

[38] Nunis, Doyce B. *The Bidwell-Bartleson Party: 1841 California Emigrant Adventure: The Documents and Memoirs of the Overland Pioneers*. Santa Cruz, CA: Western Tanager Press, 1991.
* The party's name was reversed since Bidwell wrote the first published account of the overland trip.

needs of a large emigration with families. Although as yet unknown, this breakthrough was on the cusp of becoming a reality as the next season of overland travel to California would prove to be the turning point for wagons over the Sierra.

It was the Stephens-Townsend-Murphy Party of 1844-45 that would make the final breakthrough establishing the first feasible wagon route into the heart of California—but just barely.[39] Traveling on information from previous wagon trains, they left Council Bluffs, Iowa Territory in the spring guided by an elderly but highly experienced mountain man, or trapper, named Caleb Greenwood. They followed the Platte River to Fort John (previously Fort William) which was a replacement structure built of adobe bricks—a huge renovation over the cottonwood logs of the old post. As they continued on beyond South Pass to a place later named the Parting of the Ways, the emigrants were convinced by Greenwood to take what he believed was practical cutoff through 53 miles of waterless, nearly grassless, sage-covered terrain to the Green River.[40] It was difficult (about 30 hours to the next water source), but it saved three days of travel opposed to turning off toward Fort Bridger, then up to Fort Hall. As a result, his alternative route was honored with his name (sometime later it was also known as Sublette's Cutoff). Upon reaching Fort Hall, those Oregon-bound departed, and the remaining forty-six emigrants, twenty-three men, eight women, and fifteen children, attached to eleven wagons, set out to make their way to California.

Beyond the fort, eighty-year-old Greenwood again persuaded members of the Stephens Party to take what he thought was a better route to the Humboldt River. This must have been based on his earlier travels during his younger days. His alternative course passed through what became known as the City of Rocks (in southern Idaho) named so because of the area's many odd-shaped formations. Again, Greenwood's past experience and guidance paid off. It also helped that the emigrants he led were equipped with good wagons, most carrying light to moderate loads, and pulled by hardy animals that could take the abuse of this cutting-edge journey.

Reaching the Humboldt intact, they followed its sandy banks lined with stunted willows. Monotonous as it was, they realized every day how indispensable this waterway was; travel would be impossible across the bleak Nevada desert without its life-giving gift. Furthermore, to the emigrants' amazement, when this sluggish body of water ran out of energy some 300 miles from its source, it simply ended in an extensive meadow-like "sink" choked with grasses, reeds, and deep muck. Unlike a typical river that drained into a larger one and eventually out to sea, this one just soaked into the sand of the desert floor.

Adding to their anxiety at this point, they faced a crucial decision to either work their way south of the Humboldt Sink to find Walker Pass as the Chiles-Walker Party had attempted the year before, or they could head directly west to a gap in the Sierra that held the possibility

---

[39] From here the Stephens-Townsend-Murphy Party will be referred to as the Stephens Party.

[40] Wyman, Walker D. *California Emigrant Letters*. New York: Bookman Associates, 1952.
* An unidentified traveler states that Greenwood or Sublette Cutoff was measured by "roadometers" at 53 miles.

of a suitable alternative. Their choice was somewhat alleviated when they befriended a Native American whom they called Truckee. He was able to communicate to Greenwood, through drawings in the sand and sign language, the existence of a river flowing from the mountains directly west from where they sat. It was a tempting option and was promising enough to do some reconnaissance on horseback. Encouraged by what was reported, it was decided to be worth the risk. Leaving the sink, the trail entered the unavoidable expanse of desert forty miles in length. Watered by only one sulfur-infused boiling spring at the mid-point, there was no other way to reach the steep eastern slope of the snow-scarred peaks of the Sierra Nevada. But after two days of hard driving around the clock in heavy sand, they arrived at the river they named Truckee in honor of the man who assisted them in their venture.

Having rested by the cold, clear water of the Truckee and its meadows (where modern Reno sits), they continued on. There is little doubt that the formidable mountain barrier they were about to enter intimidated just about every emigrant who cast eyes upon it—let alone anyone who sought to bring wagons through. Unknown at the time, the Stephens Party was about to pave the way for wagon travel over a mountain summit into California—the same route that the Donner Party would face the following year.

After another short pause, Caleb Greenwood took the opportunity to scout a way to bypass some of the Truckee River canyon through Dog Valley, while emigrants crisscrossed an increasingly difficult path farther into the Sierra. Still, while harness leather stretched, battered wagons creaked, and iron-wrapped wooden wheels scraped against rocks, they knew they were making history as their powerful oxen lurched forward with each tormented step into new territory.

As the party inched its way toward the summit of the Sierra, blustery November clouds began releasing snow that became increasingly deeper in the higher elevations. This warned of the real possibility of entrapment in the icy holds of the mountains. Having followed the Truckee River west in hope of finding an obvious pass to the western slope, the river now bent to the south where critical decisions had to be made.

The Stephens Party's ordeal was not over. With winter weather looming, and the newfound confusion to locate a pass that would admit their wagons was of pressing importance and with good reason. If winter snows sealed any or all possible avenues across the Sierra, they would be all but doomed. A consultation was held, and it was decided to split up in search of a way to cross the spine of the mountains. The group concluded that half a dozen emigrants (including two women) would go on horseback with two pack animals loaded with supplies and head up the main stream to find a pass. While encamped, the remaining members of the wagon party would search for a suitable gap around the snow-encrusted rocky cap of what is now Donner Summit. At this junction near the end of Truckee Lake, a number of emigrants gave up on getting their wagons across and six were left behind. A difficult trail had worn down some of their animals to near exhaustion. It was better to leave some of the wagons here until the following spring or risk losing everything. They were to be guarded by three volunteers one of whom was seventeen-year-old Moses Schallenberger.

Schallenberger and two others were soon busy building a crude cabin measuring twelve by fourteen feet, about eight feet high, and rooved by rawhide and pine brush.[41] On and off snow storms had left snow two feet deep by now, and was increasing by the time they finished the shelter two days later. The rapid accumulation of snow indicated that they might be getting into more danger than they bargained for. Discouraged, it was decided to get out while they could, but the physical endurance of the escape proved too much for Moses and he returned to the cabin alone. Amazingly, the winter turned out to be less severe than it could have been, and he was able to survive chiefly on the coyote and fox that he trapped until rescued by his friends months later in late February 1845.

At the same time the Schallenberger ordeal was beginning to play out, members of his company on horseback had been diligently following the Truckee River until coming upon its exit from what is today known as Lake Tahoe. It must have been amazing to see this huge span of the purest water on Earth in its most pristine state. However, there was no time to waste and the group began working their way through canyons where they eventually stumbled upon the American River headwaters. With great difficulty, they managed to twist their way down the western slope of the Sierra toward the Sacramento Valley. Slowly distancing themselves from snow higher up, the hazards were still many as they descended the fast, deep, and steep canyons of this river system. It would have been futile had wagons attempted to go this way; besides, they hoped to connect at some point along the way with their companions who had hopefully found a wagon pass, and if not, make their way to the Sacramento Valley and send out the alarm for help.

After two days of reconnaissance, another detachment of the Stephens Party that was actively bringing up five wagons, found a way to get over the summit into California, but it wasn't easy. They had to work their way along the north side of Truckee Lake and up over a series of steep, slick, granite cliffs and ledges partially covered with wet snow two feet deep in places.[42] The demanding pass through the Sierra became even more difficult when they reached a ten-foot wall of rock that could not be avoided. To deal with this latest obstacle, wagons were unloaded, animals unhitched and led through a narrow slot in the rock to the top of the wall. Chains were then connected to the animals, and the remaining links lowered for attachment to a wagon tongue. Each vehicle was then pulled up the vertical face. Contrary to popular legend, wheels were not removed (at least not in this situation). Then the empty wagon was literally rolled up to the top of the precipice as animals pulled and men lifted and pushed until the task was accomplished.

Repacking and yoking their animals once again, they left the summit behind and continued west down to the headwaters of the Yuba River. A milestone had been reached; they were the first to bring wagons into California on November 25, 1844. That night in camp sitting

---

[41] This cabin was discovered the following year much to the surprise of the Breen family, of Donner Party fame, who made use of it during their entrapment.

[42] Kelly, Charles, and Dale L. Morgan. *Old Greenwood; the Story of Caleb Greenwood: Trapper, Pathfinder, and Early Pioneer.* Georgetown, CA: Talisman Press, 1965.

by blazing campfires, they must have been comforted somewhat by their hard-won success proving that as difficult as it was, it could be done. And not only that, they did so during the (relatively moderate) winter and were, no doubt, extremely fortunate to have made it down the Sierra's western slope before the pass was completely blocked by snow.

They were still above the snowline; over-worked animals were still pushed to their limits, and food was alarmingly low. It was, therefore, decided to leave their remaining battered wagons behind with only six women and two men to care for more than a dozen children. The seventeen men that remained were to make their way to Sutter's Fort and return with supplies and fresh animals as soon as possible.

Those left behind suffered greatly, but their crossing of the Sierra that began in mid-November would end happily with the return of rescuers by the end of February. Wagons to be retrieved in the spring. Future emigrants now had a way to enter California with their families, necessities, and possessions in tow linking dreams with reality. The 1846 travel season would see hundreds of emigrants using this newly developed access across the Sierra. This would include a group of emigrants who would become indelibly linked with the pass to the point of overshadowing the achievement of the Stephens Party, but with a much different outcome. They were the Donner Party.

****

With all of the history behind the development, and on-going evolution of the Oregon and California Trails, access was wide open for aspiring emigrants who had the advantage of information from those who came before. But the journey could still be very consequential either in rewards or hazards or both. Having spent nearly a year in preparation for their journey, the Donner-Reed parties departed the filth-strewn muddy streets of Springfield, Illinois on April 14, 1846. With thirty-one members and their caravan of nine vehicles in line, it was only the second season emigrants set out to cross the Sierra with wagons.

Distinguished historian David McCullough provides a perfect description for the undertaking the Donner-Reed families were about to commence in a single sentence: "Imagine packing up an entire household, saying goodbye to all you've known, and setting off to walk, essentially to walk, to California a continent away, little knowing what was in store."[43] As adventurous and final as McCullough's statement rings, it echoes a candid reality. For families committing to more than 2,000 animal-powered miles to the Pacific Slope in the 1840s, it virtually meant a one-way destination with little chance of ever going "home" again. As difficult as the trip would become physically, it was also connected emotionally by relationships of those left behind bound only by irregular letters. One such optimistic missive early on provides a glimpse into the early progress of trail life. Written to a friend by Tamsen Donner on the Platte River dated June 16, 1846, the following excerpt was published in Springfield's *Sangamo Journal* a month later. She wrote:

---

[43] The Donner Party. Videocassette. Directed by Ric Burns. 1992; WGBH/Boston: Steeplechase Films, 2001.

"Indeed, if I do not experience something far worse than I have yet done, I shall say the trouble is all in getting started. Our wagons have not needed much repair, and I can not [sic] yet tell in what respects they could be improved. Certain it is, they can not be too strong. Our preparations for the journey might have been in some respects bettered."

As with a majority of emigrants starting out, the first weeks were filled with excitement and adventure as they passed over the gentle undulating grasslands of the plains. But as the companies of wagons proceeded west into the Rockies, the real hardships of trail life began to emerge. This soon tested the endurance and spirits of all who committed to make such a trip. This would be especially true of the Donner Party whose "preparations for the journey [that] might have been in some respects bettered" would be revealed in the form of overloaded wagons combined with the additional factors of lost time and choosing to take Hastings Cutoff. Beyond that, there awaited the demands of advancing over the spine of the Sierra Nevada in the footsteps of the Stephens Party who had opened the way for wagons on the ever-fluid California Trail.

4. Death and a Change of Plans

A year before the Donner-Reed party set out, Robert Cadden Keyes, one of James Reed's brothers-in-law, had set out for Oregon but had changed his mind along the way at some point and had gone to California instead. Traveling with the William B. Ide company, he wanted to see this highly promoted paradise for himself. When he arrived, he did not find California to his liking so he went to Oregon. While in Oregon City, he wrote to future Oregon emigrants in an article published by a local newspaper before heading home to Illinois. Keyes knew of Hastings' plans to promote emigration to California, and the main purpose of Keyes' article was seemingly to aid Oregon promoters and downplay California's chief advocate, Lansford Hastings, thus keeping any emigration surge moving toward Oregon. Keyes makes his short-term observations and preferences known in an article from the *Oregon Spectator*:

"To the Oregon Emigration:
"I arrived at this place today, and at the request of some friends, I make this statement to you concerning California, and the operations of men there: Captain Hastings left on the 4th of May to meet the company from the United States, for the purpose of persuading them from their path, and enticing them to California. Now this I can say to you that may hear Hastings tell of the wonders of California, there is a scarcity of timber and water, and though the hills are set with oats and the valley with clover, it is all short feed, as the sun burns the clover down by the 15th of July, and the stock have to live on the seeds in the winter. I have seen enough of Oregon to perceive that it is the best grazing country of the two, and for agriculture they won't compare.["]
Robert C. Keyes
Oregon City, June 17th, 1846

It is of interest that Robert "Cad" Keyes commented that timber and water were scarce. The pine trees of the Sierra Nevada and the redwoods of the Coastal Range were covered with high-quality forests that he certainly could not have missed. Albeit it was not yet economically feasible to harvest these trees profitably at the time. Still, an early attempt was made in 1848 with an agreement between John Sutter and James Marshall to build a water-powered sawmill on forested land higher up on a branch of the American River. This, of course, would lead to the gold discovery that triggered the rush of 1849. Water would also be a vexing issue to make agricultural gains productive throughout the semi-arid Great Central Valley during the dry summer months until seasonal rains came. And it was Sutter, proprietor of the trade fort New Helvetia (modern Sacramento), who had already begun developing northern California's first irrigation system in 1841 setting the example for the future of California's unsurpassed agriculture dominance in the coming decades.[44] Keyes certainly observed the dried grasslands

---

[44] Hurtado, Albert L. *John Sutter: A Life on the North American Frontier.* Norman: University of Oklahoma Press, 2006.

that thousands of fat cattle thrived on, and native Californios who profitably ranched them. Yet, perhaps it was surprising to him that while cattle in the east fattened on grass that remained green with regular rainfall throughout the summer months, it might not have occurred to him that western cattle could do just as well on dry fodder. It's also possible that he just simply preferred Oregon as its climate and resources were similar in many ways to his native Illinois.

****

At the same time the *Oregon Spectator* publication came out, it is notable that Lansford Hastings was heading east from California to examine Fremont's new Salt Lake route. His intention was to extend it to Fort Bridger where many California and Oregon bound wagons could be engaged to take his planned cutoff. Adding to the soon to be interaction of events, the Donner-Reed party had just left Independence, Missouri eleven days beyond Hastings' recommended departure date of May first. One hundred miles and seven days into their journey, they would catch up with the large Russell Party and join them. Most of who would become known as the Donner Party attached themselves to this group that now made up about 80 wagons.

As Robert Keyes made his way back to Springfield, Illinois from Oregon, his travels would naturally take him through Fort Hall. Unbeknown to him at the time, his strong-willed mother, seventy-year-old Sarah Keyes born in the year of America's Declaration of Independence, was determined to make the journey with her daughter, Margret, and son-in-law James Reed even though her health was fragile due to her losing bout with "consumption" (tuberculosis). According to Edwin Bryant, who traveled with the Donner-Reed contingent part of the way, he recorded that she wanted to see her son Robert one last time as she may not have the opportunity again. Despite the odds of not surviving such a trip, her desire was honored and had a direct impact on the design of the large "family wagon" that Reed had built with details in mind to accommodate her. Sarah's decision to head west with her family would have far reaching influence—more than anyone could have realized at the time.

Years later her granddaughter, Virginia Reed, believed that she did not want to stay behind as she might never see her only daughter, Margret Reed, ever again. She hoped to connect with her son Robert at Fort Hall, and then would have gone all the way to California to remain with Margret. Unfortunately for Sarah, she became weaker as the Donner-Reed caravan worked its way west toward the Platte River. However, heavy rains filled the Big Blue River to flood stage causing the wagon train to halt and wait for the river to subside before crossing. It was at this point of the journey near Alcove Springs in modern Kansas that Sarah passed away. In death, she released the emotional bonds and tangible comforts of her family's care. The rugged advance of her remaining family's quest to seek a better life would still go on, but for Sarah, with a touch of irony, she would be left behind, surrounded by a lonely prairie wilderness, far from her family.

---

* The Sacramento Valley receives less than twenty inches of rain per year. Sutter was the first in Northern California to realize that sending river water into irrigation ditches was key to successful agriculture. His pioneering efforts to divert water began as early as 1841.

Sarah's death is of interest for two reasons. First, there is the sobering drama of her last days and her prairie funeral as recorded by family and fellow travelers. Unlike a formal nineteenth century funeral and burial in the family plot, a trail ceremony was a somewhat different affair. It was of course similar in the emotions of permanent loss, but very different in the sense of abandonment and isolation in a remote wilderness where a loved one would likely never be visited by family again. It was a heart-wrenching disconnect from tradition, often followed by strong feelings of guilt. On May 20, eight days into the journey and nine days before Sarah Keyes died, James Reed wrote a telling letter to a brother-in-law in Illinois. He stated that Sarah "will not stand it" for she "is so blind that she cannot take her coffee or plate if it is set near her. She cannot eat anything [and] I am of [the] opinion a few days will end her mortal career." Reed's observations proved to be true. Sarah died on May 29 surrounded by loved ones and the boundless open prairie while waiting to cross the swollen Big Blue River.

Traveler Edwin Bryant goes on to say that a cottonwood tree was felled and planks shaped from it to form a coffin. A stone was then procured and fashioned into the shape of a tombstone engraved with the words "Mrs. Sarah Keyes, Died May 29, 1846: Aged 70." And finally, J. Quinn Thornton wrote that "death in the wilderness—in solitude of nature, and far from the busy abodes of men, seemed to have in it a more than usual solemnity."

Another reason her death is of particular interest, and perhaps the most significant, is that the Donner-Reed parties were now free to choose any new trail variation or cutoff they felt was best. All plausible options were now open as there was no mandate to go to Fort Hall in order to intercept Sarah's son Robert. At this juncture on the trail no one yet knew of Hastings new wagon road. They did, however, have a vague idea before they left Independence of government explorer Fremont's recent mile-saving deviation to California directly below the Salt Lake. By the time they reached Fort Laramie, it is no coincidence then, that James Reed had all but determined to take it. At the "parting of the ways" beyond South Pass, the nine wagons of the Donner-Reed train and the eleven vehicles of seven other families would leave the main caravan. George Donner was elected captain, and the new wagon train veered off on the left-hand trail toward Fort Bridger and Hastings Cutoff.[45] The remainder of the wagons they had been traveling with diverged to the right under the leadership of William M. Boggs, and headed across the sage-covered desert landscape of Greenwood Cutoff on their way to Fort Hall.

---

[45] At the Parting of the Ways, a number of families and individuals joined the wagons under the elected captaincy of George Donner. Others would join at Fort Bridger. The Graves family with their three wagons were the last to catch up with the Donner Party as they followed the new trail through the Wasatch. A total of twenty-three wagons and 87 emigrants made up the caravan; it was as large as the wagon train would ever be.

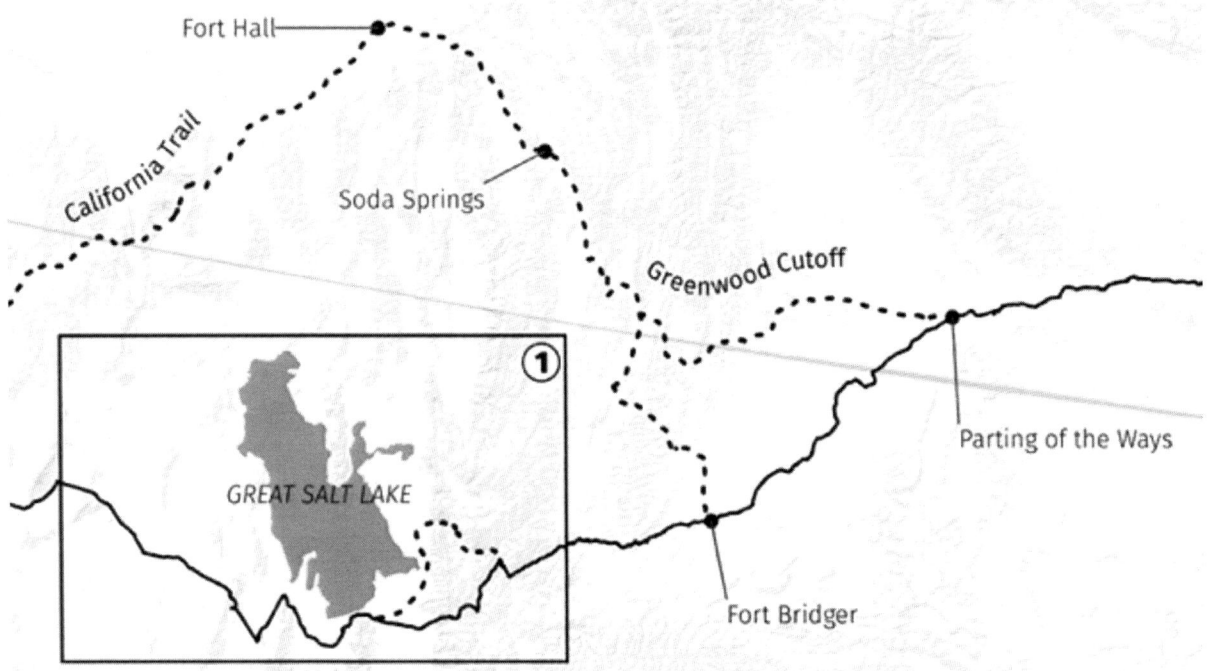

At Fort Bridger, emigrants could still easily access the route to California via Fort Hall or choose to take the new Hastings Cutoff south of the Great Salt Lake.

5. Cutoffs and Calamities

Cutoffs were always a part of the Oregon and California trails from their beginnings. In fact, the Oregon Trail never existed as a discreet single road. Historians have called it a "trail corridor."[46] Trappers turned wagon guides, as well as emigrants themselves, actively sought improvements with every new season of travel. Make no mistake, most every cutoff had its own specialized risks, especially the ones that were a work in progress, but all were balanced with a worthwhile or perceived advantage. For example, in 1844, mountain man Caleb Greenwood's Cutoff, at the Parting of the Ways in Wyoming, was a deviation that offered no water or grass for animals across a fifty-three-mile stretch, but saved nearly three days travel to reach Fort Hall; therefore, considered worth the hazard.

The next year, Greenwood again established another significant alternative through the Sierra when he explored a detour that bypassed the rugged Upper Truckee Canyon by way of Dog Valley. This longer but easier variation was a welcomed amendment for the 1846 emigrants ascending the wheel-smashing, axle-breaking Truckee River Route. The same year, to avoid the steep wall at Donner Summit, the Joseph Aram Party scouted another way wagons could pass over the spine of the Sierra via Cold Stream Canyon just south of Truckee (Donner) Lake.[47] And all of this was happening as the Donner Party themselves closed in on their desperate scramble up the Sierra in their losing battle with time and weather.

Contrary to the popular perception that Hastings Cutoff was the most dreadful route ever attempted west of the Mississippi, there are a number of genuine disasters with severe consequences that came before and after Hastings enterprising cutoff. The first of these fiascoes, known as Meek's Cutoff, took place on the Oregon Trail in 1845. Stephen Meek, unlike Hastings, is a perfect example of a trail leader who had *never* been on *any* part of the cutoff he proposed, yet he convinced a large group of emigrants to do just that as he led them blindly into the unknown.

Meek professed to having made some earlier peripheral explorations as a trapper where his alleged cutoff ended at The Dalles (rapids) on the Columbia River. However, other than the regular Oregon Trail, the fact was he had never been across any other part of the broad expanse of Oregon Country that he asserted to know. And when emigrants on the Oregon Trail arrived at Fort Boise on the Oregon-Idaho border, Meek lured over 800 emigrants and roughly 200 wagons into believing his deceptive claim that he could lead them on a shortcut that he was familiar with eliminating 150 miles of travel. He also capitalized on the emigrants' pending fear

---

[46] Chaffin, Tom. *Pathfinder: John Charles Frémont and the Course of American Empire.* First ed. Norman, OK: University of Oklahoma Press, 2002.

[47] Graydon, Charles K. *Trail of the First Wagons over the Sierra Nevada.* Tucson, AZ: Patrice Press, 1994.

that hostile Indians may be encountered if they stayed on the regular route. And he expected to be paid a guide fee of $5 per wagon for those diverging with him, which bolsters a degree of suspicion for his motivation.

Meek's proposed cutoff of fourteen days quickly turned into an ordeal of five weeks and more than 400 unnerving miles of mountainous, desert-like, rugged terrain. Clearly lost, Meek appeared bewildered even to the people he led as he irresponsibly placed these travelers through unwarranted and inexcusable danger. The ensuing venture resulted in trail confusion, difficulty finding water, starvation food rations, sickness, and the eventual split-up of the wagon train. Loss of life would climb to the tune of at least twenty-four emigrants before the affair was over.[48] His own life was threatened on two different occasions for his lack of knowledge and blame for the death of an emigrant's son—both of which he managed to avoid. Many others would never forgive him. A year later, Joel Palmer wrote a terse account for the *St. Joseph Gazette* July 10, 1846 regarding the cutoff:

> "It was a man named Stephan L. Meek, from Jackson county, Mo. who induced the company to take that route. He stated that he could shorten the distance 150 miles over the old road, and that he was perfectly familiar with the route. But it unfortunately proved otherwise."

Another example resulting in a lapse of good judgment was the handcart experiment of 1856. It was an effort by Mormon elders to move as many late-arriving European emigrants as cheaply and efficiently as possible to the Zion of Salt Lake City.[49] The Mormon faithful who were part of this effort included two large groups of about one thousand emigrants each and were known as the Willie and Martin Handcart Companies. These mostly poor emigrants were willfully endangered by the Mormon bureaucracy and stands as a grim reminder of what can go wrong by ignoring sensible preparation practices in conjunction with *known* trail dangers. The decision to set into motion this incredulous undertaking included construction of inferior two-wheeled handcarts not powered by beasts of burden, but by humans in order to reduce costs. Only seventeen pounds of personal belongings per person were allowed, and a food ration was limited to one pound of flour per day for each man and even less for every woman and child.

To be fair, there were small herds of beef cattle following support wagons that carried bulky items such as tents and heavy bags of flour, but it wasn't anywhere near what was needed. It is almost incomprehensible to believe that this was thought adequate for a journey starting from Iowa City destined for Salt Lake City 1,200 miles away. Without question it was an acidic test of religious devotion, and all but doomed to fail. Church officials adopted a risky disregard for the traditional season of travel that began in April or May, in favor of the dangerously late departure month of August that would bump up against the winter season, and it was certainly

---

[48] Although there was much suffering, no emigrant died of starvation or thirst. Illness due to poor nutrition, and typhus or "camp fever", a bacterial infection from insect bites, are associated with deaths on the cutoff.

[49] Roberts, David. *Devils Gate: Brigham Young and the Great Mormon Handcart Tragedy*. New York: Simon & Schuster, 2008.

avoidable.

Leadership mismanagement resulted in the hasty declaration to start the two handcart groups on the Mormon Trail just north of the firmly established westbound Emigrants' Trail below the Platte River.[50] This decision would end with its victims becoming snowbound during their ascent into the Rocky Mountains near the famous Devil's Gate landmark in modern Wyoming. It was a huge miscalculation that ended in horrific consequences. The two groups of emigrants, already exhausted from weeks of travel, and gaunt from a limited food supply, were caught in an early October storm complete with sub-zero temperatures and over a foot of windblown drifting snow. All told, this incident resulted in the deaths of over two hundred individuals—more than four times the dead suffered by the Donner Party tragedy of 1846-47. It was the worst trail disaster of all time in the American West, and still stands as such today. Sadly, it could have been averted. Unlike Hastings' successful challenge to personally lead emigrants across the difficult geography of his cutoff, he had traveled within a reasonable timeframe. On the other hand, the ill-prepared handcart companies had little chance of a favorable outcome. There is a huge differentiation between calculated risk and simple foolhardiness.

Lastly, among notable calamities, was John Charles Fremont's Fourth Expedition. Starting out from Bent's Fort in eastern Colorado, he was warned by local traders and trappers that it was not a good idea to attempt a crossing of the Rockies in winter conditions. But that is not what Fremont wanted to hear as his interest was to find a year-round pass through the Rockies for a future transcontinental railroad line. Nothing was going to deter his purpose. His disaster came about as a result of deliberately chancing a mountainous winter traverse in 1848-49 through the Sangre de Cristo Range via southern Colorado's 9,700' Mosca Pass then into the San Juan range where real trouble began. Fremont, like Hastings, had previously ventured a successful winter crossing of the Sierra a few years earlier, and he played the odds again hoping for a continuation of his previous luck. That gamble, or more precisely his poor judgment based on his personal motive, would abruptly end the expedition for him and his 33 men.

As weather conditions worsened, Fremont split his men into groups to escape below zero temperatures, fierce winds, and entrapping snow, but it was too late. Their ordeal became a route to fight their way out of the mountains complete with all the suffering and severity of hardships they had to endure. In all, ten men would die from over-exertion, starvation, and hypothermia. All 120 mules of their pack train were either eaten or lost. Some of the remaining survivors turned to cannibalism in order to subsist before relief arrived.[51] Upon their rescue, the emaciated remnants of his men soon exposed the spectral details of their ordeal—a situation

---

[50] The Mormon Trail was established to keep the Mormons separate from other travelers who followed the south side of the Platte. Of interest is that the Mormons used the same trail through the Wasatch as the Donner Party had opened in 1846 to reach the settlement of what would become Salt Lake City.

[51] Hafen, LeRoy Reuben., and Ann Woodbury. Hafen. *Frémont's Fourth Expedition: A Documentary Account of the Disaster of 1848-1849 with Diaries, Letters, and Reports by Participants in the Tragedy.* Vol. XI. Glendale, Cal.: Clark, 1960.

created by the leadership of Fremont who openly disregarded the high probability of an unstable mountainous environ that could, and did, go awry obstructing what he hoped to accomplish.

Comparatively, Hastings and his cutoff was an overwhelming success alongside the aforementioned blunders. Hastings *had* been on a majority of the cutoff he proposed, and he at least had a good idea of what to expect on the section he had not personally examined that involved circumnavigating the Ruby Mountains. Hastings was also cognizant of the window of time when crossing the Sierra should not be attempted due to the blizzardly arms of snowstorms that could stop emigrants in their tracks. He self-promoted in print and in person; yet, he was true in keeping to his own advice. Even in the light that he himself had risked in a successful December winter crossing during 1845, it all added up to increase his knowledge base of when *to*, or when *not* to travel. He was painstakingly aware that any attempt to cross the Sierra Nevada after early fall (as stated in his guide book) could mean unpredictable disaster in the mountainous altitudes, which is exactly what befell the Donner Party as it did Fremont.

In contrast to Hastings, Stephen Meek's actions were genuinely misleading. The Mormon handcart companies' late start was outright reprehensible resulting in an appalling loss of life. And lastly, the deadly personal bravado of famed explorer John C. Fremont's notorious Fourth Expedition brought failure and death to others as a consequence of his venture. The bottom line is that although Hastings Cutoff was difficult and did not preclude substantial risk and mileage confusion, he could claim a more than satisfactory degree of experience and trail knowledge. Combined with his leadership and measured guidance, it made his cutting-edge trailblazing wagon route more worthwhile than not. Notwithstanding any assurances that would spare emigrants hardships, there still remains one overpowering distinction of Hastings Cutoff when compared among the three aforementioned disasters, and that is not a single human life was lost among those who followed him in 1846 nor any others until his cutoff was abandoned in 1850.[52]

---

[52] Bagley, Will. *With Golden Visions Bright before Them: Trails to the Mining West, 1849-1852*. Norman: University of Oklahoma Press, 2012. (Pages 279-280).

* By 1847 it was well-known that Hastings Cutoff was difficult and not recommended. There was limited use in 1848-49, and in 1850 it went into favor one last time triggered by the desire to reach the California gold fields as quickly as possible. Out of more than 300 gold seekers who used it, (most with pack animals) there were ten who died *on* the cutoff. The trail itself did not cause their deaths per se. It was from illnesses they possessed *before or when* they entered the cutoff. One death is claimed to be from "fatigue" which was noted by a passing guide, but it's just as likely that the individual suffered from a previous disease, and his death was simply accelerated from debility. The fact remains: No one died as a direct cause of Hastings Cutoff before it deserted for good.

6. The Most Direct Route and a Savings of 350 to 400 Miles

While the Donner-Reed parties moved among the many wagons of the Russell caravan in 1846, travel across the vast prairie to the Platte River was relatively easy. The loss of Sarah Keyes began to slowly fade away over the next several weeks as the routine of each day blended together. Yet, the tedium was often broken by a novel event such as the excitement of seeing a buffalo herd for the first time. Some of the more adventurous braved this opportunity to participate in the dangerous game of chasing down one of the huge beasts just for the thrill of killing it. Everyone else simply looked forward to tasting its lean flesh which helped supplement an already monotonous diet. And with the same head-shaking grin then as today, the meat was cooked using the dried dung of the buffalo themselves as there was a shortage of wood along the river Platte.[53]

As the wagon trains ambled into the wide-screen landscape of the undulating Great Plains, subtle changes were taking shape with every mile in this noticeably arid western land. Indistinctive points on the trail ahead soon revealed themselves to be unique isolated landmarks starting with the blocky appearance of Courthouse Rock, and farther beyond, the exotic funnel-shaped cone of Chimney Rock. Due to the clarity of atmosphere, the distance to reach them was often misjudged by miles, much to the surprise of emigrants. Almost imperceptibly, the land was beginning to give rise to the yet unseen Rocky Mountains whose peaks were still hidden behind a far-reaching horizon over 300 miles away.

The next milestone of the caravan was the approach of the trade forts Bernard and Laramie a few days ahead. Halting at an evening camp along the way, perhaps below the castle-like rock formation of Scotts Bluff, it's not hard to imagine fellow traveler, George McKinstry, pulling out his copy of Lansford Hastings' *Emigrants' Guide* published a year earlier.[54] The booklet's wrapper that once covered the dog-eared pages of small print was missing, but a hand-written replacement replete with the most basic title information was substituted. He may have read aloud to those who gathered about the potential "direct route" to California that caught most everyone's attention with particular interest. Was it somehow connected with Fremont's new route he blazed during his 1845 expedition? Could the rumors and accounts picked up by newspapers hailing it as a major cutoff to California be one and the same? The vague, almost

---

[53] Odor-free and tasteless, the main inconvenience of using "buffalo chips" was the burnt pepper-like ash that filled the air and landed on everything—including food.

[54] George McKinstry was originally from New York where he received medical training before moving on. He eventually became a merchant in Mississippi before going to California for health reasons. His original copy of Hastings' *Emigrants' Guide* survives and is kept at the Bancroft Library.

insignificant passage on pages 137-138 in Hastings' guide was now even more intriguing:

> "The most direct route, for the California emigrants, would be to leave the Oregon route, about two hundred miles east from Fort Hall; thence bearing west southwest, to the Salt Lake; and thence continuing down the bay of St. Francisco, by the route just described."

Those forty-five words Hastings' wrote almost as an afterthought only alluded to a direct connection to California, and at the printing of his book, he only related what he had gleaned from other sources and his own common sense. He merely suggested the conjectural possibility of such a passage. If there is any question as to why he didn't take the "direct route" on his return to California in late 1845, the answer is simple, no one had done it. If he had any ambitions about developing this tantalizing prospect south of the lake, it was a fanciful idea that existed only in the back of his mind. Nevertheless, it would soon become the focal point of Hastings' tarnished future with the Donner Party. Yet, as a testament of his book's value, it would be subsequently reprinted during the years 1847-49 and lastly in 1857. At any rate, his guidebook was not intended to be used as an actual trail map marking off distances, the best camping places, watering holes, and pastures for animals. His promotional guide revolved around preparations, expectations, and the general routes to Oregon or California. It was also laced with the convictions of Manifest Destiny, occasional hyperbole, and political commentary that excited the curiosity of anyone who read it.

Unknown to Hastings in 1845, a coincidence of history was unfolding at the same time he was en route to California. Fremont's Third Expedition pack train was actually pioneering for the first time an intimidating desert route that lay directly west of the Great Salt Lake. A few weeks later, upon Fremont's arrival at Sutter's Fort on December 10th, word spread quickly among Californians about the new route south of the Salt Lake.[55] During Fremont's short stay, news ran wild as the claim was made that the cutoff would shorten the distance to California by up to 400 miles. Just how this mileage savings was determined is somewhat of a mystery, but its source likely came from speculation by Fremont himself or his men who shared information about what they had just accomplished back in October. Adding to the flurry of events, Hastings, who reached Sutter's Fort on December 25, would soon meet with Fremont in mid-January 1846 (and perhaps again with some of his men toward the end of March).[56] There, at Sutter's Fort, Hastings confirmed that the geographic theory of the "direct route" was now a reality, and it was this encounter that propelled his initiative to develop Fremont's recent

---

[55] With a streak of amazing good fortune just shy of disaster, the Stephens-Townsend-Murphy wagon train made a winter crossing of the Sierra in 1844 bringing wagons across the barrier for the first time. Fremont's Second Expedition also made a winter crossing two months later in their wake. The following year he navigated the Sierra during winter once again in 1845 with his Third Expedition, and was trailed the same season by Lansford Hastings' small group. The next year would not be so forgiving for the Donner Party. Even Fremont's luck would finally come to an end during his 1849 Fourth Expedition while attempting a winter passage of the southern Rockies.

[56] Andrews, Thomas F. "Lansford W. Hastings and the Promotion of the Salt Lake Desert Cutoff: A Reappraisal." *The Western Historical Quarterly* 4, no. 2 (April 1973): 133–50. https://doi.org/10.2307/967168.

breakthrough into a wagon road. He realized this would entice an increase of emigration into the resources, wonders, and political realm of Upper California with the added bonus of getting there quickly.

An example of this excitement is captured in a letter sent by Californian Jacob Leese to his friend Thomas Larkin in Alta California's capital, Monterey dated January 12, 1846. It contained a tangle of second-hand news derived from both Fremont and Hastings: [57]

> "Captain Hastings has jest arrived at Sutter, from the U. S. by land with 10 men through the Stoney Mountains [term for the Rockies] 400 miles shorter than has ever been traveled. [Fremont had just completed his new salt flat cutoff that was allegedly 400 miles shorter; Hastings traveled the regular route via Fort Hall.] A Larg [*sic*] Emigration will be through this summer." [News of the "Larg Emigration" came from Hastings.]

His letter is interesting on two counts. The first is that news of the Salt Lake desert cutoff was still based upon Fremont's original mileage saving estimate, but subsequent hearsay and communications from other sources would fluctuate widely over the next several months from an incredible 900 miles to as low as a one-hundred-mile advantage.

The second interesting detail in Leese's letter is the "Larg Emigration" he referred to. This may have been in reference to the Mormon leaders who planned a move west, and who could conceivably send forth a massive migration of their faithful to California. And those emigrant hopefuls might be tempted to take a cutoff that purportedly shaved off hundreds of miles on the way to a new homeland far from the persecutors of their religion.

Contradictory or hearsay reports blended with a mixture of partial or actual facts were commonplace during this turbulent time, and is embodied in a communication written by Thomas Larkin just two months later. A merchant by trade, he was appointed by the United States Government to keep the President informed about events in California. In an excerpt from his correspondence sent to Washington, D. C. dated March 6, 1846, he states an incredibly large mileage benefit derived from Fremont's desert route:

> "Captain Fremont passed three degrees South of Fort Hall, having taken a route supposed to be a desert, which made his distance to California, eight or nine hundred miles less...He describes the new route he followed as preferable, not only on account of the less distance, but less mountainous, with good pasture and well watered."

How Larkin ascertained the wildly unrealistic 800 to 900-mile savings is all but inexplicable since no authority is mentioned. On the other hand, it is interesting that Larkin reasonably approximates the latitude Fremont traveled south of Fort Hall. He also parrots a similar description of the Great Basin as conveyed by Fremont in his January 24 letter to his wife—parts of which would be revealed in the Maryland based *Nile's National Register* newspaper

---

[57] Larkin, Thomas Oliver, and George P. Hammond. *The Larkin Papers: Personal, Business, and Official Correspondence of Thomas Oliver Larkin, Merchant and United States Consul in California.* Vol. IV 1845-1846. Berkeley: University of California Press, 1953.

two months later in May.[58] Nonetheless, it is clear that unsubstantiated rumors integrated with reasonably accurate details were still floating around weeks after Fremont and Hastings had gone their separate ways.

****

Wagon trains arriving at Fort Laramie, about a half day's travel above Fort Bernard, had now advanced nearly 700 miles with relative ease. From this point forward, however, the geography would change dramatically as they approached the distant snow-slashed peaks of the Rockies through the corridor of South Pass. The trail leading to the Pacific flank of the Continental Divide was greatly anticipated as it was the undeniable signpost that they had entered the West proper. But for now, the relative convenience of trading outposts and being able to send mail, trade for necessities and wants, or make repairs was a welcomed respite.

At the first trading post, Fort Bernard, Edwin Bryant, George McKinstry, William Russell and several others, nine in all, decided to exchange their wagons for horses, mules and pack saddles at the smaller establishment.[59] Since they had no families or merchandise to hold them to wagons, this faster mode of travel would allow them to escape the constraints of slower-moving vehicles.[60] But while the partners of the newly formed Bryant-Russell mule train were wheeling and dealing for their outfits, there was an unexpected encounter taking place eight miles ahead among the massive jumble of emigrants, wagons, and Native Americans who encamped around the adobe-walled bastion of Fort Laramie. It was here the chance meeting between James Reed and James Clyman, who was going back to Missouri, took place. A few weeks earlier he had just traversed the newly plotted Hastings Cutoff with the promoter himself and while at Laramie he recorded the following words in his diary for June 27:

> "we met numerous squad of emigrants untill we reached fort Larrimie whare we met Ex govornor [sic] Boggs and party from Jackson county Mi[ss]ouri Bound for California and we camped with them[.] several of us continued the conversation untill a late hour. And here I again obtained a cup of excellent coffee at Judge Morins camp the first I had tasted since in the early part of last winter...."

Although Reed is not mentioned in Clyman's diary, he was likely one of those who

---

[58] Fremont, John Charles., Mary L. Spence, and Donald Jackson. *Expeditions of John Charles Fremont., v. 2: The Bear Flag Revolt and the Court-Martial*. First. Vol. 2. Place of publication not identified, IL: University of Illinois Press, 1973.

[59] They backtracked from Laramie realizing they could get a better deal at Bernard where their transaction took place. The short-lived trade post opened in 1845 to compete with Laramie, but burned down the following year under suspicious circumstances. By now Russell had resigned as leader of the wagon train and was replaced by William M. Boggs. Clyman camped with the newly outfitted Bryant-Russell pack train after leaving Fort Laramie.

[60] The Bryant-Russell mule train quickly outdistanced their former wagon train on their way to Fort Bridger. When news of Hastings new cutoff was confirmed, they would be the first group to take the cutoff guided by Hastings' partner James Hudspeth. Emigrants with wagons, including the large Harlan and Young companies, would be led by Hastings himself as he pledged in his open letter.

"continued the conversation untill a late hour." Clyman, who had originally gone west for a more healthful climate years earlier, had become a revered mountain man. Among his more adventuresome exploits, he and a small group of trappers became the first to circumnavigate the Great Salt Lake before he wandered back to Illinois.[61] There, Clyman and Reed became acquainted when they enlisted for duty in the Black Hawk (or Sauk) War under the leadership of a future president, Abraham Lincoln. After the war, the two men went their own ways following their individual pursuits. Clyman continued his western ventures and offered his services as a seasoned guide. Reed, on the other hand, forged ahead with his many enterprises involving various businesses in Springfield. Their encounter many years later at Fort Laramie must have been a pleasant surprise for both men as they relived their past and present times. As the evening drifted into night and the campfires dimmed, there is little doubt that a discussion of the new cutoff Clyman had just completed became a topic of interest.[62]

On a historical level, there is some controversy as to what exactly came up during the late-night conversation, and who specifically was there on June 27. It must have included James Reed, yet he never mentions him, nor is there any reference to Hastings Cutoff. He was more impressed by the excellent coffee he enjoyed. However, twenty-five years later, Clyman provided a renewed clarity of that day stated in a biographical sketch of his life as recorded by R. T. Montgomery on May 8, 1871. The interview included a number of interesting specifics that were not noted in his diary during his short layover at Fort Laramie:

> "Mr. Reed, while we were encamped at Laramie was enquiring about the route [Hastings Cutoff]. I told him to "take the regular wagon track, and never leave it—it is barely possible to get through if you follow it—and it may be impossible if you don't." Reed replied, "There is a nigher [closer] route, and it is of no use to take so much of a roundabout course [meaning going all the way to Fort Hall]." I admitted the fact, but told him about the great desert and the roughness of the Sierras, and that a straight route might turn out to be impracticable."

Clyman's much more detailed recollection of his conversation with Reed two and a half decades later is a little puzzling and warrants a number of questions. It seems as though Reed already knew about the cutoff Clyman had just crossed when they met at Fort Laramie. If Clyman's memory is to be accepted at face value, he recalled that Reed did not say *if* there is a nigher route; he said there *is* a nigher route. Reed, therefore, seemingly appeared to have some knowledge of the cutoff and had made up his mind at Fort Laramie to take it even before

---

[61] The career expectancy of a mountain man until death by a wide variety of causes was about four years. Many found that life was much easier by setting up small trading posts or offering their services as guides. Those who beat the odds like James Clyman, and Jim Bridger for example, were celebrated.

[62] A day later on June 28, another topic of interest quietly takes place. Virginia Reed becomes a teenager, but no birthday celebration is observed as we know it: no cake, no cards, no gifts. There was perhaps only a simple mention of her entrance into the world by her mother. Americans in the mid nineteenth century simply did not celebrate birthdays as we do today.

speaking with Clyman who conceded that Fort Hall was a "roundabout course."

For those in the 1846 emigration to California, the seed of an improved mile-cutting route might well have been gleaned a full year before the Donner-Reed party had even formed. Persistent, optimistic information abounded and was temptingly available before any company set out on the trail in 1846, and the most famous explorer of the time, Fremont, was on the cutting edge of new geographical knowledge leading newspapers to suggest his purpose and intentions with alluring statements. The scene was set for what would seem to be a logical risk for the Donner Party in the coming months. A 300 to 400 mile savings to California would soon be stated by Fremont, unwittingly crowed by others, and echoed by Hastings who seemed to have some reservations of the distance saved, but would soon promote the advantage of the new route south of the Great Salt Lake and make it a reality for wagon travel.

So what led Reed to think there was a cutoff south of the Salt Lake before meeting Clyman? He knew the logical prospect of the alleged cutoff based on Hastings' description in his *Emigrants' Guide*. More importantly, accounts from Fremont's scientific expedition had also trickled in filling newspaper columns in frontier towns as well as states east of the Mississippi.

The Independence, [Missouri] *Westport Expositor* reported, according to the *Missouri Reporter* that on June 26, 1845, its understanding of what Fremont intended to do on his third exploring tour of the West. It is stated that he will "complete the survey of the great Salt Lake." The newspaper also states that "It will probably eventuate in the discovery of a new and straight road both to Oregon and California, passing for the most part through our own territory, diminishing the distance some three or four hundred miles and the time two months."

It is very likely that the Donner-Reed company had ample access and opportunity to have read the contents of those papers or discussed with others the implication of Fremont's expedition. This very likely influenced Reed and others in their decision to consider Hastings Cutoff. Reed himself would later write to his brother-in-law stating that he understood Hastings Cutoff to be a savings of "350 or 400 hundred miles."

Another such enticing report came from E. A. Farwell, a returning emigrant to New Orleans from California by sea via Mexico. The content of the April 22, 1846 *Picayune* likely did not go unnoticed by James Reed and others when it reported the following information:

> "… having had the pleasure of conversing with a gentleman [Farwell] who arrived in town on Monday direct from California … The most important intelligence he had brought related to Fremont, who had reached Sutter's … with a force of about sixty mounted men, and who had been so fortunate as to discover a new route, or pass, by which California can be reached by emigrants in sixty days less time than by the old route via Oregon. This new route is perfectly practicable for wheeled vehicles, and when it comes to be generally known, will give a renewed impetus to emigration to California."

The new "route, or pass" Farwell speaks of is the future Hastings Cutoff. However, his claim that "California can be reached by emigrants in sixty days less time" was a gross exaggeration. The entire journey typically took 120 days, and there was no way a single cutoff was going to reduce travel time by half. It wasn't long before other newspapers such as

Missouri's *Jefferson Inquirer* of April 29 printed that Fremont had "discovered a good wagon road," or the *Missouri Republican* of May 5, 1846 that repeated similar news. It is clear that a variety of media sources were accessible and read by emigrants like the Donner-Reed party before they headed out across the frontier.

There is also the tantalizing possibility that Reed may have known of Fremont's letter to his wife that appeared in the *Nile's National Register* May 16 edition, even though Reed's group left Independence four days earlier.[63] The article disclosed Fremont's explorations of the Great Salt Lake and crossing the Great Basin in October 1845 (on the soon to be Hastings Cutoff). Fremont also states that the basin itself is not barren in general but is lined with ranges of mountains, covered with grasses of the best quality, wooded with trees, and full of deer and mountain sheep. He paints a disarming picture leading one to believe that the route he had just traveled was relatively straightforward while glossing over the difficulties posed by an extensive desert of salt.[64] Fremont even goes as far as to say that "for wagons, the road is decidedly far better."

****

When the Bryant-Russell mule train resumed their journey beyond Fort Laramie into South Pass on their way to Fort Bridger, they came across the lone horseman Wales Bonney on July 10 carrying Hastings' open letter regarding his new cutoff. Bryant recorded that he would "not recite the main contents of the letter" but affirmed it hinted that the California Government (still under Mexican control at this time) would oppose American emigrants and "invited those bound to California to concentrate their numbers and strength, and to take the new route which had been explored by Mr. H., from Fort Bridger via the south end of the Salt Lake, by which the distance would be materially shortened."

Moving quickly, on a late July evening six days later, Bryant's small pack train happened upon the promoter himself, Lansford Hastings, and his partner James Hudspeth who had made camp near Fort Bridger. The two men had just been beyond South Pass to meet emigrants on the trail encouraging them to take the new route and send off Hastings' open letter with Wales Bonney previously encountered by Bryant. Passing the night with Hastings and Hudspeth, Bryant put into words what they said about their recent trip from California as "having explored a new route via the south end of the great Salt Lake, by which they suppose the distance to California is shortened from one hundred and fifty to two hundred miles." This must have been in reference to emigrants heading to California from Fort Hall. Hastings' proposed mileage savings was perhaps the distance they believed to be gained by not going to Fort Hall from Bridger, plus an additional one hundred miles or so directly attributed to the cutoff itself. It's important to point out that no one, including Fremont, had actually measured the distance of the new trail, so estimates were just that and variations would be expected.

---

[63] It was not unusual for current news to catch-up with emigrants who were already on the trail by someone either returning or starting out days later.

[64] Kit Carson, another member of Fremont's Third Expedition and one of the very first to cross the Salt Desert, stated years later that he "travelled on about sixty miles [and found] no water or grass."

The day after Bryant met Bonney, the wagon train of Charles L. Putnam of Kentucky intercepted the solitary courier and took the opportunity to send a letter to his father Joseph under the heading "Sweetwater 220 miles from Fort Hall," July 11, 1846."[65]

> Dear Father [,]
> "There is a gentleman in our camp [Wales Bonney]. He arrived late this evening bringing a letter from Mr. Hastings, which stated that he, (Mr. Hastings) would wait at the Salt Lake 60 miles from Fort Hall [Putnam appears to be misinformed here as Hastings planned to meet emigrants at Fort Bridger.] & from thence take us a new route to California which would make a difference of 300 miles nearer. But if it is his design to aid in Revolutionizing the country and to get us to aid him in immortalizing himself, he will find himself, vastly mistaken." [He also relates:] "If there is any danger we will not go to California. But to Umqua river in Oregon 250 miles from Suitor's [Sutter's] settlement in California a beautiful valley which is spoken of highly by Hastings & everyone who has seen or written about it."

When Charles Putnam read Hastings' open letter, it suggested that his new cutoff would not only entice emigrants to go to California over Oregon on an expedient cutoff for which Hastings was actively recruiting, but also to appeal to American boosterism—in effect, the Manifest Destiny of California. Putnam seems to imply that this was in reference to Hastings' siren for American influence in the vulnerable Mexican province of Alta California. Hastings again urged these emigrants to reach California quickly and to be on the ready for action if necessary. If Hastings was attempting to "immortalize himself," Putnam was having none of it. He makes it clear in no uncertain terms that he would head to Oregon for land, not conflict in California. In fact, Putnam outright rejected Hastings' new cutoff with the rejoinder that "If hereafter we find it would be to our advantage to go [to] California it is but 250 miles [to Fort Hall] over a road which has been often travelled."[66]

This is about as far as Hastings would be immortalized. He never had any real intentions to make himself the leader of a California revolution let alone "President" of the upper Mexican province. Besides, by the time Hastings had arrived in California, after departing from the wagon trains he led to the Humboldt River, war in California raged and would once and for all close the window for anyone's supposed ambitions.

Those "ambitions" were rooted in Bidwell and Sutter's distrust of Hastings who spoke

---

[65] Morgan, Dale. "New and Nearer Routes." In *Overland in 1846*. Reprint, Lincoln: University of Nebraska, 1993.
[66] ibid

* Eight days ahead of Putnam, John R. McBride gives us the only physical description of Hastings stating that "on the morning of the 3rd of July, 1846, we met about twenty miles east of the summit of the South Pass, Lansford W. Hastings, [who] had come all the distance from Sutter's Fort on the Sacramento River, California to meet the emigrant trains and pilot them by a new route, discovered by himself [actually Fremont "discovered" it], to the paradise of the Pacific—as he insisted California was. He had but a single companion, and a Mexican vaquero. His companion's name was Hudspeth, and he was about as repulsive in manner as Hastings was attractive. He was a coarse, profane creature, who seemed to feel that loud swearing was the best title to public favor." [McBride went on to describe Hastings as] "a tall, fine-looking man, with light brown hair and beard, dressed in a suit of elegant pattern made of buckskin, handsomely embroidered and trimmed at the collar and openings, plucked with beaver fur... an ideal representative of the mountaineer."

freely about his not so subtle American expansionist viewpoint. Hastings was not one to hide his opinions, and Sutter remained wary of his politics even though he always cordially greeted him and joined him in various partnership agreements. By being so overt as to where his loyalties lay, Sutter saw him as a forcible threat to the stability of his frontier outpost. This may also be one of the key reasons why some of the assimilated foreigners residing in California, for example Thomas Larkin, disliked his book. He viewed Hastings' guide as a veiled menace to upset the current Mexican regime in Alta California whereas sympathetic Californios might otherwise be won over to achieve the same end peacefully.

Nevertheless, talk is just talk, yet Bidwell seemed to be particularly bothered by Hastings. He unjustifiably blamed Hastings of plotting to be the game-changing leader of an American takeover, and making himself a would-be president ruling over an independent California republic.[67] It was Bidwell's accusations which has caused the most damage to his reputation by perpetuating an image of the man that Bidwell, whose unidentified source, he later admitted, was hearsay. Unfortunately, this unfair judgement of Hastings has been solidified by authors and historians who persist in promulgating it to this very day.[68]

****

On July 16, shortly after Charles Putnam sent off his letter, Edwin Bryant arrived at Fort Bridger the same day the Harlan and Young wagon trains pulled up to decide whether or not to take the cutoff. In his spare time, Bryant vividly described the outpost as "two or three miserable log-cabins, rudely constructed, and bearing but a faint resemblance to habitable houses."[69] More importantly, in addition to Hastings, mountain man Joseph Walker was there

---

[67] Like Bidwell, Larkin was very cordial in his correspondence with Hastings and seemingly befriended him, but behind his back Larkin was a different creature. He determined that Hastings' guide was "very untrue and absurd" and that "No general reader will read one quarter of the book." He presumably disregarded everything but the hyperbole in his publication. He was also wary of Hastings' intentions, quoting his book that stated "The tide of emigration…is unparalleled in the annals of history. The eyes of the American people are now turned westward, and thousands are gazing with the most intense interest…upon the Pacific shores." U. S. Consul Larkin informed the government about Hastings' innuendo as if President Polk did not have similar thoughts on the inclusion of California.

[68] Andrews, Thomas F. "Lansford W. Hastings and the Promotion of the Salt Lake Desert Cutoff: A Reappraisal." *The Western Historical Quarterly* 4, no. 2 (April 1973): 133–50. https://doi.org/10.2307/967168.
* Many years later Bidwell acknowledged that his evidence about Hastings possible motives in California was based on hearsay. The evidence supporting this is found in the document *"California, 1841-48," [dictation for H. H. Bancroft, 1877], 110-111, MS, Bancroft Library, University of California, Berkeley*. Bidwell's damning judgment has led to countless suspicions about Hastings and accepted as fact by writers and historians alike making it nearly impossible to separate the man from what he never did or would never do.

[69] Edwin Bryant, a physician of some training and a journalist residing in Kentucky, decided to go see California for himself with the hope that a better climate would benefit his health. He also kept a journal of his entire trip with the intention of publishing his experiences out west. Arriving in California, he participated in the War with Mexico, and afterwards became a judge of the courts for a short time until he returned to Lexington, Kentucky. Just missing the Gold Rush before he went home, his publication based on his western travels entitled *What I Saw in California*

too. If the two men spoke to each other, nothing was recorded even though it would seem likely that they did. Walker was a guide during Fremont's Third Expedition and had been in the group who crossed the Salt Lake desert via Secret Pass to the Humboldt River where the regular California Trail intersected. Walker, although he personally did not care for the cutoff, may have been the one who reiterated that the distance saved in reaching California was 350 to 400 miles. This must have been questionable in Hastings' mind having just traveled the route himself, and Hastings was more conservative in his estimate of the 300 mile savings that he promoted.

When Bryant was introduced to Walker, he noted that he spoke "discouragingly" of the cutoff. This reinforced Bryant's similar unfavorable impression of the cutoff as well, but pack trains had already traversed the route twice and perhaps there was room for improvement. Wagons would complicate matters, yet they kept arriving at the fort intent on taking the cutoff as they waited for Hastings to make the call to start. Stragglers, if any, would have to catch up as best they could or simply take the regular route to California via Fort Hall. By this time, Bryant concluded that wheeled vehicles, especially with families in tow, was too risky an endeavor and felt that they should stay on the regular Fort Hall road. Because of his conviction, he consequently wrote letters to his friends who he anticipated might be farther back on the trail, including one for James Reed, with the advice that he should not "hazard experiments" with his family on the new untested wagon path. It was a letter Reed would never receive.

By mid-July, most of the wagons on the forefront of Hastings' new road had gathered at Bridger. While waiting at the ramshackle establishment crowded with more than 300 persons, it is Hastings who appears to have reduced his original three-hundred-mile savings he promoted down to 250 or perhaps 200. These figures may have come from different conversations with two men: Doctor T. Pope Long and an unnamed "correspondent." Long may have got his information based on the idea that circumnavigating the Rubies could add about 50 miles to the journey (It would actually add about 127). Thus, it would reduce 50 of the 300 mile savings. On the other hand, in a separate exchange with the unnamed correspondent, it was believed to be a savings of 200 miles. This may have been based on the subtraction of miles from Bridger to the base of the Wasatch which was about one hundred miles and where the cutoff extended into the Great Basin proper. Regardless, Long shared his newfound information gleaned from Hastings himself when he wrote to his brother in Missouri from Fort Bridger on July 19, 1846:

> "We arrived here on Thursday, and are now waiting for a sufficient number of wagons, in order to take a nearer route crossing the country on the south end of the great salt lake. This route will cut off at least 250 miles, and is the one through which Capt. Fremont passed last season. Mr. Hastings...reports the route perfectly practicable for wagons.... About forty wagons are now with us waiting to take the cutoff....We have received news that war is raging between the U. States and Mexico....We will arrive in California, I think, about the middle of September...."

---

was printed in 1848. It quickly became very popular capturing the imaginations of Americans throughout the country. He comitted suicide in 1869.

Of additional interest, are the words of the unnamed correspondent at Bridger whose letter was published in the *Missouri Republican*. He wrote that Hastings planned to "conduct them in by the new route, by the foot of the Salt Lake [near the base of the Wasatch], discovered by capt. Fremont, which is said to be two hundred miles nearer...."[70]

Both writers mention Fremont, one of the most popular and celebrated explorers of the time lending credibility and putting to rest the improbability that this route would fail to be advantageous. Long and others were aware of this. Having taken the route via Secret Pass in reverse, Hastings understood the mileage savings by mule train on that route, but realized that Secret Pass was in no way practical for wagons. He would have to find a way through or around the Rubies as Fremont had done. This awareness undoubtedly led to a more conservative revision of the mileage savings anticipated. He touted the route as "perfectly practicable for wagons," but three algebraic factors remained to be integrated into Hastings' proposed route from Fort Bridger. Exactly what would be the best wagon descent down the Wasatch from Bridger into the Great Basin? How much additional time would slower moving wagons add to the long desert stretch overall, and where would the Rubies be intersected? Hastings could not be sure. No one was. But he knew enough to know that it could be done.

Long was certainly aware of Hastings' open letter proposing that his cutoff would be a 300 mile advantage. At Fort Bridger, Hastings was undoubtedly the source of the more conservative 50 mile deduction. And if anything indicates the ongoing modifications of a work in progress. He could only base his revised estimations on the route that he took himself via Secret Pass on the northern end of the Ruby Mountain Range, and upon reassessment, reduced the savings. Since this pass was not practical for wagons, Hastings would have to guide them on an alternate route south along that range until he could find either an admissible gap somewhere along the way, or, if necessary, go completely around the Rubies. He knew Fremont had pursued a similar course before turning west, so Hastings was not blindly leading through sheer guesswork even though he had never been on that stretch of Fremont's road (and has been heavily criticized because of it). As far as he was concerned, logic dictated that this variation for wheeled vehicles would still reduce miles, but just how much of a gain would be unknown until it was explored. Possibly it would be within a 50 mile difference from Secret Pass, and an overall improvement of the Fort Hall route by 200 miles depending on where the starting point was assumed.

In another letter, an unknown sender wrote to the *Missouri Republican* in July 1846: ..."the new route, by the foot of Salt Lake, discovered by capt. Fremont... is said to be two hundred miles nearer than the old one, by Fort Hall."[71] This would still be a significant mileage

---

[70] Morgan, Dale. *Overland in 1846*. Lincoln: University of Nebraska Press, 1993.

[71] Korns, J. Roderic, and Dale L. Morgan. *West from Fort Bridger: The Pioneering of Immigrant Trails across Utah, 1846-1850: Original Diaries and Journals*. Logan: Utah State University Press, 1994.

savings in contrast to the Fort Hall route if true. Nevertheless, the statement "which is said to be two hundred miles nearer" is important as it expresses uncertainty, keeping in mind that events were very fluid and could change rapidly. The letter does not dispute a mileage advantage for those considering the cutoff, at least with pack animals, but wagons would be much slower—especially when breaking trail and then having to reroute along the Ruby Mountains to avoid Secret Pass which would add extra miles to some degree. And as noted in the letter, Fremont's trail started "by the foot of Salt Lake." It was Hastings who extended the cutoff up the Wasatch to Fort Bridger.[72]

Regardless of the risk, the Bryant-Russell pack train, unencumbered by wagons, decided that they would take the cutoff. Leaving the fort on July 20, they were led by James Hudspeth and his three companions on horseback. (Hastings would set out the same day leading wagons). In lieu of Hastings current appraisal of the cutoff's advantage of 150 to 200 miles, the proprietors of the trade post, Bridger and Vasquez, would repeat Joseph Walker's more glowing assessment that, although difficult, it supposedly stripped off 350 to 400 miles to California. And of course, they did not want to deflect any business the new cutoff would bring. Since Fort Hall would be bypassed altogether by the California bound, anything they could say to emigrants to make it sound favorable was expressed—even to such late arrivals as the Donner Party who rolled into Fort Bridger a week later.[73]

****

Upon leaving Fort Laramie, the Boggs (formerly Russell) caravan still included the nine Donner-Reed wagons. Traveling about two hundred miles farther west, they reached the famous granite landmark of Independence Rock in modern Wyoming. There, near the whale-shaped feature, they too came across the mounted wayfarer Wales Bonney who once again shared Hastings' open letter encouraging emigrants to take his new cutoff boasting a 300 mile advantage and that he pledged to guide the emigrants himself. At this point, if Reed had any reservations about the cutoff after speaking with Clyman, the contents of the public letter put them all to rest.

Continuing west, the wagon train ascended the corridor of South Pass leading into the Rocky Mountains and over the Continental Divide where the watersheds now drained toward

---

* This is interesting because the information seems to be a hybrid of Hastings' assessment in his book suggesting that emigrants leave the trail "about two hundred miles east from Fort Hall" combined with the fact that Fremont had opened a new route south the Salt Lake the previous year. The unknown person who is the source of this information could not have known that Hastings was, in fact, going to make Fort Bridger the departure-point for his new cutoff. Thus, the writer could only surmise that the new route starts "by the foot of Salt Lake."

[72] Fremont's 1845 approach to the Great Salt Lake came from the south. He did not enter the Wasatch Mountains at any time unlike Hastings who planned to meet emigrants at the Fort Bridger-Hall junction within that range.

[73] Gilbert, Bil. *Westering Man: The Life of Joseph Walker*. Norman, OK: University of Oklahoma Press, 1985.
* It is interesting that Walker actually met the Donner Party east of Fort Bridger. He was told they were heading for Hastings Cutoff of which Walker warned them not to take, but his advice was ignored.

the Pacific. Eighteen miles beyond the pass, a fork in the trail was encountered that would later be called the Parting of the Ways. Here, the emigrants of the Boggs wagon train were invited to pause for a decision. Wagons heading to Oregon (or California) could split to the right taking Greenwood Cutoff to Fort Hall. Those veering left set their bearing toward Fort Bridger and the start of Hastings Cutoff about a hundred miles away. From there, they would still have the option of taking the California Trail to Fort Hall which was another 85 miles away if they chose to do so. Subsequently, nineteen wagons made up of eleven families (two more would be added later), and a number of single individuals, decided to break left.[74] Soon thereafter, an election was held for the captaincy of the new caravan. It ended in James Reed's defeat perhaps due to his somewhat overly presumptuous personality in contrast to the more popular, easy-going George Donner—and with his leadership, the emergence of the Donner Party.[75]

When the newly formed Donner Party arrived at Fort Bridger on July 28, they learned that Hastings had left eight days earlier. Even so, they spent the next four days resting and acquiring replacement oxen that Reed and both Donner brothers lost from drinking pools of bad water. New animals were purchased from Bridger and Vasquez who Reed referred to as "excellent and accommodating gentlemen." The fort's proprietors also greeted the Donner Party with a more generous cutoff estimate of 350 to 400 miles. Reed was already allured by the savings claim of 300 miles carried by Wales Bonney, and now the cutoff took on an additional contradictory bonus of up to 400 miles. There might have been some suspicion of exactly how many miles the cutoff actually saved in Reed's mind, but Vasquez and his partner were very persuasive and obliging so Reed's guard was down; he knew that this cutoff was a work in progress, and it was not unusual for information to change over the course of a short period of time. However, with the advantage of the cutoff being even better than initially anticipated, it was an easy choice to make. Besides, Hastings was far ahead leading dozens of wagons, and Reed was more determined than ever to take it.

Surprisingly, the letter Bryant left for Reed warning him to avoid Hastings Cutoff was not forthcoming. It somehow escaped the attention of Vasquez (Bridger was illiterate) to hand over the letter which lends to the suspicion that the missive might have been read by Vasquez and then accidentally "forgotten." After all, the success of Hastings new route would attract emigrants who would normally have gone to the British outpost Fort Hall via Greenwood Cutoff— it was a motive the two shrewd mountain men shared and they used every opportunity to keep their establishment relevant. On July 31, 1846, the same day the Donner Party set out on the trail following Hastings' tracks, Reed sent off his own letter to his brothers-in-law back in Illinois. The letter's contents would eventually be shared in his hometown *Sangamo Journal*

---

[74] The eleven families, excluding singles, were made up of the Reed, George Donner, Jacob Donner, Breen, Eddy, Murphy, Foster, Pike, Keseberg, Fosdick, and Wolfinger. The McCutchens joined at Fort Bridger. The Graves family with their three wagons would be the thirteenth and last to join the Donner Party when they caught up with them in the Wasatch.

[75] George Donner was the wagon leader in name only. James Reed, although annoying to a number of emigrants in the party, was still valued for his decisiveness and natural ability to lead. Thus, he was the de facto leader.

newspaper in which Reed's communication details a relatively optimistic picture of Hastings' new "better route."

> "I want to inform the emigration that they can be supplied with fresh cattle by Messrs. Vasques & Bridger...and they can be relied on to do business honorably and fairly... They are the only fair traders in these parts. On the new route we will not have dust, as there are about 60 waggons ahead of us. There is, however, or thought to be, one stretch of 40 miles without water; but Hastings and his party, are out a-head examining for water, or for a route to avoid this stretch."

As for the "40 miles without water," Vasquez was at least partially correct informing Reed. He was also correct in that James Hudspeth was, in fact, "out a-head examining for water." This search was driven by his earlier experience with the eastbound Hastings-Clyman pack train where it was determined that the brackish water at Redlum Spring was not adequate for large numbers of emigrants and their animals. Hudspeth was unable to find adequate water on his way out with Bryant's pack train all the way to the summit pass of the Cedar Mountains. There he said goodbye to the nine members of the Bryant-Russell train and loudly proclaimed with outstretched arms "Now boys, put spurs to your mules and ride like hell!"[76] And with that melodramatic scene, Hudspeth and his three companions headed back to assist Hastings in leading emigrant wagon trains down the Wasatch. On his return, however, Hudspeth, through close observation and good fortune, did locate a large group of springs—Hope Wells—10 miles east from Redlum and 13 to the Cedar Mountain crossing that led to the salt flats. The springs would more than adequately address the immediate needs of wagon trains, but there still remained a large span of desert without sufficient water before reaching Pilot Spring. This meant carrying water for the first 40 miles to where the next 40 or so would be the actual "dry drive." It is of little wonder then, that a complicated crush of information exchange led to misevaluated confusion with serious consequences that the Donner Party would soon realize. Nevertheless, events were well into motion, and there was no turning back.

---

[76] While at Fort Bridger, Bryant was able to ascertain that the "Salt Plain" was somewhere between 60 and 80 miles (75 according to Joseph Walker's estimate). This begs the question as to why the Donner Party did not know this as well? Reed knew about the 40 mile "waterless" section, but was unaware that the total desert length was 60 to 80 miles. Before the members of the Bryant-Russell group crossed the Salt Desert, they filled the only vessel they had in their possession: A gallon-sized empty powder keg filled with some camp coffee topped off with impure sulphur-tasting water taken from a very small unnamed spring (Redlum) that they had to "excavate" by hand to obtain. The bottom line is that the Hastings Cutoff mileage advantage was not clear cut, and it should not be surprising that it was constantly being revised.

7. Clyman's 40

When Lansford Hastings and his eastbound mule train left Sutter's Fort during April 1846, he had one goal in mind: Open a wagon route south of the Salt Lake in the wake of Fremont's explorations. At Johnson's Ranch just before crossing the Sierra, Hastings' small group was joined by several others that included frontiersman James Clyman. A few weeks later they had reached the headwaters of the Humboldt River and worked their way to the northern end of the Ruby Mountains where they slipped through the narrows of Secret Pass. While there, Hastings no doubt took note that westbound wagons would have to skirt the Rubies to the south at that point since Secret Pass would require too much road work to justify the effort. Moving at a brisk pace, it wasn't long before they arrived at the base of Pilot Peak and the spring below it that was variously named Bonnark, Pilot, and eventually Donner Spring. Here, they could view for the first time the massive floor of an extinct lake; a seemingly limitless salt plain far beyond the reach of sight which was not as adequately described by Fremont as Hastings had envisioned during their brief acquaintance.[77]

The peril that lay ahead certainly caused everyone in the Hastings-Clyman pack train to soberly confront what they were about to get into.[78] But if the cutoff was to be a success, crossing the formidable Salt Desert had to be overcome in order to continue reconnaissance all the way to Fort Bridger where emigrants could be met. Filling anything that held water, the small troupe moved forward with single-minded urgency mixed with genuine fear under the reserved confidence of James Clyman and the resolute determination of Lansford Hastings. It was here that a cutting-edge wagon route would be forged upon Fremont's conviction that this was a major improvement deviating from the traditional California Trail.

There has been much discussion as to the actual length of the Salt Desert. Accounts range from as high as 90 miles to a low end of about 60. Hastings himself claimed it was 55 miles having traveled the route in reverse although his figure was a guess since he had no way to accurately measure it, but surprisingly, his reckoning was not far off the mark.[79] Others, such

---

[77] Andrews, Thomas F. "Lansford W. Hastings and the Promotion of the Salt Lake Desert Cutoff: A Reappraisal." *The Western Historical Quarterly* 4, no. 2 (April 1973): 133–50. https://doi.org/10.2307/967168.

[78] Hastings may not have realized how intimidating the Salt Desert was until he witnessed it first-hand. Fremont never mentions any difficulty in crossing it, and doesn't seem to provide Hastings with any concerning information when they met. Joseph Walker, who was with Fremont, later spoke "discouragingly" of it when Bryant met with him at Fort Bridger. By then Hastings had already crossed it himself and decided that it was doable. Years later members of Fremont's Third Expedition recalled that the desert stretch took two days to cross, the road had become muddy, and the expedition lost ten mules and several horses.

[79] Korns, J. Roderic, Dale Morgan, Will Bagley, and Harold Schindler. *West from Fort Bridger: The Pioneering of Immigrant Trails across Utah, 1846-1850: Original Diaries and Journals*. Revised Ed. Logan, Utah: Utah State University Press, 1994. *Hastings' thought the Salt Desert was 55 miles. This conclusion may have been in

as Virginia Reed, a young member of the Donner Party, asserted years later that "Haistings [*sic*] said it was 40 but i think it was 80 miles." She, as well as other members of the Donner Party, were told there would be a 40-mile section of waterless desert, but what was not foreseen was the *overall* distance of the desert. As it turned out, it would be about 80 miles based on where the Donner Party would later take their final water at Hope Wells. This, however, was not clear until their arrival at that point of their journey. This uncertainty would contribute to considerable suffering for the many wagon trains ahead of them, and it would be even worse for the Donner Party who continued to fall farther behind.

Hastings was gone by the time the Donner Party arrived at Fort Bridger, so the source of Virginia's second-hand information came from Vasquez or Bridger who had either spoken with Hastings directly, or conversed with emigrants who had spoken with Clyman while on his way back to Missouri (as he did with James Reed at Fort Laramie). Clyman's belief that the "dry drive" of 35 to 40 miles long was based upon his experience without water when he crossed the "great desert" with Hastings. In the ensuing report provided by the proprietors of Fort Bridger, members of the Donner Party seem to have misunderstood that the "dry drive" was not the overall distance of the Salt Desert, but only a defined portion of the cutoff. Mystifying the situation even more was Reed's convoluted mileage in a letter to his Illinois brothers-in-law when he stated that he is just 250 miles from California "while by the way of Fort Hall it is 650 or 700 miles—making a great saving in favor of jaded oxen and dust…"[80]

The source of the "dry drive" which was intermingled with the total distance of the Salt Desert can be found within James Clyman's eastbound trek with Hastings as recorded in his personal journal. He wrote in his diary on May 28, 1846, that they left their camp at the base of "Pilot Peak," crossed a desert plain, passed an "Island of rocks" [Silver Island] and made a "bold trot" until dusk where camp was made for the night at Grayback Mountain without water or "one spear of vegetation." In his diary he notes that he had been told that if Fremont's trail could be followed, there would be no more that 20 miles between water.[81] Unfortunately, this optimistic hope proved to be elusive, and the dry stretch was now based upon an understanding that when you "carry" water, you *have* water until it runs out, and only then does one calculate the distance without water *to* water.[82] The seasoned frontiersman revealed that when Hastings'

---

conjunction with James Clyman when they traveled across it together. Based from Redlum Spring to Pilot Spring, the mileage is about 70 miles.

[80] Morgan, Dale L. *Overland in 1846: Diaries and Letters of the California-Oregon Trail. Vol. 1.* Lincoln, Neb.: University of Nebraska Press, 1993.

[81] Clyman, James, and Charles Lewis. Camp. *James Clyman, Frontiersman: The Adventures of a Trapper and Covered-Wagon Emigrant as Told in His Own Reminiscences and Diaries.* Portland, OR: Champoeg Press, 1960.

[82] This is conjecture, but it may help explain the discrepancy of how a 70 to 80-mile stretch was reduced to a 35 to 40-mile waterless stretch. Hastings did not represent the entire distance of the desert as 40 miles, but the distance after carried water was gone. However, the Fort Bridger proprietors repeated the 40 mile "dry drive" that came from Hastings or Clyman who spoke to emigrants on the trail.

pack train crossed Fremont's desert route, they suffered through a 35 mile "dry" crossing. He was not referring to the length of the entire desert, but only a waterless segment.

As an experienced mountain man who had been in this area years earlier, Clyman certainly shared his wisdom with Hastings as they traveled. Leaving the spring at Pilot Peak with carried water, they likely ran out about 20 miles before reaching Grayback Mountain where Clyman believed that the distance from Pilot Peak was "40 miles." The next day, May 29, after spending a long waterless night at Grayback, the group continued their trek across "one more plain" before traversing the pass of the Cedar Mountains. Descending the eastern side of the same range, the waterless stretch finally ended at Redlum Spring (also known as Dell or Sulphur) about 15 miles from where they started out that day. Clyman records being without water for a total of about 35 miles, so they "unpacked for the day" at the spring having traveled "20 hours and 30 hours without water[.]"[83]

Clyman assessed the waterless segment at about 35 miles but may have included an additional five miles to err on the side of prudence since the mileage he calculated was based solely on experience. By Clyman's reckoning, the entire Salt Desert crossing from Pilot Spring to Redlum was estimated at 55 miles but was actually closer to 67. Moreover, it was Clyman's calculations of traveling without water that would become confused with the overall distance of the Salt Desert as evidenced by Virginia Reed's statement. Nevertheless, the ultimate mileage would be based on variations between water sources on either side of the Salt Desert that would determine how the distance was calculated. For example, Thomas Hemings Jefferson, a map maker and one of the first to cross Hastings Cutoff by wagon, measured the stretch for the first time using some type of wagon wheel odometer. He gauged the distance starting from Hope Wells where the caravan he traveled with took on water for the last time. From there it was another 13 miles to Redlum Spring (which was not used), and another 3 miles to cross the pass at the head of the Cedar Mountain Range where the extensive salt flat was exposed in all of its frightful glory. At this point, the sand and salt-encrusted plain that Jefferson was measuring

---

[83] Clyman, James. James Clyman, Frontiersman: Definitive Edition. Portland: Champoeg Press, 1960.332n194

*The eastbound Hastings-Clyman pack train eventually worked their way up various canyons of the Wasatch Mountains taking into consideration the best way to blaze a wagon route. They arrived at Fort Bridger in early June only to find it vacant. At this juncture, Clyman and some others took leave and headed up the trail toward Fort Hall where he met his former trapping partner Louis Vasquez. He was on his way to meet his partner Jim Bridger for the travel season when he encountered Clyman. He could have easily informed Vasquez that the dry drive across the desert he had just completed was 35 to 40 miles without water. At the same time, Hastings with his partner James Hudspeth were on their way to South Pass encouraging emigrants they met along the way to take the cutoff they had just charted. About two weeks later, however, Hastings and Hudspeth returned to find that Vasquez and Bridger had arrived just before the wake of emigrants who began streaming in by droves waiting for Hastings and Hudspeth to lead them. Most were already familiar with Hastings' open letter and perhaps versed with additional details about the route shared by Clyman's contact with westbound emigrants.

terminated 67 miles later at the next water source, Pilot Spring, but the entire stretch was 83 miles from where they last watered at Hope wells.[84]

Like the 70 wagons Hastings guided well ahead of the Donner Party, they too, took on their last water at Hope Wells which was the last practical water station before crossing the emptiness of the Salt Desert.[85] Hastings, no doubt, led wagons to these springs because of Hudspeth's recent reconnaissance with the Bryant-Russell pack train. He also determined at this juncture to leave a note for trailing emigrants that was more alarming than reassuring. It revealed that the next segment of their journey was going to be devoid of water not just 40 miles as thought, but twice that distance starting from Hope Wells, to Pilot Spring which became known as the "fearful long drive."[86]

Since the emigrants would not be able to acquire any of the precious liquid until arriving at Pilot Spring, this meant they would run out of carried water long before reaching the western end of the Salt Desert. They knew that at least 40 miles would be devoid of any relief, but an 80-mile desert stretch with the only life-sustaining spring found on the farthest edge of the Salt Desert was a recipe for budding disaster. Transported water could only last so long—perhaps running out 20 to 30 miles before reaching the life-saving spring at the base of Pilot Peak. To make things worse, it was barely possible for many to carry enough water for themselves not to mention their animals that were worn with fatigue and stress. Still, they pulled wagons—some

---

[84] T. H. Jefferson published a small guide and map in 1849 just in time for the Gold Rush. He recommended that at Hope Wells three to four gallons of water per animal should be carried for the 83 mile stretch he measured. Heinrich Lienhard, who traveled with Jefferson across Hastings Cutoff, provided each of his animals with one and a half gallons a day that held out until the final ten miles before reaching Pilot Spring. All of his animals survived through what he called the "limitless plain" over what he thought was at least 70 miles and perhaps up to 90.

* Trail historian Roy Tea's detailed measurement using T. H. Jefferson's map compared to United States Government Survey quadrants measured the distance at 67 miles. There are also other longer distances from 75 to a maximum of 90 "measured" miles as claimed by other emigrants of the period. It is unclear as to how exactly this mileage was calculated other than an estimated "measurement" starting from a point further east, and stopping for water at more than one spring but counting the mileage between each one before reaching Hope Wells. It could also be anecdotal.

[85] Redlum Spring was used by the Hastings-Clyman party on their way east to Fort Bridger. Clyman describes it as a small spring of brackish water which did not run more than four rods (66 feet). This relatively small spring was bypassed by the wagon trains Hastings led as well as the Donner Party as Redlum Spring was considered inadequate. The discovery of Hope Wells changed that. Redlum was small for the large number of wagons it would need to service and so ignored. However, holes could have been dug to enlarge the spring's capacity without too much effort, and putting up with the water's sulphur-impregnated taste would produce the added bonus of gaining nearly a day's travel (about 13 miles from Hope Wells to the pass through the Cedar Mountains) before crossing into the Salt Desert proper. This would have reduced the overall distance of the "fearful long drive" from 83 to 70 miles.

[86] Bypassing Redlum Spring may have been an error as it could have provided some water to replenish reserves one more time before running out somewhere on the salt flats but closer to Pilot Spring. Reed, ahead on horseback, knew it was there, but the poor quality of the brackish, sulphur-tainted water turned him away. Gold seekers taking Hastings Cutoff on their way to California in 1850, found Redlum Spring to be poor quality as well but somewhat adequate by digging holes and allowing the water to seep in.

overloaded and all much heavier carrying a crucial supply of water.[87]

Hudspeth as well as Hastings must take some of the blame for the confusion here, too. Not because of the 35 to 40-mile dry stretch, but the fact that Hope Wells was about 16 miles farther east than the original path Hastings had tracked from Redlum Spring. Until Hastings reunited with Hudspeth and learned of Hope Wells, only then would he have a good idea of the distance to water. It would now be at least 80 miles between taking on water at Hope Wells and reaching the spring at the base of Pilot Peak. With only hauled water available from this point, there remained the potential for devastation of animals and property alike. But the cutoff was in full swing, no one could realistically turn back, and without a suitable water source between Hope Wells and Pilot Spring, the practicality of the cutoff was falling into question. The only viable salvation of Hastings Cutoff that remained was the proposed mileage savings to California, and even that would soon come into question.[88]

---

[87] Water is heavy weighing about eight pounds per gallon. If a number of receptacles were available to take on 50 gallons, about the amount of an average bathtub, the weight added to just one wagon would be 400 pounds not to mention the added burden that overly stressed wagon animals had to endure.

[88] In the confusion of opening the new cutoff, the mixed intelligence from Hudspeth, Clyman, and Hastings was the best that could be obtained at the time. Hastings was not a villain putting emigrants into an unrealistic position, but simply reacting to the difficulties of his cutoff in real time. The bottom line is that it could be done, but geography would determine the practicality of the cutoff in the end.

8. Time Lost and Gambles

Delays. We're all familiar with them. We expect them in our everyday lives and deal with them in a variety of ways. Some are self-imposed, others cannot be controlled. Variable in duration, most are benign and all but meaningless in the larger scheme of things. Yet others change the future irreversibly. We attempt to limit delays by being aware of time. We actively seek intelligence, weigh the advantages of options, and consider long-term factors in order to foresee or forestall potential impediments. Some delays are necessary, but others accumulate into an assortment of layers that have far-reaching consequences.

The most unalterable delays are built upon an insidious chain of events that slowly gathers momentum. Delays, and the circle of time associated with them, are especially relevant as they influence decisions and judgments that, more often than not, aggravates an already progressing situation. Hope then becomes the empty promise that struggles with determination to believe that success can be achieved. In the case of the Donner Party, when they reached the valley of the Great Basin, a host of factors rooted in delays and time began converging into the sudden epiphany of what had been happening far too long, and what had become far too late to reverse.

The emigrants, who planned to leave Fort Bridger on Hastings Cutoff in 1846, were confident they could endure the hardships associated with establishing a wagon-blazing trail that would significantly shorten the distance to California. There was a 40-mile dry spell, but that stretch might be lessened if a new spring could be located. Unfortunately, due to a problematic misunderstanding, the desert span would end up being double what was expected and water had to be carried to bridge the gap.[89] Besides, anyone who had earlier taken the imposing Greenwood Cutoff in order to avoid the longer Fort Bridger road to Fort Hall had to push through a grueling sweep of 53 waterless miles to save three days' travel time. Therefore, the prospective difficulties of Hastings Cutoff did not deter the caliber of emigrants who had gathered at Fort Bridger waiting for Lansford Hastings to give the order to ship out. With the travel season well under way, combined with the exciting prospect of reaching California through a more direct route, there was strong motivation for Hastings to move. To wait indiscriminately for straggling emigrants who might or might not show up was not a sensible option. It would be more prudent to move along in case there were unforeseen delays ahead instead of wasting travel days sitting idle.

As Hastings contemplated departure, he may have recalled his own ominous warning on

---

[89] Hudspeth, while guiding the Bryant-Russell pack train ahead of Hastings, found a better water source—Hope Wells. It was superior over the inadequate Redlum Spring. Unfortunately, Hope Wells was 10 miles east of Redlum, thus making the waterless span of the Salt Desert longer. Mapmaker T. H. Jefferson would nonchalantly christen this waterless stretch he measured at 83 miles as the "fearful long drive" which would require transported water to reach the next oasis at Pilot Spring covering approximately 20 miles per day.

page 144 in his guide that stated, "unless you pass over the mountains early in the fall, you are very liable to be detained, by impassable mountains of snow, until the next spring, or, perhaps, forever." With the consequences of those words and roughly 700 miles to California, he made the decision to leave the fort on July 20. Hastings' partner, James Hudspeth, headed out first with three companions leading the faster-moving nine man Bryant-Russell pack train.[90] Over the next few days Hudspeth took them on a semi-exploratory mission looking for an alternative route down the Wasatch, and to find a better water source than Redlum Spring.[91] At the crest of the Cedar Mountains, Hudspeth sent Bryant's party over the final intimidating 67 miles of salt flat desert to Pilot Spring before turning back to find Hastings and help with the wagons he was guiding.[92]

On the same day that Hastings gave the command to start, one hundred miles east of Fort Bridger the Boggs Company stopped just before reaching Little Sandy Creek at the Parting of the Ways.[93] According to Oregon-bound emigrant J. Quinn Thornton, who recorded in his journal as the Donner Party formed, everyone was "elated and in fine spirits, with the prospect of a better and nearer road to the country of their destination." The exception was Mrs. George Donner who was described by Thornton as "gloomy, sad, and dispirited in view of the fact that her husband and others could think of leaving the old road, and confide in the statement of a man of whom they knew nothing, but was probably some selfish adventurer."[94] Aside from Tamsen's lone voice of opposition, her husband soothed her doubts and because of his likeable, gregarious personality, he was elected captain of the new wagon train that branched off onto the left-hand road toward Fort Bridger, Hastings Cutoff, and California.

When the Donner Party rolled into Bridger, it was discovered that they were eight days behind Hastings, yet the option to follow him, or stay on the traditional trail to Fort Hall and

---

[90] Hudspeth's three companions were John Minter, James Kirkwood, and J. C. Ferguson.

[91] The limited brackish water at Redlum Spring was a chief reason Hudspeth was doing reconnaissance while guiding the Bryant-Russell train. This led to the discovery of Hope Wells. In 1849 California-bound gold-seekers taking Hastings Cutoff used the small spring at Redlum and expanded upon it by digging pits along the sixty-foot runnel of water. Nevertheless, it would never be able to adequately supply large numbers of emigrants.

[92] The Bryant-Russell pack train crossed the Salt Desert in an amazing 17 hours covering about 67 miles at an average clip of four miles an hour. From there the group followed the path of Fremont's expedition and the tracks of the Hastings-Clyman caravan via Secret Pass to where it intersected with the regular California Trail. Following the land-locked Humboldt River to its terminal end, they soon met their last major obstacle: Crossing the Sierra Nevada up the Truckee River Route then down into the Sacramento Valley.

[93] The Parting of the Ways was actually a point on the Oregon Trail where it veered off to the right putting emigrants on the start of the more difficult Greenwood Cutoff but reduced the mileage to Fort Hall by about 53 miles. Keeping to the left was the traditional route to Fort Hall, but emigrants would first have to reach Fort Bridger (where Hastings Cutoff began). From there they could head up to Fort Hall where emigrants had the option to set out specifically for Oregon or California.

[94] Houghton, Eliza Poor Donner. *The Expedition of the Donner Party and Its Tragic Fate*. Truckee, CA: The Sierra District of California State Parks, 1996.

California both remained viable.[95] Their arrival behind the main emigration had been due to a variety of seemingly benign delays that were now quietly adding up: Some were necessary as in waiting for the Big Blue River to subside from flood stage followed by the death of Sarah Keys. Others were self-imposed. For example, taking an extra day beyond the traditional halt for the Fourth of July celebration. No one seemed to be overly alarmed, in fact, they laid over four days at Fort Bridger recruiting themselves and their animals before starting out after Hastings on July 31. The Donner Party undoubtedly believed the cutoff was risk worthy even without his direct guidance.[96] After all, about seventy wagons and 300 emigrants were ahead of them leaving a well-marked trail, and if it crossed anyone's mind, the advance emigrants would have taken care of much of the necessary roadwork on the new route by the time the Donner Party followed in their wake. There were also a number of overly optimistic notions and partially understood information offered by Bridger and Vasquez who encouraged the use of Hastings Cutoff. In the coming weeks, their incautious promotion would contribute to an escalation of hardships the Donner Party would soon endure.

No one could have been overly surprised that Hastings had already left. His guidebook stated that companies should leave Independence, Missouri no later than May first, but like many others, the Donner-Reed families had broken that advice by starting on May twelfth. James Reed was still much in favor of the new cutoff along with others in his group, and concerns about falling farther behind must have begun creeping in. The letter that Edwin Bryant left for Reed advising him to avoid the cutoff was never handed over to him which would have at least given him one final chance to reconsider what he was getting into. The emigrants also began to feel the strain of knowing they were near the tail end of the emigration which certainly factored in the decision to take the cutoff. So, the real blame for the Donner Party's tailspin of related events, if one is inclined to support it, accelerates not with Hastings, but with the overly optimistic proprietors at Fort Bridger. There is also no doubt that James Reed's influence certainly played a powerful role in choosing to follow Hastings as evidenced from an excerpt of a letter he sent back home to relatives.[97]

> "The new road, or Hastings' Cut-off, leaves the Fort Hall Road here, and is said to be a savings of 350 or 400 miles in going to California … There is, however, or thought to be, one stretch of 40 miles without water.… We are now only 100 miles from the Great Salt Lake by the new route,—in all 250 miles from California; while by Fort Hall it is 650 or 700 miles… The rest of the Californians went the long route—feeling afraid of Hastings' Cut-off. Mr. Bridger informs me that the route we design to take, is a fine level road, with plenty of water and grass, with the exception before stated… [the 40 waterless miles]. It is

---

[95] With the arrival of the Donner Party at Vasquez and Bridger's fort, James Reed, having conversed with the rumor-prone proprietors, stated in a July letter to his brothers-in-law that Hastings and his party were examining ahead for water or for a route to avoid the waterless portion of the road which Reed felt could not be eluded.

[96] Several others joined the Donner Party while at Fort Bridger.

[97] Morgan, *Overland in 1846* Vol 1, Pp 203-204n10.

estimated that 700 miles will take us to Capt. Suter's Fort, which we hope to make in seven weeks from this day."[98]

Unfortunately, what the Donner Party could not know was going to change everything as Hastings' partner, James Hudspeth, made a critical route change on his return from the Bryant pack train to help guide wagons through the Wasatch. Heading back up the range, he met the lead group of the Harlan and Young wagon trains who were part of five strung-out emigration parties working their way through a less demanding stretch of trail (near modern Henefer). There, he persuaded them to go down an entirely different path of canyons than he and Hastings had originally scouted two months earlier. Hastings at the time was assisting slower caravans farther back and had no input in Hudspeth's decision to veer away from the initial planned route in favor of the Weber River drainage. Why he did this may have been inspired by his recent probe through the Wasatch with the more agile pack train he had just guided. By working through the Weber canyons, he may have been seeking a better connecting route to the Bear River up to Soda Springs. The trail to Hastings Cutoff would then follow the western base of the Wasatch from Soda Springs rather than intersecting the range through Fort Bridger. There was also the temptation to take advantage of the available manpower that seventy wagons would bring to cut through or around obstacles.

Regrettably, the Weber River canyons and tributaries did not cooperate with Hudspeth's exploratory plan. The pathway he pursued turned out to be much too rough, rocky, brushy, and at times so narrow that wagons could barely squeeze through. There were also places where vehicles were forced up canyon walls so steep that one wagon pulled by two struggling yokes of oxen lost their purchase and all were smashed to atoms using the vernacular of the day—fortunately without loss of human life. This decidedly impractical deviation would have a major impact on the Donner Party resulting in them having to cut their own way down Hastings and Hudspeth's original track in the vicinity of Echo and Emigration canyons. Hastings undoubtedly looked upon Hudspeth's decisive action with apprehension, but it was too late to change course. Unwilling to forsake emigrants who might be straggling behind, he hurried back to the junction where Hudspeth had directed wagons away from the original prescribed route to warn potential late-comers by leaving a message attached to brush with instructions to avoid the bad road ahead, find him, and he would show them a better way down the Wasatch into the Salt Lake Valley.

---

[98] The "250 miles from California" is puzzling, but a possible explanation is that if Reed subtracted the 400-mile savings anticipated via Hastings Cutoff, in comparison to Fort Hall's 650-mile figure. That would leave 250 miles to reach California according to Reed's reasoning. Arriving at Sutter's Fort in seven weeks would be a stretch, but reaching the Sierra by mid-September was still possible before leaving Fort Bridger. Years later Reed would have a very different view of Vasquez and Bridger as stated in the *Pacific Rural Press*, March 25, 1871: "Several friends of mine who had passed here with pack animals for California had left letters with Mr. Vasquez—Mr. Bridger's partner—directing me to take the route by way of Fort Hall and by no means to go the Hastings Cutoff. Vasquez being interested in having the new route travelled, kept these letters. This was told me after my arrival in California." Edwin Bryant or a member of the pack train undoubtedly informed Reed of the letter.

Historians and writers have argued that Hastings should have come back to personally lead the Donner Party as "promised" (a word he never used). An equally fair counterargument could just as easily be made that the Donner Party had already made the decision to aggressively chance their lot regardless of whether Hastings came back or not. Six days out of Fort Bridger they still had the option of simply turning back to the traditional Fort Hall road. Instead, having found Hastings' note, the group committed to a loss of momentum with another delay. All in the Donner Party knew that Hastings' proposed wagon route was a work in progress involving dozens of wagons and hundreds of emigrants ahead of them. Yet his missive did more to confuse rather than clarify, that is why the Donner Party decided to send James Reed, Charles Stanton and William Pike on horseback to find him.

Even with the advice Hastings provided in his general guide, the Donner Party was slow to grasp the cumulative effects of their choices that had been building up from the beginning (think of Donner wagons overloaded with merchandise, or Reed's heavy oversized wagon). There were still serious obstacles to be reckoned with regardless of the cutoff's mileage advantage, and a growing anxiety as the consequential sum of their delays began to race toward uncontrollable fruition. Entrenched in time lost, they slowly became entangled in their own web of poor decisions, acceptance of overly optimistic encouragement, and the unknown that lay ahead, all of which would leave them reeling at the base of the Wasatch.

****

By the time James Reed had found, conferred with Hastings, and returned to his wagons on a borrowed horse, four days had elapsed (Stanton and Pike were to catch up later after resting their animals from hard use). The news Reed brought back was optimistic. He had caught up with Hastings' wagon trains near a spring and formation known as Adobe Rock on the southern tip of the Great Salt Lake. Upon their meeting, the two men immediately admired each other as they were very similar in leadership qualities that housed a never-failing assertiveness that drove their endeavors.

Although it was impractical, unnecessary, and too late for Hastings to go all the way back to guide the awaiting Donner Party, he was more than willing to assist Reed in clarification of the route he should take. Riding back a surprisingly long distance to a prominent peak (Big Mountain) in the Wasatch, Hastings pointed out the way he had explored two months earlier. The conversation between Reed and Hastings is not recorded, but his advice was not of a con artist as some have concluded. It's hard to imagine Hastings wringing his hands with malevolence in anticipation of getting a few hundred Americans to the Pacific shore at any cost for his own selfish reasons. Dead emigrants would not help anyone's political or financial designs in Upper California.

Hastings was certainly unequivocal in that his original exploration through the Wasatch would be much easier than the wheel-busting Weber route; Reed was agreeable, and always free to reverse course back to the regular California Trail. However, with renewed confidence, Reed headed back on the would-be path marking trees with a hatchet and observing first-hand what the wagons of his company would have to pass through.

Unaffected by the obstacles Reed encountered, he was resolved to take the new route. Without compromise, he "reported in favour [sic]" to his company and encouraged their consent. The path would be more direct and less than half the distance of Hudspeth's roundabout debacle, but it would require a significant amount of roadwork to get wagons through. This included hacking through tangles of underbrush, felling pine and aspen trees choking the way, and rocks—not to mention descending and ascending mountains and canyons. Reed, confident of the gamble he was so freely advocating, was assuring in his ability to persuade; after all, he had just traveled the route. He would know. Satisfied with his salesmanship, he recorded in his journal that night "induced the Company to proceed."[99] The net was now cast as the Donner Party set off to trailblaze Hastings' original cutoff down the Wasatch into the valley of the Salt Lake.

****

From the time they found Hastings' note, it would be 16 days in all that included a grind through 35 miles of difficult trail building to get through the Wasatch. That did not bode well for the Donner Party. They had become their own advance emigration—the indirect result of Hudspeth's offhanded decision to depart from the original route. Of the able-bodied males, only 28 (14 years and older) were on hand to do the back-breaking work of cutting a wagon path.

A few days into hacking their way through the Wasatch, there was an unexpected surprise. It was the three wagons of Franklin Graves, his twelve-member family, and hired teamster, John Snyder, who rolled up having decided to take Hastings Cutoff. Perhaps they were hurried along by the emphatic reports and partial information that Vasquez and Bridger continued to spew while at their fort. Heading out, they were fortunate in choosing the correct track to join the Donner Party and not veer off into the Weber Canyons. Nevertheless, there they were, the last wagons on the trail for the season, a stark reminder that time was of the essence, and the Donner Party thankful that three more hands were available to help cut trail.[100]

The Donner Party's roster was now complete with 87 members and 23 wagons. As they neared completion of the new trail, there was just one more taxing push that required the multiple teeming of their animals that struggled to pull a single wagon up the last summit. At the top, they were greeted with the fantastical sight of the Great Salt Lake soaking up the jet-blue atmosphere of the heavens, and the demoralizing mountain-studded expanse of the Great Basin. Far ahead and still unseen remained the Salt Desert, and hidden much farther away, the snow-splintered granite peaks of the formidable Sierra Nevada silently awaiting their arrival. Effecting their final descent, they ultimately emerged into the Salt Lake Valley on August 22.

---

[99] Hall, Carroll Douglas. *Donner Miscellany: 41 Diaries and Documents*. Book Club of California, 1947. Page 20.

[100] The three extra hands were Franklin, his seventeen-year-old son William, and Snyder. All other members of his family were females tending to essential duties, or were children too young to meaningfully assist in trail clearing. It is also worth mentioning that heavier wagons requiring frequent double or triple teaming must have caused some grumbling among members of the Donner Party as they trudged up and down the canyons of the Wasatch. Reed's wider family wagon would almost certainly require some extra trail work at times.

Years later in 1871, James Reed still defended the route he promoted down the Wasatch declaring that "I here state that the number of days we were detained in road-making was not the cause by any means, of the company remaining in the mountains during the following winter."[101] Reed echoed a pragmatic responsibility for his influence, and it is notable that he did not blame Hastings nor criticize him in any way. Writers and historians after the fact would take up the pen and interpret vague evidence that Hastings had purposely misled them—which he clearly did not.

Halfway into their journey across the Great Basin, as they leap-frogged water sources, bridged mountain ranges, and rolled over the sage-covered plains toward the Salt Desert, they finally arrived at the last practical oasis to take on water. Hope Wells was a cluster of inviting springs surrounded by acres of lush grasses superior in quality and quantity compared to what the Hastings-Clyman group had made use of at Redlum. While resting among the essential resources, a wagon board was noticed with the bird-shredded remains of a second note left by either Hastings or Hudspeth.[102] The message pieced-together by Tamsen Donner revealed the unwelcomed news that there would be no significant spring to break up the lengthy desert from here on out until reaching Pilot Spring. The disbelief that the distance to water would be decidedly longer than expected, and the implication that water and grass for animals must be transported from the springs here, must have been demoralizing to say the least.

The note stated in somewhat cryptic terms "2 days—2 nights—hard driving—cross—desert—reach water."[103] Seemingly more of a directive than suggestion, the note may have been deliberately terse as to leave the logistics up to the emigrants themselves regarding how they would best approach the algebra of time, distance, water, and stores of fodder for their animals. Two days and nights implies four segments of twelve-hour intervals to make the entire crossing based on information gleaned from pack trains and adapted to wagon travel on the fly. Wagon trains covering 15 miles a day was typical, and over a 48-hour period would total about 60 miles. "Hard driving" implied about 20 miles per 12 hours or 80 miles in 48 hours to cover the distance to the next water—a formidable undertaking. Either way, it was much farther than the 40 mile "dry drive" the Donner Party had anticipated. Perhaps this was the misunderstanding

---

[101] Korns, J. Roderic, Dale L. Morgan, Will Bagley, and Harold Schindler. *West from Fort Bridger: The Pioneering of the Immigrant Trails Across Utah, 1846-1850*. Logan, UT: Utah State University Press, 1995. Pp 220n24

* Taking into account that Reed was speaking in hindsight, he was correct. There was still time to cross the Sierra ahead of winter snows, but a host of complications further up the trail would begin narrowing that possibility.

[102] Hastings wrote in a very verbose style that the shredded note lacked. It seems plausible then that someone else may have left the bare-boned script pieced together by Tamsen Donner (if in fact that was the entire content of the directive). James Hudspeth seems a logical possibility as author of the note since he was Hastings' co-leader and knew the route as well. The distance from Hope Wells to Pilot Spring is about 83 miles.

[103] Houghton, Eliza Poor Donner. *The Expedition of the Donner Party and Its Tragic Fate*. Truckce, CA: The Sierra District of California State Parks, 1996.

that failed to clarify that water hauled from Hope Wells meant there would be water until it ran out leaving an actual waterless drive of 40 miles or so across the entire 80-mile stretch.

Shocking as this realization was, it was all they had to go on. On the favorable side, it was not unreasonable for animals on a scheduled pace with strategic rests and care to accomplish such a task. Also, taking into consideration that the Salt Desert was generally flat, slower-moving wagons would have the ability to travel at a steady pace—the key to successfully "reach water" on the western side of the desert. The rationed use of water, conceivably for the next 80 miles of this difficult stretch, was of critical concern. They would have water for roughly the first half of the route; however, the second 40 mile stretch of the daunting white-swept plain would embody a harsh challenge for those who made better choices and worse for those who did not. There was, however, at least some degree of comfort knowing that Hastings and the emigrants of seventy California-bound wagons were ahead somewhere in the distance having successfully passed over what the Donner Party was now confronting.[104]

Having absorbed the reality of the second note, any former confusion was now decidedly put to rest. Water loaded in each wagon would vary in quantity depending on how many receptacles were filled (which may have been an issue for some), and there was the additional stress on animals now pulling the dead weight of the life-sustaining liquid. A serious depletion of transported water was to be expected by the time they reached the halfway point of the Salt Desert, and for many, there would be a complete lack of water by the time they wheeled somewhere beyond the Grayback Mountain with some thirty plus miles remaining to reach the God-send water of Pilot Spring.[105] As unsettling as it may have seemed, the span across the Salt Desert could be done. Hastings had proven it. He never faltered, made excuses, nor sent emigrants to their deaths, difficulties were to be expected, and he was doing exactly what he set out to do. Even with the added complications of water rationing, wagons pulled by increasingly weakened or inadequate animals all eventually made it across the cutoff.

The emigrants of the Donner Party left Hope Wells with mixed feelings about what lay ahead as they continued their journey. Ten miles into their trek they passed a barely visible green patch in the distance that was Redlum Spring. Reed himself rode out to examine it but decided that the brackish seep of water was not worth the effort for wagons to top off their supply. Three miles farther, the wagon train began its ascent across a pass in the Cedar

---

[104] Hastings had to adapt his calculations to the minimum realistic time it would take for wagons to cross the Salt Desert. Based on his former experience, his reverse crossing with Clyman was 20 hours, so doubling the travel time for wagons compared to mule trains made sense. Prudent as it seemed, he was certainly close to the bone regarding the lengthy distance wagons had to struggle across to get water. Slower vehicles, especially very heavy ones with weakened or overly stressed animals, would lead to irrevocable losses for some.

[105] The Breen family (as well as others in the Donner Party) seem to have hauled a reasonable amount of water and provided faithful attention to their animals. They had apparently equipped themselves with the most critical of supplies: food stuffs, clothing, bedding and other typical domestic items of necessity without overloading any of their three wagons. Vehicles containing many non-essential worldly goods, as in the case of George Donner, including James Reed and perhaps Louis Keseberg, created disproportionate stress on their work animals.

Mountains where the summit horizon slowly revealed the snow-like expanse of the Salt Desert proper.

Peering from the top of the Cedar Mountains, the emigrants faced what must have seemed like an illimitable waterless barrier. It projected an unnerving panoramic emptiness and the uncertainty that lay ahead. At the farthest extremity they could see their goal: The towering summit of Pilot Peak standing 10,700 feet on the other side of the desert plain harboring the critically important spring at its base. Transported water was now low or gone for many, and the next stretch was unmistakably the alleged 40 mile "dry drive" soon to be better known as the "fearful long drive." To make matters worse, they were crossing the realm of the Great Basin in late August which is a high desert with an average elevation of 4,000 feet. Temperature extremes encompassed everything from triple digit heat, to windy nights that dropped to near freezing. Even though they were aware that the most difficult section of the desert crossing was about to begin, the wagons ahead of them left few signs that suggested they would suffer unduly. Unknown to the Donner Party, however, their first bout of serious loss on the long, waterless stretch was about to close in on them.

****

Crossing the Salt Desert more than two weeks ahead of the Donner Party, Jacob Wright Harlan was among the vanguard led by Hastings. Over four decades later in 1888, he published his experiences about getting to California. Originally from Indiana, when he was eighteen, Harlan ended up joining his uncle's family from Michigan who decided to head for California. At Fort Bridger his company was induced by Hastings to take his new cutoff. Of special interest is Harlan's vivid description of crossing the Salt Desert as he recalled the ordeal which occurred on or about August 15 through 17.

> "…we laid in a supply of fresh water [at Hope Wells] for the ninety-mile desert. We started our passage over the desert in the early morning, trailed all day and all night, and on the morning of the third day our guide [either Hastings or Hudspeth] told us that water was still twenty-five miles distant. Our teams were so exhausted that they could not haul the wagons [subsurface muddy areas undoubtedly contributed to their difficulties]. We had to unyoke them and drive them to the water, and then back again to fetch the wagons."[106]

Several emigrants lost animals that collapsed or were unhitched to wander off and die, but no wagons were left behind. Everyone was able to either revive their animals at Pilot Spring and go back to get their vehicles, or lend their animals to more unfortunate emigrants for that purpose. This prevented any property from having to be left on the desert. Upon reaching Pilot Spring himself, Harlan adds that "After passing the desert, we found it necessary to rest our animals for three days, they were so exhausted and spirit-broken."

The Donner Party's traverse of the Salt Desert would almost mirror what happened to

---

[106] Harlan, Jacob Wright. *California '46 to '88*. Reprinted. LaVergne, TN: Bibliolife, 2010.
*This also suggests that Hastings and/or Hudspeth were actively out on the desert informing and encouraging emigrants to push on instead of simply waiting for them at the relative comfort of Pilot Spring.

Jacob Harlan's wagon train with a few notable exceptions: Some required four to five days to make the crossing to Pilot Spring; more animals drifted away never to be found; four wagons would be left behind, and five days were spent at Pilot Spring recuperating, searching for animals, and bringing up wagons. If Hastings is the regulation villain that he is so often portrayed, it is on the Salt Desert section of his cutoff that he must share some criticism. Historian Stanley Kimball may have said it best when he suggested that "Perhaps Hastings' culpability should be limited to the fact he tragically failed to realize that oxen hauling heavy wagons across a desert is far different from men crossing on horseback."[107] There is certainly truth in that statement, but there is also truth in that even though Hastings pushed the emigrants to the edge of disaster—it never materialized, nor did anyone die as a result of Hastings' determination to succeed in moving Americans west carrying the ideals of Manifest Destiny he so sincerely believed in and hoped to expand upon.

Nearly all emigrants and their animals suffered on this section of the cutoff, but one small band of five Swiss emigrants two days behind Jacob Harlan, namely, the single wagon of Heinrich Lienhard's party prepared very carefully before crossing what he called the "limitless plain"—and it paid off. He states a big reason that his group suffered less is that "Every vessel that could hold water was put into readiness to be filled, before our departure, with this indispensable liquid." Doing that, and taking "great care" of their animals, would contribute to their passing without any loss all the way to Pilot Spring (just barely, but make it they did). They seem to have had a lightly loaded wagon compared to many others, and being in the rear of Hastings' escort, may have been able to take advantage of wagons before them that had taken the best path. Lienhard later wrote that "The journey from the last place with good grass and water [Hope Wells] to this spot [Pilot Spring] had lasted from [about] nine o'clock in the morning on the seventeenth until a little after four o'clock on the afternoon of the nineteenth of August [a fifty-five hour push including rests]."[108] Along the way, they passed 24 abandoned wagons (about one-third of the total) at various intervals on the final stretch of desert. Those emigrants unhitched their animals to get to water as quickly as possible and return. Every wagon would eventually be recovered, so when the Donner Party passed about fourteen days later, they saw no unoccupied wagons but may have seen a number of dead oxen scattered here and there which would not be an uncommon occurrence.

****

As the Donner Party left the Cedar Mountains behind for the final push across the Salt Desert, stunted trees and sage began to disappear. They were now making a beeline for a split in the distant "rocky hill" called Grayback Mountain where travel was generally uneventful even though devoid of water and grass. About ten miles west of the broken outcropping, shards of

---

[107] Clayton, William, et al. *The Latter-Day Saints' Emigrants' Guide: Being a Table of Distances ... from Council Bluffs to the Valley of the Great Salt Lake ...* Patrice Press, 1983.

[108] Lienhard, Heinrich, and Erwin Gustav Gudde. *From St. Louis to Sutter's Fort, 1846.* Norman, OK: University of Oklahoma Press, 1961.

grayish rock on the plain resembling shattered glass soon began transforming into a mixture of light brown, and powdery white sand complete with wind-blown dunes that had to be navigated. Beyond the drifts, the desert flat was slowly becoming dominated by patchy crusts of salt as they followed the trail of Hastings' wagons. What remained of the water carried by emigrants from Hope Wells days earlier was now coveted and was carefully rationed. Fodder offered to overworked animals was often rejected for lack of moisture which stressed the animals ever closer to their breaking point. Failing animals covered fewer miles per day which harbored the potential for greater disaster, and in a world powered by beasts, the destruction of animals guaranteed personal property loss. The temptation for some to forego adequately resting their animals in an attempt to make up time, combined with little or no water, turned out to be a no-win mistake as animals stopped, dropped, or ran off at the first opportunity. And worse, the Salt Desert held one more aggravating secret that no one warned about.

With the Grayback now far behind them, they came upon an area known as the "big bend" which was described by T. H. Jefferson as an area of "wet marl incrusted with salt, into which wheels cut and make hard pulling." This caused the emigrants to veer their wagons in a southwesterly direction in an attempt to avoid as much muck as possible. Here, few traveled in single file. Wagons began to spread out like wandering vectors seeking the most feasible line around thick sludge while keeping their animals and vehicles from becoming sporadically mired in it over the next 25 miles or so.[109]

Unknown to emigrants at the time, they had been and were passing over a massive extinct inland sea that was once filled with the meltwater from the last Ice Age.[110] It was here the water table of this ancient lakebed lingered just below the salt-encrusted surface in places and would be encountered now and then all the way to Crater Island. Wagon wheels crushed into this sticky mud making travel exceedingly difficult, and caused the greatest havoc for the heaviest of wagons that drained their animals' strength, and impeded progress on the cutoff at the most inopportune time.

When the Donner Party came upon this hidden subsurface obstacle, some were entering day three of their Salt Desert crossing while others farther ahead were within reach of Pilot Spring. Here and there the iron-rimmed tires of heavy wagons continued to punch through the salt-hardened crust into the miry oatmeal-like muck. These bogs slowed them to a mere crawl at times and pushed their animals to the absolute limit of endurance. This undoubtedly led some to lighten their loads by dumping a variety of items no longer deemed essential, yet others chose not to do so. James Reed, in an attempt to save all of his property, went so far as to instruct his

---

[109] Clyman made no mention, nor warned anyone, of the mucky areas on his eastbound trek with Hastings that caused so much trouble for heavy wagons later on. Bryant clearly noted places where mules sank to their knees, but apparently it was not overly troublesome for his mule train. This suggests that Clyman and Bryant either traveled slightly different routes, or were able to easily avoid extensive parts of it. No one would have known about Bryant's situation anyway since he was far ahead and out of contact with the wagons that followed him.

[110] The Great Salt Lake is the only remnant of this colossal geologic event.

teamsters to lead his animals to water if they failed to pull his wagons. Reed then went ahead on foot to get water more than 20 miles distant. Unfortunately, it wasn't long before his animals could go no further, and all three of his vehicles had to be left behind.

Over thirty-six animals would be lost by various families during this stretch, but Reed took the worst hit. Due to his teamsters' mismanagement of his thirst-crazed beasts, they ran off resulting in Reed losing eighteen of his twenty animals. This forced him to borrow from emigrants who were recuperating at Pilot Spring. With their help, he was able to salvage what he could from two of his abandoned vehicles but retrieve only one over the next two days. Deciding, perhaps unwisely, to keep the family wagon, Reed had to be appalled at the sudden swiftness of his loss leaving him and his entire family nearly destitute in a most distressing situation, and he wasn't alone. In addition to Reed's misfortune, George Donner, as well as Louis Keseberg, would each lose a wagon—all four standing like out of place monuments upon a glistening expanse of white salt for miles around.[111] The chief cause was due to overloaded wagons pulled by overworked animals. It took three to five days for the Donner Party to cross the Salt Desert (August 30 thru September 4), and it was a messy affair. For example, William Eddy, with his wife and two small children, arrived at Pilot Spring on day three, but he had to return for his wagon left nearly 20 miles out.

The record is relatively silent, but it appears that the Donner brothers, George in particular, stubbornly held on to much of the wide array of trade goods he carried from the start even after abandoning one of his vehicles. So, by the time everyone had crossed the Salt Lake Desert reaching Pilot Spring (today's Donner Spring), five additional days would be spent recuperating, retrieving wagons, or searching for lost animals of which none were found. They were already low on food by this time and still nearly 500 miles away from their goal.[112] This would lead to volunteers Charles Stanton and William McCutchen being sent ahead to Sutter's Fort on a resupply mission by which they would return to their fellow emigrants at some unspecified point on the trail. As for the property lost on the desert, it would soon be scoured by subsequent travelers throughout the next few years who were looking for useable goods or firewood.

Much of what still remained of the Donner Party's abandoned property on the desert was picked over and recovered by relic hunters in the late 1920s and has continued every decade since. Amateurs and professionals alike are still captivated by the Donner Party's history on

---

[111] It is interesting to observe that the Breens, as well as a number of other families, are not mentioned as having suffered unreasonably on this testy desert crossing. They seem to have taken better care of their animals and were well prepared for hard travel without carrying excessive possessions or speculative merchandise. On the other hand, one of George Donner's three wagons was weighed down with goods specifically to be profited upon in California. Keseberg, his wife, daughter, newborn son (the only baby born on the trail), and hired hands were reduced to a single vehicle at this point as well.

[112] It is an odd coincidence that the Harlan as well as the Donner Parties realized that they had underestimated the amount of food required for their journey at Pilot Spring. Both groups sent men forward to bring back provisions from Sutter's Fort.

Hastings Cutoff, and their curiosity is fueled by the enduring amazement in which nineteenth century travelers so boldly crossed this formidable geologic feature.

In 1986, a wave of renewed interest regarding Hastings Cutoff emerged due to concerns about a water diversion project which led to a formal excavation. Because the rising water level of the Great Salt Lake was threatening structures near the shoreline, water would need to be pumped over a section on Hastings Cutoff which would flood and destroy it in the process. A professional archaeological team was organized to record and recover any remains or evidence related to this historic trail before it was potentially lost forever. Even though the sites have been altered multiple times in the past, small mounds of blown salt and sand still indicated where the wreckage of abandoned wagons once stood. And as one might imagine, the ensuing excavations revealed some fascinating finds and insights—in particular regarding James Reed's family wagon.[113]

Through careful archaeological methodology, one of the sites revealed wagon ruts impressed into the desert crust which had been covered and preserved by blowing sand. The wagon that made the impressions had an atypical wheel base of eighty-six inches or slightly over seven feet wide. The tire marks of this unusually large vehicle were ten inches wide, and the rusty remains of an exfoliated iron tire hoop indicated a wheel diameter of five feet which is highly suggestive of Reed's family wagon.[114] This is especially interesting as it provides additional information about the actual width of the family wagon and the massive wheels that supported it. At other sites, wagons with a fifty-nine-inch (about five feet) wheelbase were uncovered which was in the range of a standard wagon possessed by George Donner, Louis Keseberg and James Reed as well. All three families abandoned wagons, at least in part, because they stubbornly held on to articles of trade and personal value at the expense of their animals. The result: longer recovery stops, slower progress, and finally loss.[115]

****

---

[113] Hawkins, Bruce R., and David B. Madsen. *Excavation of the Donner-Reed Wagons: Historic Archaeology along the Hastings Cutoff.* University of Utah Press, 1990.

* During the 1986 excavation of the Donner-Reed wagons, a fragment of a blue transfer print shell-edged plate was uncovered. The 2004 Alder Creek archaeological excavation found a similar fragment indicating potential evidence of dumping some property.

[114] Ibid

* A wagon "tire" is the iron ring on the outside of the wheel that protected the curved wood felloes that supported the spokes protruding from the hub. Reed would leave behind both of his "standard" wagons in favor of keeping his large "family" wagon. Perhaps the tire that was excavated was part of an extra wheel left behind.

[115] Evidence for the excessive weight of the Reed's larger family wagon is based, in part, on the fact that it took eight oxen to pull it and later in the journey complaints from others that it required double teams to get the wagon over even the most moderate grades. The Donner brothers appeared to have kept many of the numerous trade goods they started out with. When the Second Relief party reached the Donners' Alder Creek camp in early 1847, they auctioned items on the spot to help offset rescue expenses. A later "salvage" party mentioned numerous goods that were not essential or practical for a long journey west. In essence, trade goods and unneeded items (furniture for example) were grudgingly held onto creating a contributing factor to the Donner brothers' misfortune.

There is little doubt that George and Jacob Donner equipped their wagons with the suggested supplies for a long journey west as advised in Hastings' *Emigrants' Guide*; however, George and his brother also loaded their wagons with profitable goods before departing for California. Eliza Donner (Houghton), only three-years-old in 1846, later wrote a book that was published in 1911—much of which likely came from Donner Party survivors she spoke with. She did, however, list quite a selection of trade items her parents brought (as mentioned in the introduction) "to be used in exchange for Mexican land-grants…"

From all appearances, it is likely that even after George Donner's loss of a wagon and perhaps some trivial property left on the Salt Desert, he still held on to most of the valuable goods he and his wife started out with. That means at least one of his two remaining vehicles was filled beyond practical capacity with many unneeded goods.[116] If that was the case, his optimism to keep material goods may have been influenced by the belief that the cutoff he was taking put him closer to California than he actually was, and therefore, worth the risk he put upon his strained animals. With the additional anticipation of Stanton and McCutchen returning with provisions, holding on to as much property as possible was not discouraged, but justified. However, it also kept his overworked animals in a constant state of stress and decline which would become very apparent by the time he reached the Humboldt River.[117]

Having rested a full five days at Pilot Spring, the Donner Party was ready to move on. Stanton and McCutchen were already in motion to bring back supplies from Sutter's Fort anticipating a diminished food supply. Skirting the Toano Range by way of Silver Zone Pass, they soon reached a gap in the Pequop Mountains that led them to Warm Spring where a critical juncture would define Hastings Cutoff to California. Heading northwest towards the narrows of Secret Pass was only practical for pack animals, so the circumnavigation of the Ruby Mountains was the only option for wagons. This meant that every mile moving south along the Rubies was wasted time and added mileage that abated the "most direct" advantage on the cutoff, but there was no other choice.

Flanking the Rubies was the only real possibility for wagon travel. It was the only section of Hastings' evolving cutoff that he had never explored himself after realizing that Secret Pass was not viable for wagons, and he has received much criticism for it.[118] However,

---

[116] Hawkins, Bruce R., and David B. Madsen. *Excavation of the Donner-Reed Wagons: Historic Archaeology along the Hastings Cutoff*. University of Utah Press, 1990. p. 113.

[117] Houghton, Eliza Poor Donner. *The Expedition of the Donner Party: and Its Tragic Fate*. Reprint ed., Sierra State Park Foundation under supervision of the Arthur H. Clark Co., 1996.

* Eliza Donner Houghton claimed her father, George, cached some of their valuable property at a place she calls Geyser Springs. It was apparently somewhere along the Humboldt River. She recalled leaving behind "several large cases of books and other heavy articles belonging to my father", and that the wagon was lightened "through pity for our oxen." It is a wonder that George only lost one wagon on the Salt Desert while holding on to the aforementioned heavy items. Nevertheless, valuable goods still remained in his vehicles.

[118] Limburg, Peter R. *Deceived: The Story of the Donner Party*. Pacifica, CA: IPS Books, 1998.

having previously spoken with Fremont, who had traversed the range himself just a few months earlier, Hastings knew it was possible to work around them. He would have been unsure of just how many miles and days this detour would require, but he did not waver nor blindly lead emigrants into the complete unknown. The only question on the downside of this deviation was how much distance this alternative would erode from his original line to California? So, as Hastings and Hudspeth guided wagons south along the Rubies, they kept a constant lookout for a suitable pass that would allow wagons to intersect the range before reaching its terminal end. There were some promising possibilities, but none were acted upon until modern Overland Pass, was crossed. Before being able to loop back up the Pacific side of the Rubies in a northwestern arc, about ten days and more than 127 miles of travel were used up before reaching the California Trail and the Humboldt River watershed. Emigrant Heinrich Lienhard sarcastically called it "Hastings Longtripp." Nevertheless, skirting around the Rubies was the only logical route to pursue by wagon, even though it negated a significant portion of the mile-saving, more direct line of travel via Secret Pass that afforded the cutoff's original advantage.[119]

By now it was clear that Hastings Cutoff would never be the "most direct" route for wagons without the assistance of Federal Government intervention to develop it.[120] One must also keep in mind that the basic geography of the West was just being understood, comprehensive maps did not exist, and GPS was undreamt of. Still, Hastings made the best of what he set out to do, again without incurring a single death. As for the Donner Party, due to their lateness, they continued to lose control of events they held in check before leaving Fort Bridger. They followed in Hastings' wake around the Rubies, but still continued to lose time at a critical point, thus increasing the risks the Donner Party had already taken upon themselves.

Unfortunately, with the exception of Secret Pass, the irony is that the cutoff really offered little in reduced mileage for wagon travel since the Rubies had to be circumnavigated. And as a result, it was nearly as long as the Fort Hall road to California but with more difficulties along the way: Water sources were too spaced out at a critical time; the shimmering expanse of the Salt Desert and the mucky areas it hid would always be challenging; extended recovery delays took away time on the cutoff that did not impede travelers on the traditional trail. All of these factors stacked up to defeat the perceived advantage of the cutoff that it was once thought to hold. Lansford Hastings tried to make it work, but in reality, without more development on his cutoff, which was not forthcoming, only pack trains taking Secret Pass would have a significant edge over the regular trail to California.

---

[119] Unknown to Hastings, the circumnavigation of the Rubies, just beyond Warm Springs to the Humboldt River, would take about 127 miles of travel to complete. Comparatively, Secret Pass would cover about 65 miles and two days of travel to reach roughly the same point on the Humboldt River where the Donner Party emerged. Although the circumnavigation of the Rubies was still shorter in distance compared to the regular California Trail, the difficulty of terrain made the route longer, more time consuming, and of little mileage value over the long haul.

[120] Government map-making surveys were an acceptable use of federal funds as it benefitted the entire country. On the other hand, making road improvements that would only help a specific part of the country with tax payers' money was often frowned upon as a misuse of federal purse strings by Americans in general at this time.

****

At last the Humboldt River Basin was reached uniting the regular California Trail just west of the modern town of Elko. It was somewhere at this point that Hastings and Hudspeth took leave from the scores of emigrants they led across the new cutoff. The emigrants would be on their own from now and would safely enter California on the time-line prescribed by Hastings. By crossing the Sierra within the margin of safety as stated in his book, they avoided being trapped by snow. This was all due to his credit as an experienced guide who encountered and overcame many adverse conditions along the way. It can be said then, that he practiced what he preached even though his new cutoff did not fare well overall.

By the time the Donner Party reached the Humboldt, they remained completely isolated from all other emigrants. The life-giving Humboldt River that made travel across the Nevada desert possible would soon unveil its own unique set of challenges. They were now passing over the homelands of Native Americans who quickly discovered that the emigrants' stray or unattended animals were an easy food source to be exploited. In the resource-limited environment they survived within, this would cause misunderstanding and occasional conflict between the two opposing cultures.

Two weeks of travel along the Humboldt continued to take its toll among the emigrants. After everything they had been through, intense heat and thick dust still remained constant tormentors. Stress never really took a backseat, and the Sierra Nevada loomed in the distance. As they moved along the slow, almost stagnant meander of the Humboldt, it sometimes twisted in a way that was easier for wagons to travel away from the river. The downside is that it often took wagons over deep powdery hills of sand. Petty issues among the emigrants, which were typical in every wagon train, would normally never evolve much further than a minor dispute with a quick end. But this would not be the case with the Donner Party when an argument boiled over into a physical confrontation on the afternoon of October 5, 1846. Out of control tempers would lead to deadly consequences between John Snyder and James Reed at a location known today as Iron Point (Station).

As the Donner Party wagons began their ascent up the long sandy hill at Iron Point, it required double and sometimes triple teaming to get their wagons over. It was a tedious process: hitching additional animals, going up, bringing the beasts back down again for the next wagon, re-hitching, and in between, a lot of waiting. On this particular day, teamster John Snyder was in no mood to wait. With a single yoke of oxen that pulled one of Franklin Graves' wagons, Snyder began lurching his vehicle up the slope. Failing to move his wagon with enough power, he became stuck. Reed's teamster Milt Elliott commanding Reed's larger family wagon then decided to pass Snyder, and in the process the two rigs became entangled. Hot words were exchanged between Snyder and Elliott. This was soon followed by Reed getting involved himself which only enraged Snyder to violence as he sporadically began to batter Reed's struggling animals with the handle of his whip. Reed tried to distract Snyder from his invaluable mish-mash of borrowed cattle and oxen he defended. He even tried to goad Snyder into settling the issue at the top of the hill away from the animals, but Snyder would have none of it. He continued to escalate the situation by threatening Reed whose exasperation only inflamed Snyder's rage even more. He was not going to entertain any possibility of ending the matter as he continued hitting Reed's bewildered beasts. In a futile attempt to stop him, Reed came close enough to Snyder who then struck Reed's head a number of times before he pulled out his hunting knife, lunged forward, and plunged it into Snyder's chest. It was a mortal wound that instantly ended the fray and, in a few minutes, Snyder's life as well.

It may have seemed as though this incident was a classic example of self-defense. It was not. It might have been the pent-up frustrations and passive-aggressive anger some held toward Reed, and the dissatisfaction of his overbearing influence that had put them through the difficulties of Hastings Cutoff. This was an opportunity to put Reed in his place. At first, things took a turn for the worse as friends of John Snyder took one side and Reed's the other. Some wanted to hang him as a murderer on the spot. Reed's supporters stood fast with the reasoning of self-defense. Reed himself, although injured, appeared to have taken what had transpired with deep remorse, and even helped bury Snyder. In the end, banishment was grudgingly imposed as the punitive measure of choice. Reed only agreed to it if his family was taken care of which was granted, and he probably justified his castigation as more of a relief effort instead of a punishment.

Unknown to anyone at the time, what started out as a harsh judgement, would end with Reed becoming a godsend not only for the rescue of his family, but for all surviving members of the fragmented Donner Party who would be trapped in the Sierra for months. For now, Reed took his leave on horseback with friend Walter Herron heading toward Sutter's Fort. They soon caught up with the Donner families who were farther ahead oblivious of what had transpired two days earlier. Reed likely did not say much if anything to George or Jacob about the Snyder incident, and for the rest of his life he rarely mentioned it and refused to speak of the regrettable altercation.

****

With the Snyder incident left behind, difficulties still remained. Not long after leaving Iron Point, the Reeds' family wagon was abandoned. Could it have been the loss of borrowed or weak animals, or did it just become impracticable to go on with a wagon that was simply too cumbersome to deal with on every hill they encountered? What happened to it? No one knows for sure to this day. The family wagon would not be the only one lost. Due to Indians chipping away at wounding or killing their unguarded animals during the night, the emigrants suffered additional diminished animal power which forced William Eddy and his small family to abandon their wagon as they worked their way down the Humboldt.

The bathtub-like Great Basin possessed another curious feature at the terminal end of the Humboldt River that no one in the Donner Party had ever witnessed before. Instead of running into a connecting body of water or finding its way to the ocean, the Humboldt became more sluggish with every mile until its waters were engulphed by desert sand creating a massive muddy bog filled with tall reeds, grasses, and tangles of stunted willow trees at a place known as the Humboldt Sink. It was, however, a place to take a final brief rest before committing to the last desert stretch of their journey, later to be named Forty Mile Desert. While preparing to depart, German emigrants Mr. Wolfinger and his wife Doris, having lost too many of their animals to justify keeping their wagon, decided to abandon it. This was the third and final vehicle given up along the Humboldt, but Wolfinger in an attempt to avoid a total loss, determined that he would cache, or bury, his most valuable possessions with the expectation of retrieving them at a later date. Sending off his wife to join the main group of emigrants, he remained behind with two other German travelers, Reinhardt and Spitzer, who were to assist him before setting off to reunite with her.[121]

By the time the Donner Party was ready to cross Forty Mile Desert, they had decided to set off at dusk and travel through the night as much as possible to avoid the sun's blazing heat. Unlike many desert stretches, this one offered a small respite in the form of a boiling spring about half way through. It was of poor quality—being tainted with sulphur—but it was better than nothing. Still, this desert remained just as difficult as any other they had encountered due to deep sand that relentlessly fatigued their hard-worn animals. The toll exacted from this difficult crossing resulted in the deaths of six more oxen before reaching Truckee Meadows. This was the much-anticipated destination that meant desert travel was over for good. Only three years later, gold seekers feared this leg of the journey. Some recalled it in vivid words stating that the trail could be easily followed at night as the stench of decay filled the air and animal corpses lined the road nearly every step of the way.

The lush pastures of Truckee Meadows were a welcomed contrast after all they had endured. It was mid-October as they camped by the clear crisp water of the Truckee River bordered by miles of grasslands and strings of trees. At last there would be no more waterless stretches to hurry through, or thick dust coating everything exposed to air. This would be their last gathering as a group at the base of the Sierra. After resting a few days, individual families and their extended associations began to leave more or less independently when inclined to do

---

[121] With the exception of Sarah Keyes, there were no other deaths associated with the Donner Party until they reached the valley of the Great Basin. The next to die was a solo traveler named Luke Halloran who was taken in by George and Tamsen Donner while at Fort Bridger. He was suffering from advanced tuberculosis and soon died somewhere near modern-day Grantsville, Utah. This was followed, as discussed earlier, by John Snyder's death a few weeks later after a violent confrontation with James Reed. Louis Keseberg, in an attempt to relieve the burden of his animals pulling his one remaining wagon, compelled the elderly Mr. Hardcoop (first name unknown) travelling with Keseberg to walk. He increasingly lagged behind all in the Donner Party over the next few days, and was abandoned to an unknown fate. The next death is linked with the apparently well-to-do husband (first name unknown) of Doris Wolfinger. They gave up their wagon at the Humboldt Sink. Sending his wife ahead, he prepared to cache possessions with the help of Joseph Reinhardt and Augustus Spitzer. The next day they caught up with the rest of the emigrants without Wolfinger claiming he was killed by Indians. Thirty years later Leanna Donner, George and Tamsen's eleven-year-old daughter, recalled that "Joseph Rhinehart [sic] was taken sick in our tent [at Alder Creek mid-December 1846], when death was approaching and he knew there was no escape, then he made a confession in the presence of Mrs. Wolfinger that he shot her husband; what the object was I do not know." The final fatality before leaving the Great Basin occurred while the Donner Party was recuperating at Truckee Meadows. It was caused by the accidental discharge of a pepperbox pistol that struck William Pike leading to his agonizing death.

so. But for now, it was a place where they could exhale a brief sigh of accomplishment during this much-needed chance to recuperate body, soul, and animals one last time before taking on the last major obstacle of their journey—the ascent of the Sierra Nevada.

At this moment, they were about a month behind Hastings' recommended window to cross the mountains in relative safety. But as a result of an accumulation of delays over the last few months that had slowly recoiled their advance, they invited a potential gamble with disaster. While at Truckee Meadows, evidence of changing weather was telling. Billowy clouds of rain and snow flurries tumbled down on their encampment between streaks of sunlight that shot across the Sierran heights. It was an unnerving indication that there might be little time to lose. The balance of simple hope, teetering with the ever-present risk of uncertain mountain weather, was truly becoming a race against the inevitable consequences that swirling flakes in a snow-filled sky would bring. Having reflected upon the success of their desert crossings, they prepared to leave the Great Basin toward the white-dusted peaks of the Sierra.

****

We encounter obstacles every day, and most will never change the course of our lives in any meaningful way, but some can change it forever for the simple reason that we want to get someplace fast. Lansford Hastings discovered this during his overly optimistic quest to open a new wagon cutoff that was thought to shave off hundreds of miles to California. En route, however, he soon realized that he was pushing the cusp of human and animal endurance, yet his leadership was successful. As it turned out, Hastings was not a villain, nor hero. He did not take advantage of emigrants for selfish reasons. In the end, his cutoff just wasn't worth the effort to save a few scores of miles that were slowed by a number of geographic hardships. These included irregular water sites, long stretches of desert, wagon-stopping muck, and too many recovery days. The belated Donner Party played into the indifferent hands of fate by making the poor decision to take a new trail still in development. They found out far too late that they had gone way over their heads in their expectations to get to California quickly. It led to a continuing series of delays that culminated into an irreversible ordeal in the Sierra that changed the course of their future endeavors forever. But such was the elusive pursuit of Manifest Destiny that drove emigrants to the Pacific shores bringing with them a cannot fail attitude that was as contagious as the risks they took.

9. Misunderstood Man of Manifest Destiny

Lansford Warren Hastings has been branded with the extremes of scoundrel to visionary. However, scoundrel seems far too accusatory and visionary much too noble.[122] Unlike the terms themselves, the man himself lies somewhere in between. "His own man" might be the best descriptor. In the realm of history there are those who possess the leadership to move into action; those who watch events without the determination or ability to make things happen; and finally, those who try to explain what happened. Lansford Hastings is a perfect example of the first construct; Mexico's rule of Upper California the second; writers and historians the third.

Although Hastings set the standard for leadership and was at the forefront of travel and promotion of the West, there remains an almost impervious dislike of him by others. Hastings is often viewed in a misappropriation of prevailing harsh judgments starting with his contemporaries and continues to this very day based chiefly on a lengthy historiography of unfair assessments and biased interpretations. There is a consistent portrayal of Hastings that has run wild in historic literature. For example, historian Bernard DeVoto claims Hastings was "recklessly ambitious." Author George Stewart claims that Hastings' new cutoff was not "bold" but "idiotically foolish." Another labels him a "dictator."[123] One even goes as far as diagnosing him with an "almost psychotic need to control others."[124] The list goes on.

However, in more recent times, there has been some reluctance to paint him exclusively as an untrustworthy rogue. It may have started with historian Dale Morgan's simple, yet poignant, observation who stated that "My personal feeling is that since 1930 Hastings has had a bad press in re. [regard to]1846, everybody (myself included) fashionably jumping on him. It is time to redress the balances and re-examine this history from his point of view."[125] The complexity of who Hastings actually is, and what motivated him must be countered against a wall of past and on-going mythology that surrounds the man. Setting aside hasty evaluations, the assorted sources that survive written by him and others provides enough evidence to view the man more objectively. Wrapped within the ideals of Manifest Destiny, and as a man of his period, his pro-American stance, and motivation to move Americans west is decidedly a man apart from the singular selfish gains and single-minded desires alleged by his critics.

---

[122] Bagley, Will. "Lansford Warren Hastings: Scoundrel or Visionary?" *Overland Journal* 12:1 (Spring 1994): 12-26.

[123] Stookey, Walter. *Fatal Decision*. Salt Lake City, Utah: Deseret Book Company, 1950. P. 72.

[124] Lavender, David. *Westward Vision*. New York, NY: McGraw-Hill, 1963. P. 353.

[125] Andrews, Thomas. "The Ambitions of Lansford W. Hastings: A Study in Western Myth-Making." *The Pacific Journal Review* 39 (1970): 474.

Hastings, a young attorney from Ohio, would wear many hats when it came to western migration. In 1842, at the ripe age of twenty-three he was Oregon bound. Only a few weeks into the journey, he was chosen as company leader of the caravan after emigrants had a dispute with the original captain. It was his first endeavor leading others, and he was apparently quite good at it as he remained at the helm for the remainder of the journey. He made mistakes, but was quick on the learning curve, adapting to the do's and don'ts of trail life. At Independence Rock for example, he and one other man made the error of lagging behind their company one morning. Native Americans took advantage of the situation and relieved them of all their belongings, including clothes. The incident was more comical than threatening, but it lends evidence that he had an adventurous human side. He also had a business mind. Upon reaching Oregon Country, he was soon hired as a surveyor of Oregon City while also engaging his law degree as a land claims lawyer. He was a unique combination of trail-hardened traveler and educated professional who was able to fit in just about any situation he came upon or desired to undertake. Like many in his day, he never seemed to be satisfied with only one iron in the fire, and it is no surprise that he was constantly on the move for new opportunities.

During the following spring of 1843, Hastings left Oregon leading a California-bound pack train among other small parties heading south to Sutter's Fort (that included James Marshall, the man who would trigger the California Gold Rush). Arriving at the fort, there is little doubt that he observed the provinces' economic possibilities that invigorated his personal ambitions as well as his country's. California appeared to have it all during his four-month stay, and compared to Oregon, it was unsurpassed based on the potential advantages of untapped resources, agriculture, industry and trade laid out in front of anyone with any kind of an imagination.

Long before Hastings had any idea that an explosive chain of events would unravel his long-term plans, he had already contemplated the political climate of California. He envisioned that if a large flow of emigrants spilled into California, the ineffective Mexican Government could either be convinced to support the advantages that Americans would bring, or be easily overpowered.[126] He took note of the weak grasp California's Mexican authority held which certainly sparked his desire to accelerate changes that he felt Americans would make if they

---

[126] Lewis, Donovan. *Pioneers of California True Stories of Early Settlers in the Golden State.* San Francisco, CA: Scottwall Associates, 1993.
* American John Marsh, who had settled in California by 1837, slowly became disenchanted with the political infighting among Mexican authorities. By 1845 he was prepared to recruit men and organize an effort to overthrow the fickle California government. If things went well, Marsh considered that he might end up as governor or even president of the new republic as a result. It is interesting to note that it was Marsh who entertained the idea of becoming "president" of California, not Hastings as John Bidwell claimed years later based on hearsay. Unfortunately for Marsh, any aspirations he may have held were quickly squashed beginning with the Bear Flag Revolt, followed by the presence of John C. Fremont, and the efforts of President Polk who was determined to bring California into the fold of the Union. Even American trader Thomas Larkin who kept an eye on developments for the U. S. Government in Monterey thought the Californios would peacefully side with an American takeover.

could just see it for themselves.[127] So, in 1844 he left for the states by way of Mexico and New Orleans armed with ideas for a guide that bolstered Oregon and in particular California—regardless if all of it was accurate or not. He soon reached Ohio determined to bring others into the fold the following year and published his promotional guidebook entitled *The Emigrants' Guide to Oregon and California*. It encouraged West Coast emigration and provided practical advice.

****

While Hastings was in Missouri preparing to return to California in 1845, he learned that the Latter-Day Saints were planning to go west in 1846 to find a place where they could practice their religion unencumbered. Hastings stated "that several thousands of Mormons were making great preparations in the states to steer their course [the] ensuing summer to the Promised Land which they say is California." Hastings carried this rumor to the Pacific Coast, and wild talk of a massive emigration was rife. The rumor quickly spread to the Mexican governor in Monterey suggesting that thousands of Mormons were already on the road. Hastings went as far to predict that California emigration would be much closer to "fifteen or twenty thousand."[128] In reality, about 500 emigrants would actually enter the province by land, and they would not be Mormons. Still, it is telling that even before emigrants came in large numbers, his resolve and prominence as a promoter and believer in Manifest Destiny was apparent. Hastings perceptions are powerfully exemplified in the following passage from his guidebook on page 151:

> "I can not [sic] but believe, that the time is not distant, when those wild forests, trackless plains, untrodden valleys, and the unbounded ocean, will present one grand scene, of continuous improvements, universal enterprise, and unparalleled commerce: when those vast forests, shall have disappeared, before the hardy pioneer; those extensive plains, shall abound with numerable herds, of domestic animals; those fertile valleys shall groan under the immense weight of their abundant products: when those numerous rivers, shall team with countless steam-boats, steam-ships, ships, and barques and brigs; when the entire country, will be everywhere intersected, with turnpike roads, rail-roads and canals; and when, all the vastly numerous, and rich resources, of that now, almost unknown region, will be fully and advantageously developed."

It's almost too easy to claim that Lansford Hastings was visionary, and he is clearly a man in lock-step with the ideals of Manifest Destiny. But in order to advance his farsighted

---

[127] Morgan, Dale L. *Overland in 1846: Diaries and Letters of the California-Oregon Trail. Vol. 1*. Lincoln, Neb.: University of Nebraska Press, 1993.
* See pages 38-41 in *Overland in 1846* to read letters from Hastings and others tying in Manifest Destiny. Alluding to freedom and "unbounded enterprise." Overwhelming the Mexicans was rooted in the absence of respect for Mexican authority, and a perceived lack of industriousness that a flood of emigrants would change. This was to include thousands of Mormons totaling an overly optimistic 15 to 20 thousand new arrivals entering California. Unfortunately, the leader of the Mormons, Brigham Young, had other plans and decided that the isolation of settling his followers near the Great Salt Lake would better suit his ideal of a Zion in the wilderness.

[128] Bagley, Will. *Kingdom in the West: The Mormons and the American Frontier*. First ed. Vol. 3. 16 vols. Kingdom in the West Series. Spokane, WA: A.H. Clark, 1997. Pages 84-85.

endorsement, he would first have to persuade as many emigrants as possible into heading directly toward California's wonders and favorable prospects in a way yet to be championed by Americans.[129] Little did he know that in the coming months a man he knew of, but had never met, was about to alter his imagined enthusiasm into bold action.

At the age of twenty-six, Hastings was no stranger to long distance travel west of Missouri, and in 1845 he set out once again. This time it was an overland journey exclusively for California by way of Fort Hall.[130] Upon approaching California's mountainous barrier via the recently opened Truckee River Route in early December, the small pack train he led risked and eluded the potential disaster of a winter Sierra crossing. Snowstorms might have easily entrapped them and ended Hastings' place in history. But luck was on their side, and Hastings' party of nine crossed the summit safely and descended the pine forested western slopes to the foothills that bordered the open plains of the Sacramento Valley.

At this juncture they entered a surprisingly temperate climate which felt more like spring weather back east contrasted against the wintery mountain conditions they had just left behind. Here they casually paced across a park-like, oak-speckled countryside that stretched as far as one could see over summer-scorched grasslands that remained brown for lack of rain.[131]

Hardened by months of travel with few comforts, his troupe approached the distant streaks of black chimney smoke belching across the sky. Its source, the welcoming sight of John Sutter's chalk-white adobe fort reflecting the cheering glints of heaven-sent sunlight that slipped through gathering clouds. It was Christmas Day 1845. Only two days later, heavy rain soaked the valley for the first time in years, and higher up, deep snow sealed the 7,000-foot Stephens Pass over the Sierra until spring.

Two weeks earlier, Captain Fremont's men of the U. S. Army Corps of Topographical Engineers Third Expedition made their unannounced winter crossing of the Sierra en route to Sutter's Fort. Upon arrival, they brought news of an important geographic breakthrough. As formidable as the new trail was, they had just crossed the Great Basin directly west from the southern end of the Salt Lake for the first time. More significantly, it was believed to shave off hundreds of miles to California. However, Fremont's immediate concern was to reunite with his

---

[129] Influential New York newspaper editor Horace Greeley sided with Hastings' favorable view of California. He did his best to encourage emigrants to go there while discouraging Oregon emigration.

[130] This demonstrates that he had no intention of taking a "mythical" route south of the Salt Lake.

[131] Hager, Anna M., et al. *The Larkin Papers: Personal, Business, and Official Correspondence of Thomas Oliver Larkin, Merchant and United States Consul in California.* First ed., vol. 3, Univ. of California Press, 1952. *California has always been plagued by severe multiple-year droughts. "There will be no killing of Cattle this year for the hides and Tallow south of Santa Barbara, from the want of rain last winter. C [California] has been without its usual rains for 4 years. Each winter since 1840 we had but very little rain."

men who were exploring farther south, so he quickly left the fort in search of them without meeting Hastings. Their eventual encounter at Sutter's Fort weeks later, however, would bring about unrecorded conversations that triggered decisive action on Hastings' part that would soon connect his cutoff with the Donner Party forever.

****

Hastings was an acute, if not overly zealous, observer when it came to the Pacific Coastal region. His published declarations encouraging emigration to Oregon and especially California were deemed threatening and scandalous by Mexican officials at the time but no action was taken. Nevertheless, the loosely ruled populous of Alta California belied a continuing disenchantment and apathy with their own central government in Mexico City and its forced presence locally on matters that they could better govern themselves. On the other hand, Californios were perceived by foreigners to ineptly control the providence's future. Stalled by inability, lack of progress, and failure to develop anything more than a sporadic hide and tallow trade with Americans, it was obvious that the prevailing economic and political conditions in California were open to the ideals that Manifest Destiny would bring. And Hastings would play an intriguing role as an accelerator of that change.

Having acquainted himself with John Sutter and his fort manager, John Bidwell, Hastings prepared for that change by helping to survey Sutterville along the Sacramento River in exchange for prime lots of land totaling half a square mile.[132] With ready-made flood-free landings for purchase, Hastings, like Sutter, could envision extraordinary trade possibilities. With the Sacramento River running deep from the interior of the Sacramento Valley all the way to San Francisco's world-class port, California and the world beyond would be connected. Sutter understood this, and was well ahead in his ambition to actively encourage the flow of American as well as Euro-American emigrants who naturally gravitated toward his frontier fort bringing with them a variety of skills which were essential for the success of his semi-primitive fiefdom.

Although illegal under Mexican law, Sutter was selling tracts of his grant to unnaturalized foreigners and nothing was done to stop it. It was another sign of weakness in Hastings' mind justifying an American takeover. Sutter, a naturalized Mexican citizen, may have viewed Hastings as an agitator, but he was also one to move fast complimenting his own long-term plans. For example, in 1845 Hastings was part of an unsuccessful exploratory party to find Sutter a suitable location for a grist mill on the Feather River. Keeping Hastings close was in his best interest for the time being as he realized that Californios would have to be convinced that an influx of Americans would bring economic prosperity and governmental stability.

---

[132] Bidwell did not appear to care much for Hastings even though the two surveyed lots together for the future location of Sutterville in 1845-46. It is probable that while working together Hastings learned about Bidwell's navigation along the Rubies five years earlier. Bidwell's journal of his 1841 trek entitled *A Journey to California* was printed sometime in 1843 or '44 and may have stirred an adversarial rivalry. Perhaps Bidwell felt that he was not getting due credit for the first published overland guide to California. Hastings' 1845 promotional book, *The Emigrants' Guide to Oregon and California,* greatly overshadowed Bidwell's account. This may have led to the harboring of ill-feelings and the negative perception Bidwell held towards Hastings for decades to come.

Therefore, populating California with Americans was essential in order to challenge the status quo of Mexican authority before an independent republic could be realized.

Soon thereafter, Hastings learned that Fremont had pioneered a new route west of the southern edge of the Great Salt Lake. He was captivated by the rumors that it could be three to four hundred miles shorter than the regular Fort Hall route to California. It was only speculation at best, but it spread like wildfire through word of mouth and rumor. This could be the game-changing cutoff for a desirable mass emigration into California. True, the new route had only just been traveled by a government funded expedition with pack animals, but it intrigued Hastings. What better way to bring about emigration to California quickly than by a straightforward route bypassing Fort Hall's northwestern hook? It now seemed more plausible than ever.[133]

****

Lansford Hastings and John Bidwell returned to Sutter's Fort in the early evening of a chill January day. They had been surveying potentially valuable lots on the Sacramento River a mile away. Looking across the spread of Sutter's generous Mexican land grant, New Helvetia, they could see last year's wheat stubble among dormant irrigation ditches, the first in northern California, that brought water to once idle fields. The double gates of the fort were wide open exposing a flurry of activity inside. Dismounting just before the entrance, Hastings pulled off his saddle bags and handed his horse and mule laden with surveying instruments to an accommodating Indian vaquero who led his animals off to one of the fort's low adobe-walled corrals. As he passed the fort's entrance, he could not help but notice new faces standing around in conversation, many drinking the fort's home-made brandy freely poured from thick, imperfect glass bottles into battered tin cups. Suspecting that someone important had arrived, his perception was soon proven correct; the date was Thursday, January 15, 1846.

It wasn't long before Hastings found out that it was Fremont who had just returned from a failed attempt to locate a group of his men who were exploring mountain passes farther south.[134] Hastings then quickly found Sutter who relished being the fort's perpetual center of attention. Upon Hastings' request, he wished to meet Fremont as soon as possible. Fremont, who was occupying one of the many rooms inside the fort's walls had been resting undisturbed until Sutter's quick knock on a crude, ill-fitting leather-covered door broke the solitude. Cautiously, one of Fremont's men just inside swung it open. Sutter formally introduced Hastings but then abruptly excused himself feeling unwelcomed. The intention was not mistaken; Fremont did not trust Sutter, his questionable loyalties, nor his penchant for

---

[133] Hastings was becoming more determined than ever to do his part to bring in as many emigrants to California as possible. He may have thought that an overwhelming flood of emigrants would peacefully put an end to Mexican rule in California. Thus, keeping in line with the ideals of Manifest Destiny, a peaceful takeover of California would be logical since Americans had so much to offer.

[134] Eventually they would arrive at the fort.

scuttlebutt, and so he treated him with indifference.[135] Hastings, on the other hand, was asked to find a place to sit among piles of valuable tack, luggage, and stacked weapons, all illuminated by the glow of a whale-oil lamp and a small fireplace.

Thus, began the start of a long conversation that continued well into the night. Focusing on the future of California and the new cutoff, events were moving fast, and Hastings saw his contribution in the development of a wagon road over Fremont's new route west of the Great Salt Lake. It was a cutoff believed to save untold miles and streamline emigration to California. The discussion at some point was also most certainly underscored by a more pressing objective held by Fremont: To make his military presence known and to influence the future of California favorable to an American takeover. Precisely what was discussed between the two men is unknown to this day, but Hastings was impassioned to act, and he rushed to play his role in defining the potential of a wagon route for which he set out to promote in earnest.

In a letter Sutter wrote to his nearby friend, William Leidesdorff, he states, "The Emigrants from the U. States will be here this time in the month of August, because Capt. Hastings is gone so far as fort Pritchard [Bridger] to bring them a new route Discovered by Capt. Fremont which is about 3 or 400 Miles shorter as the old route over fort Hall, the foreigners will be very strong this fall...."[136] The "3 to 400" mile savings on the road to California is often repeated, but after traveling the proposed cutoff himself, Hastings would pragmatically revise it somewhat using questionable dead-reckoning calculations.

Knowledge is power and Hastings lost no time promoting this new opportunity. There was no reason to doubt its potential. Hastings was determined to see it for himself with the intention of establishing a wagon road. The once mythical passage west from the southern tip of the Salt Lake, merely hinted at in his guide, was becoming actualized. Starting from Sutter's establishment, he and partner James Hudspeth soon joined a small group who had gathered at Johnson's Ranch. It was led by mountain man James Clyman who was on his way back to Illinois. About nineteen individuals made up the party including Caleb Greenwood and his two

---

[135] Mexican officials kept abreast of events through Sutter and his frontier outpost who kept Indians in control, or in fear, and serving as a communicator of arriving emigrants or government "explorers." The growing murmurs of an American takeover that threatened to displace Mexico's fragile rule over California was becoming imminent. They knew the threat would chiefly enter from the Sierra Nevada or Oregon, so emigrants gathering at Sutter's friendly back door would be the likely source of any new revolts. Sutter himself, a naturalized Mexican citizen, held no special place in his heart for his adopted country when it came to influence, power, and profit. He had survived siding on the wrong side of Mexican authority once before during an internal revolt, and the possibility of being drawn out in the open into this new uncertain drama could alienate and shatter his tenuous stronghold for good. Therefore, he had to be cautious in his dealings with Californios who distrusted him, some of whom would like to see him expelled or even dead. He wrote worrisome letters to a network of neighboring landholders relating his suspicions of Fremont's purpose and concerns about Hastings rashness. Yet he did not inform Mexican officials until Fremont had left his fort. He knew that a wrong move could lead to the forcible loss of his holdings, but by playing to both sides, he would at least put himself in a bargaining position. If his support was thrown to the Americans, his influence and profits would likely skyrocket, but if things did not go well, he might well face the other alternative—a Mexican prison. Either way it was risky and gave cause for him to be nervous.

[136] Sutter to Leidesdorff, June 28, 1846, Leidesdorff Papers, Henry E. Huntington Library.

sons who were also headed east to seek employment as guides.

Having decided that the snowpack was hard enough to cross the Sierra still luminous with snow, the company set out on April 11, 1846 on their uneventful yet sluggish eastward journey over the Sierra's spine via Stevens Pass. Travelling along the north side of Truckee Lake, they would ironically pass the locations of the soon to be winter campsites associated with the Donner Party.[137] As they began their descent down the eastern slope of the Truckee River Canyon, they followed a route through Dog Valley previously explored by Greenwood who was with the Stephens Party the previous year forging the first wagon route over the Sierra. This was done to avoid a number of relentless back and forth traverses of the lower river canyon.

They soon reached Truckee Meadows (site of modern Reno) and worked their way to the Humboldt River sink. By the time the Clyman-Hastings party had reached the Humboldt River proper in early May, many of the Donner Party had just left Independence, Missouri only knowing of Lansford Hastings through his guidebook. They may have also read a newspaper account of Fremont's new desert crossing.[138] Traveling to the Humboldt's headwaters, Hastings would cross the northern edge of the Ruby Mountains by way of Secret Pass laid out by men from Fremont's most recent expedition.

Realizing that Secret Pass was not wagon friendly, Hastings still believed that a trail for wheeled vehicles could be worked out. As he mimicked Fremont's initial probe of the same area, he also knew that Fremont (and Bidwell in 1841) had both traveled farther south along the Rubies cutting across somewhere near the terminal end of the range. This knowledge would give him an alternative route to get wagons through. There was no malice in Hastings' conceivable analysis. He knew the Rubies could be traversed even though he had never examined that section personally. He just did not know exactly how many miles and days it would take to circumnavigate them before looping northwest on the other side to reconnect with the main trail. More importantly, the logistics of access to water and fodder for animals still had to be charted, and with that came risk.

Unfortunately for Hastings and his small band, Fremont's information regarding the Salt Desert crossing was not precise. Having reached the spring near Pilot Peak, the next cluster of miles was about to get riskier for Hastings' party. Clyman, an experienced mountain man, had been near this area in 1826 with a group of trappers and became one of the first Americans to circumnavigate the Great Salt Lake. He felt somewhat confident on this eastward work in progress and stated "…all filt incouraged as we had been enformed [sic] that if we could follow

---

[137] Stephens Pass is Donner Pass today, and Truckee Lake is Donner Lake today.

[138] Morgan, Dale. *Overland in 1846*. Lincoln: University of Nebraska Press, 1993. Vol. 1. Pages 28-29.
* Information from the *Western Expositor* newspaper was taken from the *St. Louis Missouri Reporter*, July 21, 1845, no files from the *Expositor* being known. Nevertheless, there is the possibility that members of the soon to be Donner Party may have known about Fremont's exploring endeavor south of the Great Salt Lake a year before they left Independence on May 12, 1846.

Mr Fremonts trail we would not have more than 20 miles without fresh water[.]"[139] However, the party quickly discovered that from Pilot Peak, over forty desert miles passed with no water and not a blade of vegetation for animals. Camping somewhere beyond an elevated jumble of a mountain named Grayback, they had to travel another fourteen miles the next day to reach water (at Redlum Spring) according to Clyman. This meant there was a fifty-four mile stretch and thirty hours without water.[140] The burgeoning knowledge of geography within this area was certainly in need of clarification along with the discovery of essential water and grass resources.

Upon reaching the western base of the Wasatch Mountains, there was still doubt as to the best route for wagons traversing this range. Fremont had entered the Great Basin from the south bypassing the Wasatch. So Hastings worked out his own route toward Fort Bridger through features that became known as Big Mountain, Emigration Canyon, and Echo Canyon. He could see potential, but it would not be easy.

When the party arrived at Fort Bridger in June of 1846, no one was there. At this juncture, Clyman and almost all of the original party departed on the road that led to Fort Hall. Hastings, Hudspeth, and an unnamed Indian vaquero separated and headed east until they were west of South Pass. Their purpose was to intercept some of the first emigrants of the 1846 season and convince them to take his new cutoff. From there he also sent forth a promotional open letter with a young man named Wales Bonney who was returning from Oregon. In the meantime, Hastings went back to Fort Bridger and waited.

****

Those who championed new trails to the West were the physical manifestations of the nation's idealistic ambitions. Hastings was simply an extension of that progress promoting and advancing a reality that was not without its difficulties or controversies. His part in opening the West was the tangible embodiment of how Americans were going to extend their influence over this vast continent to the Pacific and make it one country. At the same time, the philosophical ideals of Manifest Destiny were awakened by Washington, D. C.'s desire to protect the country's borders from intrigue and counter the meddling interests of foreign powers—especially England. There was also Mexico's unstable political merry-go-round of leaders who almost literally changed with the season. Those factors simply added to the uncertainty of the Pacific region in the eyes of expansionist Americans who desired stability on the continent's western shore as more Americans moved west.

Eighteen forty-six was a turbulent year for the United States. It would culminate in a treaty with England securing the border of the Oregon Country at the 49th parallel. This was quickly followed by a two-year war with Mexico ending in the cession of 525,000 square miles of land that furthered the concept of Manifest Destiny from an abstract entity into a physical

---

[139] Clyman, James. *James Clyman, Frontiersman: Definitive Edition*. Portland: Champoeg Press, 1960.

[140] So much for Fremont's "enformed" [sic] water placements.

reality. This was succeeded by the California Gold Rush, and less than a quarter of a century later, the impressive geographic accomplishment that would seal the technological aspect of Manifest Destiny—the Transcontinental Railroad. It would bind the country commercially from coast to coast opening the way for new economic opportunities and population centers across the continent for good. History was taking a decisive course, and as Bernard DeVoto appropriately titled his book, *The Year of Decision 1846*, it could not have been more so. As the United States was reviewing westward expansion and its relationships with foreign governments, Hastings was doing his part not unlike the American Government as he revised, reevaluated, and developed a new route for Americans to reach and populate California by traveling south of the Great Salt Lake. Manifest Destiny and all it represented was stretching from coast to coast with America leading the way.

****

When Mexico gained independence from Spain in 1821, they headed down a lengthy but comparable avenue of history as pre-revolutionary American colonists had done by rebelling against Great Britain a few decades earlier. After three centuries of dominating North America west of the Mississippi River, Spain could not stem the recurring uprisings and burgeoning autonomy of the soon to be Mexican nation and make them beholden to the mother country.[141] Similarly, Native Americans in Upper California were changed forever during the Spanish mission period in a bid to re-engineer their lives. After the newly formed country of Mexico was established, the mission system was abolished, but a strained relationship between its seat of government in Mexico City and its far away upper provinces, Texas and California in particular, began to show signs of tension. Rather quickly a progression of regional differences began to evolve stirring discordant animosities between the Central Government in Mexico City and the relatively isolated Tejanos and Californios. This set up conditions that led each "department," as Mexican officials referred to them, to make several different attempts at separation in less than two decades.

Debt was an ever-present problem for Mexico, and their California province was a potential source of revenue and bargaining chip for outstanding obligations owed to European nations who helped finance their independence from Spain. Groundwork for this is found in an attempt by Mexican agents and Prussian diplomats to arrange for the purchase of California for $6 million in 1841.[142] The deal fell through. The American Government had long been wary of European powers establishing strongholds on the western border of North America and made its own attempts to purchase California to help dissipate the issue. As far back as Andrew Jackson's administration, there were overtures to purchase California. Other bids were made by presidents John Tyler and James K. Polk but to no avail. Regardless, the United States was

---

[141] In addition to claiming large parts of North America, Spain also claimed large portions of South America.

[142] Hawgood, J. A., "Friedrich von Roenne: A German Tocqueville." *University of Birmingham Historical Journal* III no. 1 (1951).

simply not going to allow potential enemies to establish footholds on the Pacific Coast that would threaten the nation on some future date.[143] This was in part because of real or imagined intrigue, specifically with England and France. This was of great concern to President James Polk, who worried about the long-standing speculation that Mexico had mortgaged California to Britain as security for its foreign debt.[144]

Using California as debt security was one thing, but selling California outright to the United States was political suicide in view of Mexico City's Central Government—especially after their loss of Texas in 1836 and the United States Congress' approval of Texas statehood in 1845. On one hand, Americans were leery of Mexico's turbulent governing and instability that at one time even went as far as having the country's constitution suspended by a popular military leader, Santa Anna, who attempted to sort out Mexico's future.[145] Americans, however, saw this as an unthinkable affront to freedom. Texas and California were both caught between Mexico's neglect, rashness, and an unsettled political climate that would change hands at least thirty times in twenty years.[146] On the other hand, the Californios, between 1822 and 1846, would sift through fourteen appointed governors.[147] Disorder and disunion in Mexico City forced the government to keep most of its 80,000 troops on the ready to be used against its own people instead of dealing with protection or insurrection of their provinces far to the north.

There was also the seemingly unstoppable influence of foreigners who slowly infiltrated Mexican territory. This would eventually have long-term consequences as distrust permeated both sides. Texans would settle the issue by becoming a republic in 1836. The politically split Californios had their own evolving aspirations of self-determination but President Polk had other ideas. He attempted to pressure the Mexican Government to negotiate the sale of territory that included the Texas border, New Mexico, and California for up to $30 million. Mexico refused, and when that strategy failed, President Polk found an excuse for war when American and Mexican troops encountered each other over disputed land in Texas resulting in the deaths of American cavalry men. The American victory was relatively quick spanning only two years

---

[143] Smith, Justin Harvey. *The War with Mexico*. Vol. 1. 2 vols. New York, NY: Macmillan, 1919.

[144] Borneman, Walter R. *Polk: The Man Who Transformed the Presidency and America*. New York: Random House, 2008.

[145] Santa Anna suspended the Mexican Constitution in 1833 to strengthen the central government's power. He felt the constitution gave too much authority to individual "sovereign states." By suspending the constitution, he violated Mexican law. His actions led to rebellion in Texas and its eventual loss.

[146] Aggarwal, Vinod. *Debt Games: Strategic Interaction in International Debt Rescheduling*. New York: Cambridge University Press, 1996.

[147] Johnson, David Alan. *Founding the Far West: California, Oregon, and Nevada, 1840-1890*. Berkeley, CA: University of California Press, 1992.

beginning April 25, 1846 and ending February 2, 1848. At the conclusion of the war, the Treaty of Guadalupe Hidalgo resulted in The Mexican Cession which gave the United States 525,000 square miles of territory.[148] Thus, was the state of fluidly changing affairs during the mid-nineteenth century. It was an era encompassed by a multitude of unfolding events as governments, explorers, trailblazers, and emigrants alike entered the western arena lured by seemingly boundless land and unique opportunities.

****

Before the war, Mexico tentatively authorized a foreign population to enter Texas as it did California with the idea that by allowing additional settlers into their sphere of influence, they would become loyal Mexican citizens, increase trade connections, and of course join the Catholic church—all favorable to stability.[149] Unfortunately, future Texans also brought slaves with them. Illegal under Mexican law, it was only tolerated through a legal loophole that allowed "indentured servitude" for ninety-nine years. The influence of American settlement and accommodation was having a fracturing political affect due to a lack of assimilation and outright disregard for Mexican law.

The eventual takeover of Alta California by Americans was all but conspicuous. Hastings could see that the Mexican Government was cautiously encouraging if not outright open to inviting foreign emigrants to populate California by awarding massive land grants—as long as they were twenty-five miles from the coastline. This was to discourage illegal trade that would rob the government of tax dollars, and it would also serve as an early warning system for interior Indians resisting the encroachment of their lands.[150] Emigrants could qualify for up to eleven leagues, which is a little over 48,000 acres. To put it in a better perspective, they could get seventy-five square miles of land at *zero* cost—a fiefdom on a scale that was impossible to acquire anywhere else. Comparably, Texas land grants had been 4,600 acres, and later, Oregon homesteads were a mere 160 acres!

Therein lay the potential *and* problem. Hastings must have carefully considered the possibilities laid out in front of him. Mexico plainly could not galvanize enough of its own people to migrate into Texas let alone California. Their Spanish inherited northern lands were not destitute of colonists but limited in numbers. Immigration posed an ever-present problem because it was difficult to motivate families to settle in a far-away province where Native Americans, especially in Texas, were repeatedly trying to convince Mexicans that they were, in fact, the undisputed rulers of the land who would fight, torture, and mutilate trespassers to make their point. The Comanche, in particular, made this clear when they carried out serious

---

[148] The 525,000 square miles given up included parts of today's Wyoming, Colorado, Texas, and New Mexico, most of Arizona, and all of Utah, Nevada, and California.

[149] Most Americans, however, were Protestant and had no illusions about converting to Catholicism.

[150] Nunis, Doyce B. "Alta California's Trojan Horse: Foreign Immigration." *California History* 76, no. 2/3 (1997): 299-330. Accessed August 24, 2020. doi:10.2307/25161670. n32.Pp.65-66.

penetrations deep into northern "Mexican" territory south of the Rio Grande River.[151] They effectively weakened and overwhelmed any cohesive resistance by Mexico against Americans entering Texas and heading west to Alta California.

To strengthen Mexico's claim in its upper northern provinces, American emigration was encouraged by local authorities at first. This was in part by a somewhat disingenuous motive that would provide land grants that were in areas that would create a buffer zone between Mexican citizens and resolute Native Americans who were intent on remaining the dominant rulers of their land. Thus, the stage was taking shape as Mexican governors grappled for control of American settlers who came in such large numbers that Mexico attempted to halt immigration but to no avail. Hastings was well aware of this when he decided to promote emigration, but it wasn't going to be the kind favorable to the rule of law Mexican officials sought.

Hastings no doubt took the failure of Mexican policies as evidence of a weak, ineffective government unable to control future events. At the same time, Mexican officials in Monterey muddied the situation in California by continuing to award numerous grants and encouraging Americans to take root by making it easy to obtain citizenship and land.[152] Between 1836 and 1846, hundreds of grants had been awarded, and some forty-two percent were bestowed to non-Mexicans in order to win them over and support Mexican authority.[153] Thought to be worth the risk, this decision was designed for economic stimulation that was all but stagnant under Mexican rule. By encouraging American loyalty through large tracts of land, it seemed logical that they had much to offer in boosting the expansion of trade and everyone would benefit.

There are clues as to how Hastings perceived opportunity in California. First and foremost, unlike the Oregon Country whose land would be surveyed, sold, or homesteaded by law stemming from Washington, D. C., it would pale in comparison to the massive tracts of land that were being offered by Mexican officials in Upper California's capital of Monterey. Hastings knew that land grants would galvanize land-hungry Americans to join in.[154] Unlike Oregon's limited advantages, Hastings recognized California's potential linking commerce with interior waterways and San Francisco Bay. This could be seen with the evolution of Sutter's advantageously positioned trade fort and his agricultural endeavors with room for others to profit as well.

Territorial land ownership by the American Government in the nineteenth century was

---

[151] Gwynne, S. C. *Empire of the Summer Moon.* New York: Scribner, 2010.

[152] Weber, David J. *The Mexican frontier, 1821-1846: The American Southwest under Mexico.* Albuquerque: University of New Mexico Press, 1982.

[153] Beck, Warren A. and Ynez D. Haase. *Historical Atlas of California.* Norman: University of Oklahoma Press, 1974.

[154] Hastings himself made a weak attempt to secure his own land grant, but he never followed through.

driven by economics and politics, and was gained either through treaty, purchase, annexation or war. The system operated by three general principles. One: First and foremost, the land must be desirable for economic gain and or border protection. Two: the land must be populated with a relatively cohesive group willing to possess and maintain it. Three: The possessors must be strong enough to challenge any competitors. Thus, the platitude possession is ninety-nine percent of the law applies here. Mexico's futile attempts to maintain, win over, or develop any of the previous principles, in addition to any ambitions foreign governments might have, were stacking up for an American confrontation directed by the concept of Manifest Destiny.

Hastings perceived the abstraction of those fundamentals and was in a position to potentially influence the intentions of his government and countrymen. He did so without wildly fantasizing about becoming the president of a California republic, nor heading a military force to carry out his will as many have erroneously projected. If he did, he kept it to himself. He understood that the Californios were often at odds politically with themselves and out of touch with the long reach of the Central Government in Mexico City that could not quite capably bring their far-off northern provinces into authoritative control.

The Californios' disillusionment with their weak republic in Mexico City severely hindered any effective resistance they would have against another country that had designs to become its new claimant.[155] Suspect of possible secession from their own country or siding with the United States, Hastings was aware of Mexico's apprehensive love-hate relationship with foreigners in California—Americans in particular. And with war brewing between the United States and Mexico over the Texas boundary, California was ripe for the picking—Others felt it. Hastings was sure of it, and with the concept of Manifest Destiny proliferating, if one did not catch an opportunity quickly, someone else would and be more than happy to compete for it.

California's resources were simply there for the taking, and to put things in perspective, they would not be accelerated to advantage until gold was discovered in 1848 followed by the rush the following year. The population explosion brought forth by the Gold Rush put California's resources into play with unimaginable speed with a get in, get rich, and get out mentality. A majority of fortune seekers had just come from an agrarian environment and did not come to California necessarily to repeat that lifestyle, but that would change as many decided to make California their permanent home which was pregnant with opportunities around every corner and no one to tell you what to do. Trade goods of every type were needed to supply the miners which made San Francisco a major port of commerce. Here was a mobile society in flux, unencumbered by government regulation—a rarity in history, and Hastings was part of the leading edge that helped bring it into fruition.
****

---

[155] The government in Mexico City could offer little military protection to stop Native Americans from attacking Californios in Alta (Upper) California. Taxes were another issue. It was not uncommon for an article of trade to cost more in taxes than the price of the item! Tax monies were collected with little or no benefit to the Californios before being sent to Mexico City.

Trailblazers of the 1840s were not labeled so because they were overly cautious. They were risk-takers looking for greater rewards, and therefore, open to the ramifications of their decisions, but they did so knowingly. Hastings was on the cusp of helping emigrants get to California faster to take advantage of opportunities and undoubtedly thought that his cutoff could be developed with each season of travel and exploration. It would not be easy and everyone knew this before the first wagon rolled its wheels on what would become Hastings Cutoff, and no one would become better acquainted with its tribulations than the Donner Party. So what factors encouraged them to follow Hastings?

The Donner Party's decision to take Hastings Cutoff is not an affidavit for us to condemn, but a way to analyze why they made their choice. There was no manipulation of the Donner Party by Hastings himself, but rather a number of considerations that led to their decision to take his cutoff. So instead of looking to criticize Hastings, there are compelling reasons to examine why the Donner Party chose to follow him. First, he was an experienced trail leader dating back to 1842, so there was no doubt that he was qualified for such a responsibility. Hastings was also a trained lawyer and therefore respected as an educated man. There were two professions to quickly run up the social ladder in nineteenth century America: law and politics. Additionally, the popular guidebook he wrote offered some of the best travel preparation and advice of the day.

There was also the popular appeal of John C. Fremont whose exploits were reported in Eastern newspapers. This bolstered the validity of his newly explored route south of the Great Salt Lake to California. And Hastings, after meeting with him at Sutter's Fort, would build upon Fremont's exploration in establishing a new cutoff for wagon-based travel. Once Hastings' new route was roughly laid out, he, with his partner James Hudspeth, actively persuaded emigrants on the trail to gather at Fort Bridger to take it. He assured confidence by practicing what he preached by personally leading them.

Hastings also suggested that emigrants might encounter opposition from Mexican authorities in California since war between the United States and Mexico was known by this time. Travelling in a larger group would offer more protection based on the fear of that possibility. Dozens of wagons and several hundred emigrants had decided to take the new cutoff and were actively on the trail a week before the Donner Party arrived at Fort Bridger. While there, the proprietors of the fort, Jim Bridger and his partner Louis Vasquez, promoted Hastings Cutoff and spoke glowingly of it. Thus, they emboldened the Donner Party to take the cutoff and catch up even though they would have no guide.

The Donner Party knew they were at the tail end of the main emigration of 1846 by the time they reached Fort Bridger. Because of their lateness, it was tempting to take a route that allegedly shaved off a significant number of miles to California even though this was the first run on the cutoff with wagons. They also knew that Hastings, as well as Fremont, had made a December crossing of the Sierra the previous winter. This provided some comfort as to the possibility of an extended timeline for crossing that barrier even though early October was considered the latest prudent month to advance over the spine of those mountains.

The Donner Party's choice to follow Hastings over a demanding desert crossing of hopeful advantage was not without thought. Decisions were made on the fly. The geography and resources of the region were still being clarified, and there was no mistake, it involved risk. Because of the difficulty of the cutoff, Hastings is viewed as a cold-eyed promoter filled with unbridled vainglory. A fiend who willfully deceived emigrants causing immeasurable suffering. He is a man cloaked in a flurry of charged words strung together to unfairly implicate him with malice and negligence—all of which are simply not true. He did what he felt was best for Americans grounded in his unwavering conviction of his country's "obvious future" and led them to success. Even though his new trail would be impractical for travel other than by those using pack animals, Hastings Cutoff captures the spirit of Manifest Destiny.

10. Everyone for Themselves

By mid-October all in the Donner Party were recuperating at Truckee Meadows after a punishing drive from the terminal end of the Humboldt Sink across the sand-heavy Forty Mile Desert. This was the last place the Donner Party would be together as a whole. The next few days of rest in the meadows were a rare welcomed respite considering everything they had confronted over the last two months. Yet, even now misfortune stalked them once again with an incident involving an accidental shooting. William Pike had volunteered to go ahead with his brother-in-law, William Foster, to either intercept Stanton or go on to bring back provisions themselves. As they were sitting around a campfire preparing for the next day, Pike handed over a pepperbox pistol to Foster when it accidentally discharged hitting Pike. He suffered horrible agonizing pain, and in less than an hour he was gone.[156] He left behind a wife, two babies and the ever-present reminder that adversity can strike in the blink of an eye when least expected.

As the final days of October waned, everyone remained hopeful that winter-like conditions would hold off as it had the previous two years. However, it was becoming increasingly evident that this might not happen. Broken storm clouds were already pouring over the summits of the Sierra casting down scattered rain, sleet, and an occasional dusting of snow. They were far beyond Hastings' admonition to cross the Sierra by October 1, and their late throw of the dice would be just that. Unbeknown to the emigrants as they looked toward the steep mountain barrier between them and their goal, these individuals would soon be tested on nearly every conceivable level of human experience.

The Breens were the first contingent of the fragmented Donner company that left Truckee Meadows, and they had good reason.[157] Most of their cattle remained, and their three wagons were still intact. The Breens were also practical, and it is all but certain that their vehicles were not burdened by the excessive weight of trade items like the Donner brothers chose to haul. They appear to have chiefly carried the essential necessities for a long journey and very little else.[158] If there had been extra baggage, it was dumped long before this final push. They were also fortunate in that they had not suffered losses such as the Reeds did on

---

[156] The pepperbox pistol was a weapon with a multi-chambered barrel looking much like a downsized hand-held Gatling gun. Many models had no trigger guard and could easily go off if mishandled. The design of the firearm also had the unpleasant reputation that when fired, all chambers would sometimes discharge at once blowing off the shooter's hand or worse.

[157] Teamster Patrick Dolan, and the small Keseberg and Eddy families left with the Breens.

[158] James Breen later recalled that "Two of the wagons were loaded with provisions & the third a light wagon carried the small children and some beds."

Hastings Cutoff, nor along the Humboldt River as some other families had. Feeling confident that their animals were up for the task after three day's rest, they began their ascension of the steep fault-block mountains the Truckee River rushed down. Motivated by the constant pressure that time might be running out, it was critical to get through the next sixty miles which would put them over the summit pass and beyond. From there it would be down the much gentler western slope of the Sierra that merged into the Sacramento Valley and safety of Johnson's Ranch just forty miles from Sutter's Fort.

Others soon followed in the wake of the Breens a day or so later. At this point everyone traveled in relative independence of each other as the Donner Party was now an entity in name only. The second group to leave consisted of the largest number of individuals and families that included the Reeds, Graves, and Murphys. Meandering their way along the Truckee River, they left behind the remainder of their company: The Donners, Doris Wolfinger and a few teamsters.

Choosing to rest their animals a little longer before setting out, the Donner brothers decided to hold fast just one more day after the second group had taken to the trail. This would give their worn-down oxen more time to recuperate. And with many non-essential goods packed in their five heavily loaded wagons, their beasts would need every advantage before advancing toward the peaks of the granite-draped Sierra Nevada.[159]

Not long after the first groups of emigrants had set out on the trail, a small band of three men and seven mules laden with supplies encountered the scattered remnants of the Donner Party. It was Charles Stanton on his return trip from Sutter's Fort assisted by two Indian vaqueros Luis and Salvador.[160] This had to be one of the most uplifting moments of the last two months, and Virginia Reed later recalled that "our hearts were gladdened" with his return. Stanton, a single man, did not have to risk his life and return to the Donner Party with supplies, but, being a man of his word, he willingly carried out what he said he would do. His altruism provided an anchor of hope when there was little else to believe in.[161]

---

[159] Dixon, Kelly J., Julie M. Schablitsky, and Shannon A. Novak. *An Archaeology of Desperation: Exploring the Donner Party's Alder Creek Camp.* Norman, OK: University of Oklahoma Press, 2011.

* A few months later rescue parties, who made their way to the tragic Alder Creek camp where the Donner families suffered, saw in plain view surprising evidence of a wide variety of goods that littered their dilapidated campsite. Items the Donners so desperately held on to included many smaller items such as ceramic wares, but also surprisingly larger pieces such as household and kitchen furniture, yards of fabric, and books of which most were water-soaked.

[160] On their way to Sutter's Fort, Charles Stanton and William McCutchen passed Jacob Harlan around October 23. Stanton passed him again while heading back with pack mules (McCutchen did not return with Stanton because of illness). Interestingly, Harlan, James Reed, and Walter Herron also passed each other en route to Sutter's.

[161] The Donner Party reached a maximum of 87 members when the Grave's family and their hired hand joined them in the Wasatch. This number would be reduced on their trek across the Great Basin where five deaths occurred: Luke Halloran (tuberculosis); John Snyder (killed by Reed); Mr. Hardcoop (left behind not being able

Charged with distributing the food he brought back, Stanton also had a flurry of news to share with the various splintered groups of the Donner Party moving up the Truckee. First, James Reed and Walter Herron had made it to Sutter's Fort even though the odds were against them, so more relief was potentially on the way.[162] Stanton also reported from conversations he had with people at the fort that the mountain passes would not be blocked by snow until mid-November. He also relayed, having been over the Sierra twice now, that the mountains were steeper and more troublesome to cross than he anticipated.[163]

The Breens were the first to approach Truckee (now Donner) Lake arriving on October 31 after three days of hard travel. Advancing further, they could plainly see evidence of wagon tracks that previous travelers had taken on both north and south sides of the lake. The Breens knew with surety that little more than a year earlier the Stephens Party had plied their way through what would eventually become known as Donner Pass. They also knew from Charles Stanton's return that the recently opened Roller Pass sweeping up from the south side of the lake through Cold Stream Canyon was a viable option. This would explain the wagon tracks splitting near the foot of the lake. The Breens, however, were in no mood to take a lesser known route at this point, especially with Hastings Cutoff being relatively fresh in their minds. They stuck to the north side of the lake choosing to move up through Stephens (Donner) Pass.

Making their way from the terminal end of the lake, they must have been surprised to find a small crude cabin that had been built by members of the Stephens Party the previous year. Even more astonishing was that even though it was raining at the lake, in less than three miles there was 1,000 feet of elevation gain where rain dramatically transitioned into snow and was

---

keep up); Mr. Wolfinger (murdered by a fellow emigrant), and William Pike (accidentally shot to death). Others who left the Donner Party were Charles Stanton and William McCutchen (who rode ahead for supplies), and James Reed (banished for killing Snyder, and joined by Walter Herron). Only Stanton returned from Sutter's Fort assisted by two Indians, Luis and Salvador, making a total of 81 individuals. Of that sum, 59 began their winter encampment at the lake and 22 at Alder Creek. These numbers, however, would soon change for various reasons.

[162] Reed and Herron arrived at Sutter's Fort Oct 28th. This suggests that they must have crossed the summit pass on or about Oct 23 just before the first major storm hit the pass. Emigrant James Mathers states in his diary while at Johnson's Ranch, on Oct 29 "It commenced raining the night previous and continued to rain through the greater part of the day." That would mean snow at the higher elevations. The Donner Party did not miss crossing the summit by one day, but more likely about a week. If they had been able to cross the summit, rescue would have been more forthcoming on the western slope of the Sierra, but that was not to be.

[163] Charles Stanton, who had returned with two Indians, Luis and Salvador, may well have taken the newly opened Cold Stream Canyon to Roller Pass either on his trip to or back from Sutter's Fort. It would be Stanton who would have informed the fragmented groups of the Donner Party that Roller Pass was an option. It went up the south side of the lake to the summit of which he mentions evidence of a windlass that was used to haul up wagons. Because of Stanton, the Donner Party knew that there were two possible ways to cross the spine of the Sierra. After the Breen's aborted attempt up the fast rising Donner Pass on the lake's northern side, it is hard to believe others would attempt the same difficult pass twice unless Stanton thought it a less arduous option. The fact remains that the Cold Stream Canyon to Roller Pass route was longer and at a higher altitude than Stevens (Donner) Pass which is true. However, the emigrants of the Donner Party would only know what Stanton told them, and because of the Breen failure, it remained a viable alternative for some. When rescuers arrived at the lake camp months later, they would take Stephens Pass to the lake since it was frozen over and would be the quickest way to reach the starving emigrants.

rapidly accumulating among the granite shelves of the pass.

As they pushed up the wall-like summit rising abruptly from the west end of the lake, any remnant of the trail was covered by the accumulation of heavy, wet snow. This frustrated their animals, clogged the spokes of their wheels, and scraped the beds of their wagons making progress tiresome and dangerously difficult. It was an exhaustive, hopeful effort, but the Breens and their fellow emigrants were finally compelled to backtrack; it was the first time anyone in the Donner Party had done so. They returned to the junction not far from the east end of the lake to await the arrival of other emigrants, perhaps hopeful that Stanton held some confidence in the Cold Stream Canyon to Roller Pass alternative.

With the arrival of Donner Party stragglers, the Breens imparted crucial information regarding their aborted attempt to crest the Sierra. This was assuredly taken in with distressing interest as blunt details were revealed: The faint wagon road gave way to deepening snow shortly beyond the western edge of the lake, and quickly worsened with the wall-like rise in elevation. For some, it made no sense to attempt the same route the Breens had taken and failed, so it is reasonable to assume that some planned to reach the apex of the Sierra going south of the lake the following day by way of Cold Stream Canyon to Roller Pass.[164] Most would venture the north side with Stanton and the vaqueros whose experience may have thought a second try would be more expedient if they worked together. Regardless of who took what trail, all would either find comfort in justifying Stanton's leadership up Stephens Pass, or take a chance on Roller.

The next day, the Breen family, skeptical of surmounting the pass at all, halfheartedly lagged behind members of their former company during the final desperate thrust surrounded by increasingly deteriorating weather. It wasn't long before wagons on both routes became snowbound as they worked their way up in elevation. This led emigrants to abandon wagons and desperately try packing necessities on their remaining animals but failing miserably during a continuous soul-crushing storm. The difficulty of advancing through deepening snow eventually convinced them of the futility to get over the summit. Those on the north side found it no easier than what the Breens had encountered, and many hunkered down for the night even as Stanton pleaded with them to keep going. And as if to completely suppress their morale, an ominous, storm-charged night covered the emigrants in more snow by morning.[165]

---

[164] McGlashan, C. F. *History of the Donner Party: A Tragedy of the Sierra*. Stanford, CA: Stanford University Press, 1947.
* Evidence of the Donner Party attempting to take Cold Stream Canyon on the south side of Donner Lake to Roller Pass is limited, but William Graves many years later stated in a conversation with C. F. McGlashen that "the old emigrant road [It was actually the newer road.] followed up Cold Stream, [to] the dividing ridge. Some wagons were drawn up this old road, almost to the top of the pass, others were taken along the north side of Donner Lake, and far up toward the summit. Some of these [11] wagons were never returned to the lake, but were imbedded in the snow."

[165] The phenomenon of orographic uplift was unknown to anyone in the Donner Party. Today we better understand the mechanics of how it occurs and the effect it has on Sierran weather. It begins with vapor-charged warm air blowing onshore from the Pacific Ocean. This means rain along the coastal and interior valley regions, but as the

The objective of both groups to cross the dividing ridge had ended with the same result. In complete disarray, animals were lost and a number of wagons were abandoned on their demoralizing return to the tree protected flat where they started about a quarter of a mile from the lake. There, among the last patches of bare ground where slushy snow had melted between storms, the Breens occupied the small abandoned cabin. Others began drifting in to organize the construction of their own shelters as they settled in for a winter encampment—It was November 4, 1846, and to make things worse, more snow fell relentlessly over the next several days. They could now only hope that relief would come quickly as their race against time, the weather, and crossing the summit gap were lost.[166]

Meanwhile, the Donner wagons, much further behind, were nearing the bottom of a long mountainside pitch, when the sudden crack of hickory wood and the collapse of a front wheel sent a wagon packed with a multitude of furniture, boxes, quilts, clothing, household items, and trade goods into chaos. Stressed by a wheel-stopping rock, the strained axle of George Donner's wagon snapped buckling the stance of his worn animals in a wave of taut harnesses and twisted running gear. As the vehicle awkwardly plunged forward onto its side, it was miraculous that two of George and Tamsen's young children riding inside were not crushed among a jumble of property trapped in the wagon's cover like a net.[167]

After a panicked search by George and Jacob, young Georgia and Eliza were quickly removed from the disabled wagon followed by thanks to God that they were spared. Almost without thinking, a hired hand began unhitching the bewildered animals, as property was removed, stacked aside, and broken ceramics and bottles disposed of. Instead of abandoning his wagon, George was determined not to lose another, nor the valuable goods that it held. Gathering the appropriate tools that he and his brother needed to make the repair, both men were handy when it came to self-sufficiency, and improvising was second nature. A serviceable pine tree was located and sawed off having to suffice in lieu of durable hardwood which was not to

---

Sierra Nevada gains elevation blocking the way, clouds gather, rise, and the temperature begins to drop. Much of the precipitation falls in the form of snow on the western slope of the mountains. However, if the system is powerful enough, what remains of the storm, an atmospheric river so to speak, will extend over the dividing ridge of the Sierra and continue to discharge snow on the eastern side. This is exactly what happened to the Donner Party during the winter of 1846-47 with storm after storm rolling in leaving snow drifts more than 20 feet deep. In stark contrast of the droughts California had just experienced, a series of unrelenting storm systems mercilessly pounded the emigrants for months. This greatly hindered attempts to self-rescue or receive assistance originating from Sutter's Fort and Johnson's Ranch.

[166] Hardesty, Donald L., and Michael J. Brodhead. *The Archaeology of the Donner Party*. Reno, NV: University of Nevada Press, 1997.

[167] When the Donner families left Truckee Meadows, they were about two days behind their fellow emigrants. By the third or fourth day the lead groups had been stopped at the pass and forced to return to the lake. At the same time, the Donner brothers were dealing with a wagon repair and deepening snow that would end their advance at Alder Creek. Unable to close the gap any further, hired hands would eventually scout ahead to find out that the lead groups were encamped six miles distant.

be had in the Sierra. George held the limb steady while his brother fashioned the axle. He was using either a hammer and chisel or a hand-pulled shaving tool with a sharp steel blade. George must have thought his hands were a safe distance away as his brother shaped the thick branch to fit the hub diameter when suddenly the tool slipped instantly slicing the top of his right hand like butter. It was a serious wound, yet George tried to play it down while Jacob lamented his carelessness.

To compound this latest setback, two hired hands from the lake had come back with bad news informing the Donners that snow blocked the pass and one attempt to cross it had already failed. Perhaps quietly contemplating the recent arrival of news, George sat on a pile of possessions applying pressure to his injured hand, as his wife Tamsen hurried over among the hovering commotion of curious children. She dressed the wound for the time being with a wrap of cloth she kept in her dress pocket tying it tightly across George's hand to stop the bleeding. She then began looking for a kit of medicines among the panoply of wood boxes, trunks, books, clothing, and other material goods haphazardly piled on cowhides near the overturned wagon. She finally found the box that she sought containing the book, *Gunn's Domestic Medicine*. She then opened the dog-eared, velvety smooth index pages she had referred to many times in Illinois over the years. Finding advice on "incised" wounds, she prepared another cloth adding several drops of arnica from a corked glass medicine bottle. Returning to George, she replaced the original cloth. This was all she could do, stitches were out of the question, and infection would be an ongoing fear to be carefully monitored. This unwelcomed complication once again reminded them that potential disaster seemingly hovered over them like the bleak sky that threatened to engulf them.

At this point, camp was haphazardly made as everyone but the youngest children busied themselves with a familiar routine. Fires were made and partially melted slush from a previous snowfall was collected and heated in large family cooking pots to supply water since an immediate running source was not available. A dwindling food supply was becoming a concern, but no one distressed about getting something to eat. Their hard-worn animals fared much worse having to browse on sparse scrub and pine boughs that offered little nutrition.

Work on the repair resumed among a panoply of voices, the innocence of romping children, and the broken English from the recently widowed Doris Wolfinger. True to form, George made light of his injury and insisted that he help finish the axle while being tactfully fended off by his brother and hired men.

Early the next day, having accomplished the resurrection of the wagon and repacking it with considerable delay, the improvised repair held as the Donner families moved on through chilling rain and sleet. Slowly gaining altitude as they moved among vast bands of unaltered conifer forests, their natural spacing caused no obstructions as they navigated their five wagons among them. Chalk-swept pine boughs heavy with snow held no distinct edges as rising afternoon temperatures triggered the sudden fall of icy glitter that dropped from towering branches. The passing of sporadic water-stained boulders with snow-crowned tops indicated an unmistakable change in elevation. Occasionally being able to glimpse what lay ahead, they apprehensively focused their attention toward immense slices of towering granite mountains in the far-off reaches they inched toward.

Patches of snow that had only dappled the ground, now stretched into a continuous blanket a few inches deep as they struggled along the undulating trail. A blustery winter-like skyline, cold and vague, filled the air with storm-driven clouds. A scarcely perceptible defiant blue sky leached in and out of misty shadows as the prospect of unwelcomed shifting weather approached. By late-afternoon, between sporadic snowstorms, another grueling day had been put behind them. About a mile distant from the main trail, they could see a partially concealed valley, a meadow filled with last season's dried grasses jutting above a mantle of clumpy potato-like melting snow. It was an inviting location for a camp until poor weather ceased. Leaving the main road, they hugged the gradual edge of a hill to stay above an extent of marshy ground and to avoid a shallow creek. Heading toward the valley's irregular sweep in the half-light of a sulphur-gray sky, they reached the sparsely wooded meadow that provided their rib-lined animals with crucially needed fodder. The meadow afforded a degree protection from the elements, and furnished suitable access to a run of water named Alder Creek that meandered among the knotty roots of bushy tamarack pines.

The next day, clouds charged with moisture began sending a chilling wash of sleet and snow that fell miserably upon them. Crossing the summit remained a pressing worry, yet most remained confident that the snow would melt and this encampment would only be a temporary intermission. None were prepared to contemplate that it would turn into a stay of unimaginable duration and suffering. But with the continuation of deepening snow throughout the day with no end in sight, the denial of what might be happening slowly started to creep in. It was decided to erect a crude log cabin to protect themselves from the elements with wagons staggered as windbreaks. However, the task was quickly given up after an attempt to build it only four logs high. It was simply impractical to construct it with fresh snow accumulating fast. In its place, hastily made crude tent and brush shelters were effected for what would become a deplorable extended encampment on the level ground near Alder Creek—a name that would become synonymous with their final encampment. At the same time, six miles ahead, fifty-nine unnerved men and women, most with children, faced their own grim realization at the foot of Truckee Lake. It was truly everyone for themselves.[168]

It was in the Sierra that the full extent of all the decisions and delays the Donner Party amassed had now transformed into brutal fruition. The product of their decisions had never been the fault of Hastings, but rather their own doing. Overloaded wagons, the slow loss of time, James Reed's aggressive influence, and the lack of prudence in choosing Hastings Cutoff would

---

[168] The Breens made their attempt to cross the summit from Truckee (Donner) Lake on or about November 1. A second group of emigrants arrived at the lake on November 2. Another attempt to cross the summit with 11 remaining wagons was made on November 3. Failing that effort, they returned to the lake camp on November 4. The Donners arrived at Alder Creek Meadow with their 5 wagons six miles back on or about November 3.

all take their toll. Yet, it would be unfair to conclude that the Donner Party was completely at fault for their situation as no one can read the future. Risk is the natural engine of progress, and like the ideas behind the concept of Manifest Destiny, it is within the capacity and belief of those who take chances that make things happen. The Donner Party built their dreams upon what seemed possible, only to be stopped by complications that changed everything.

Snowstorm at sunset looking west from Donner Alder Creek campsite. Photo E. Hart

11. Battling Winter While Winning a War

It is difficult to conceive a more desperate condition of human suffering than of those at the lake camp or Alder Creek six miles farther away. Regardless of where any of the 81 Donner Party emigrants encamped, the days of November blended into weeks, then months. By February things had become desperate. During this span of time, all had endured the stress and suffering that cold, fatigue, anxiety, and the ever-increasing press of hunger could continuously impart.

Unable to cross the Sierra summit, the lead groups of the vanquished party reached the apex of their journey at the eastern foot of Truckee Lake. This was quickly followed by heavy drift-blown snow that accumulated in such astonishing quantities that it was almost beyond comprehension. Between the initial waves of storms, a number of self-rescue attempts were initiated, but all were quickly aborted due to fresh snowfall that had not yet consolidated making travel all but impossible.[169]

As howling winds warped through their make-shift camps, all made the best of their situation as they clustered together and subsisted on the limited food that remained. And if it ever crossed anyone's mind, there may have been some regret that the October 1 warning laid out in Lansford Hastings guidebook had not been heeded. One hope still prevailed, however, in the form of James Reed who had been banished from his wagon train for the killing of John Snyder. Reed along with Walter Herron had arrived at Sutter's Fort on October 28, 1846 and sounded the alarm to organize relief for the Donner Party emigrants thought to be in need somewhere on the eastern side of the Sierra.

Unfortunately, Reed's rescue attempt was thwarted on two counts. First, war with Mexico had broken out across California. Every man who could carry a gun was needed, and reaching out to emigrants who *might* be stranded was not a priority. Second, heavy snows continued to block any advances across the Sierra which countered Reed's initial effort with William McCutchan and a small band of volunteers. For the time being, since Reed did not know exactly where the emigrants were, he would have to find comfort in the belief that they might be wintering at the lower elevation of Truckee Meadows. And back at his fort, John Sutter offered his opinion that there was a good chance they had enough animals to butcher warding off starvation until the spring thaw allowed full-scale rescue efforts to take place.[170]

---

[169] Consolidation refers to snow that has warmed enough over a period of time for the ice crystals to compact. This creates a base making it possible to support weight without sinking in too deep depending on the degree of consolidation.

[170] What Reed, McCutchen, and Herron did not know, since they all left the Donner Party earlier, was that a number of their animals had been killed by Indians along the Humboldt River. This reduced their potential emergency food supply to a dangerous level when forced into their winter encampment.

****

Realizing their disheartening circumstances at the lake, shelters had been hurriedly constructed by every emigrant who could contribute.[171] The Breens were fortunate enough to occupy the previously constructed 12' by 14' cabin. It had been built to house Moses Schallenberger who was to guard the contents of several wagons left behind from the Stephens Party during the winter of 1844-45. A small fireplace warmed the interior, and drafty gaps in logs were chinked with mud, bark, moss, old newspapers, and stationary to keep chilling air from seeping in on the nine members of the Breen family.[172]

Louis Keseberg was quick to take advantage of the opportunity to build a lean-to against the Breen-Schallenberger cabin. It would require much less energy to construct, and keep him from having to deal with shelter issues other emigrants faced on a larger scale. Primitive and miserable as it was, the structure provided protection for his wife, three-year-old daughter, recently newborn son (the only birth attached to the Donner Party), and two single men who presumably helped with the construction of the refuge.

The Murphy cabin was the largest of the shelters supporting nearly twenty individuals and their essential possessions. By making use of a large boulder, just three log walls were needed to frame the cabin measuring about 25' by 18'. Like the other structures, there were no windows, and the drafty entrance was covered with animal hide. Comparable to other cabins, the floor was covered with a thick layer of pine boughs to create a barrier against the wet ground, and then laid over with a various assortment of hides, sheets of canvas, blankets, and quilts that were available.

It's not hard to imagine just how difficult it would be to live among others in the Murphy cabin. Such close proximity helped preserve warmth, but it also took away any semblance of privacy. There were many other irritations as well. Since the firepit against the boulder would not draft like a proper chimney, the atmosphere of the cabin was a continuous battle with the ever-present veil of smoke that permeated the living area reddening eyes and aggravating lungs. The occasional hint of hemlock oil was also present which was used to help remedy croup, sore throat, diarrhea, and it could also be rubbed on the scalp to help comb out lice. There was also the familiar smell of tobacco floating in the air puffed from a long-stem clay pipe. This not only fed the habit of its user, but it also helped mask the smell of body odor and the stench of urine and fecal matter from the smallest of children whose cleanliness was a constant concern.

Other than stoking the warmth of a fire that required a continuous supply of wood, the firepit was used to heat water for coffee and tea, or cooking increasingly scanty meals. To ward

---

[171] Out of 59 emigrants at the lake camp, 22 were twelve-years-old and younger. A reasonable estimate of adults who could directly assist in building shelters would be about 30 while others were taking care of children and meal preparation. Similarly, the 22 emigrants at Alder Creek would not exceed 10—a huge difference in labor ability. *See Appendix page 139.

[172] The Breen-Shallenberger cabin apparently had "two or three cot bedsteads made of poles…" according to a gold seeker who visited the site in 1849. This was unique to the other shelters.

off boredom as they huddled in their cramped quarters, some quietly conversed while others tried sleeping to forget their misery. Simple games were played to keep both adults and the younger ones engaged, and stories from memory or perhaps from the bible, were told to pass time—the only commodity of which there was no shortage. Within the confines of the room shared by its listless occupants, the dim light leaking from the firepit's thick bed of orangey coals illuminated the interior. And there were always the intermittent drips of melted snow descending from the top of the boulder's irregularly edged surface that was all but impossible to seal off. This allowed water to work its way down the fire-blackened rock until it sizzled into vapor as it neared the heat of the hearth.

The last of the structures was the "double cabin" built by William Graves and others. It was a partitioned 16' by 16' shelter that would house his family on one side and the Reeds on the other. It was constructed further away from the rest, perhaps because there was easier access to trees of the necessary diameter for the cabin's construction and would require minimal hauling. There also would have been less competition for firewood among dozens of other emigrants for this essential resource. The cabin was built on slightly higher ground in order to catch the earliest rays of sun before drifting snow ended that advantage. Graves further noted that the other cabins were on ground prone to being wet—another reason for his location of choice.[173]

All structures were about 8 to 9 feet tall and were rooved with tightly aligned logs covered with animal skins, wagon tarps, pine tree branches, and discarded clothing. However crude and cramped, each cabin provided an adequate degree of protection from the elements. The lake shelters would be the mainstay for fifty-plus members of the Donner Party as they held out for a break in the weather to send for help or receive assistance coming from the California side. What they could not have known was that both avenues of salvation would be sealed off for months. In the coming weeks, however, it would become depressingly apparent that their temporary stay would be much longer than they had ever imagined.[174]

Deep drifting snow eventually swallowed the cabins forcing the emigrants to trample U-shaped ramps to access the surface. But on dead calm days that were clear and sunny, most everyone would climb out for fresh air and look west with the hope of seeing rescuers inching down from the summit. Even with no aid in sight, at least there was the luxury of unrolling blankets to sit upon and soak up the sun's rays for a few hours which seemed very odd as it was

---

[173] The locations of most cabins are known and within the boundaries of Donner Memorial State Park in Truckee, California. The remains of the Breen-Schallenberger cabin and Keseberg lean-to rest underneath the massive pedestal of the 1918 Pioneer Monument standing 22 feet tall (representing the depth of snow in 1846-47). The large boulder that served as a wall for the Murphy cabin is also known. However, outside the park's perimeter less than a mile away is the general site of the Grave's "double cabin." It has not been precisely located, but it is thought to be close to or under the roadbed of Interstate 80 across from the high school where the old inspection station once stood. There is only speculation as to why the Graves-Reed cabin was further away from the others.

[174] Hardesty, Donald L., and Michael J. Brodhead. *The Archaeology of the Donner Party*. Reno, NV: University of Nevada Press, 1997.

sometimes warm enough to be comfortable in shirt sleeves. This was in great contrast when the arrival of a new storm plunged temperatures and dropped whirlwinds of heavy snow that was anything but mild.[175]

The Donners' Alder Creek camp beheld a significantly different scenario than the lake. They were only able to construct a cabin foundation four logs high before heavy snow impeded progress. Perhaps the project to build the more permanent structure did not resume because making the effort to cut and haul trees was thought to be a waste of effort. If help was on the way, it was going to be abandoned quickly anyway. Instead, they sought shelter in and around their wagons. But with the escalation of worsening weather, the immediate need to protect themselves more adequately from the elements became critical. This resulted in both of the Donner families making their own insubstantial shelters, and not far off three single men built a separate one for themselves. The manner in which the crude shed-like brush and tarp-covered living spaces were hurriedly built, made it all but certain that they would be a cause of endless irritation and discomfort. The misery was only softened by the hope that these shelters would be temporary. Appallingly, they would be the mainstay shelters for a long encampment with few improvements over the length of their ordeal.[176]

As late as the end of November 1846, both Jacob and George must have still believed that assistance was not far off from their Alder Creek camp. In all likelihood they may have felt that an imminent effort by California rescuers to reach them was forthcoming. Because of this, both men felt confident enough to send written requests for the purchase of food and animals from Sutter's Fort. Their appeals were to be carried by some of the single men with no family and were physically strong enough to cross the pass on foot. Other than food, Jacob specifically asked for "six yoke of work cattle," five mules to pack," and also, "four low priced active ponies suitable for women & children to ride."

It seems unusual that Jacob requested 12 work cattle as that would suggest he might salvage perhaps two if not all three of his wagons. George, on the other hand, made it clear that he wanted "5 pack mules and two horses." This would seem to indicate that he had no intention of saving either of his two remaining wagons, but in all likelihood was requesting mules to pack out most of the extensive property he and his wife had managed to get this far by wagon.[177] Feeling that relief was presumably on the way may have been reassuring in supporting their assumptions, but unfortunately assistance would not materialize, nor would relentless

---

[175] On days when the surface snow would support weight, emigrants would collect firewood, hunt, try to maintain some degree of hygiene, or visit the other cabins among other things. Some would even venture the 6-mile trek to visit the Donner camps at Alder Creek.

[176] See Appendix: Donner Party Encampments.

[177] Hall, Carroll Douglas. *Donner Miscellany: 41 Diaries and Documents*. Book Club of California, 1947. Pages 33-36.

snowstorms allow it.[178]

In the wider world, big events were also underway. The boundary of the Oregon Country had been resolved with England, and shortly thereafter, war had been declared between Mexico and the United States by President James Polk over a deadly border encounter in Texas. Polk now had an excuse to annex California, and no one could be happier to support the President's position than Lansford Hastings. Although he had no personal designs to head a revolt for an independent California, he was more than willing to help fight for its inclusion under the authority of the United States. While Hastings was helping to recruit soldiers in San Jose, a familiar person who had made the difficult trek across the Salt Desert with Hastings three months earlier, provides a little insight about the man.

If memory served Jacob Harlan correctly more than 40 years after the fact, he recalled in his reminiscent book *California '46 to '88* a brief discussion when he confronted Hastings in 1847. This would be the only record that took place in a face-to-face encounter with the promoter himself. Harlan reminded Hastings of his troubles crossing the barren desert. He then went on to say that Hastings could really say nothing but that "he was very sorry, and that he meant well." It was a very undramatic remembrance about someone who would soon be touted as an antagonist for everything from plotting to be president of an independent California, to the reckless disregard of human life on his new cutoff.

Harlan was not a man to be trifled with, and if he held any animosity toward Hastings, it would have been settled right then and there. In fact, if anyone who took his cutoff thought that Hastings was trying to put an end to his life, there was ample opportunity to discuss the irony. Hastings, an elected captain during the War with Mexico in California, openly led emigrant soldiers (a number of whom he led across his cutoff) without fear of retribution. The fact remains that no one, not even James Reed, attempted to go after Hastings for a perceived wrong which puts an end to the myth that Hastings was a hated man.

Instead, Harlan went on to state that Hastings had just finished "raising a company of eighty-seven mounted riflemen to join Fremont, and they were ready to march southward." Hastings even asked Harlan to sign-up with his newly formed company, replacing a man who was ill, and from the time of his enlistment, he would get $25 per month. This was too much of a temptation to pass up, so Harlan volunteered to serve with Captain Hastings' Company F. Within months, the fighting in California came to an end, and Harlan was honorably discharged from duty to go his separate way.

James Reed was also very busy in his movements from November to January 1846-47. He began by petitioning for land, and organizing a short-lived rescue mission that failed to reach his family. When that was put on hold, he offered his service to the United States as a soldier to fight the Mexicans. His military tour as a captain was relatively short-lived since Northern Californios were not solidly opposed to the perceived benefits of an American takeover. Thus,

---

[178] These requests were later found in the pocket of a diary Reed kept and were never delivered as intended.

resistance was limited. The only action he took part in was a minor engagement on the plain of Santa Clara on January 2, 1847. When it looked like victory was a sure thing, Reed put his energy into organizing rescue operations to reach his family as well as the other emigrants of the Donner Party. Suspense would not keep him long. Within two weeks, the worlds of James Frazier Reed and the self-rescued survivors of the snowshoe party would collide as they stumbled into Johnson's Ranch on January 17 through 19 revealing an awful truth.[179]

****

December 1846 was nearly halfway over when the lake camp emigrants organized the most aggressive initiative to get help. It took on the form of 17 individuals who were known at first as the "snowshoe party" and then later the more dramatic "Forlorn Hope." Franklin Graves greatly assisted in this self-rescue attempt by fashioning over a dozen pairs of crude snowshoes made from strips of leather and the curved wood from oxbows. The tennis-racquet-shaped devices would buoy the user without punching too far into the snow which made travel much easier.

Just a few days earlier, teamster Milton Elliot and Noah James made the 6-mile hike to the Donner camps informing them of the new plan and delivering a note from Charles Stanton asking George for tobacco and to borrow a compass before they set out. When Elliot returned to the lake camp on December 21, he learned that the snowshoe party had left four days earlier to take advantage of a break in the weather. He also reported that Jacob Donner, and three other individuals, Samuel Shoemaker, James Smith, and Joseph Reinhardt were dead. It was unnerving news that would become almost commonplace from this point forward.

On December 16 with no tent, just a few days rations, and little else other than blankets and the absolute necessities to survive, the snowshoe party began their journey across the Sierra. Hired hand Charlie Burger and ten-year-old William Murphy were the only two who did not have snowshoes, and they quickly found that they could not keep up since they plunged knee deep into the snowy trail with each step. This expended way too much energy and effort; therefore, both returned to the relative safety of the lake camp leaving the remaining 15 to push ahead.[180]

After crossing the Sierra twice, with little concern over his own well-being to help others, Charles Stanton's incredible stores of energy were about to come to an end during his third and final crossing. Claiming that he would catch up after suffering through a long cold night, he was left by the others and last seen sitting by a fire smoking his pipe—the only luxury that still afforded him a reprieve from ever-present misery. Stanton was the first to die on December 21. His body, mangled by wild animals, would be discovered by rescuers at a later date.

---

[179] Johnson's Ranch, purchased by William Johnson in 1845 (near modern Wheatland, California), was the end of the California Trail and from there the last 40 mile stretch to reach Sutter's Fort.

[180] There were 15 members of the snowshoe party: Charles Stanton, Luis and Salvador, Patrick Dolan, Franklin Graves, Lemuel Murphy, William Eddy, William Foster, Sarah Foster, Jay Fosdick, Sarah Fosdick, Mary Graves, Amanda McCutchen, Harriet Pike, and Antonio (a teamster who joined the Donner Party at Fort Bridger).

Unfortunately, conditions would continue to rapidly deteriorate for the snowshoers. Ten days out, much too far away to retreat back to the lake camp, they were caught in a severe blizzard that began on December 25, and ended 4 days later. The consequences of this bitterly cold storm resulted in the deaths of Antonio, Patrick Dolan, Franklin Graves, and Lemuel Murphy. The survivors had now been without food for more than a week. Starving, the deaths of their companions led to the first instance of cannibalism—the morbid root of fascination that drives the spellbound interest in the Donner Party story today. But the horror did not stop there.

Over the next 20 days more deaths due to starvation and exposure took their toll across the dead silence of an indistinguishable sameness of trees sticking through snow-carpeted terrain. With Stanton gone and Luis and Salvador apparently not sure of where to go themselves, a serious mistake was made when they decided to enter the American River drainage heading southwest toward their left instead of crossing over into the Bear River drainage to the northwest. The American River gorge looked to be the logical way to reach the lower elevations, but it was not. It quickly turned into a steep and wild abyss that was almost impassable. The much less challenging Bear Valley at the point of decision was hidden from their view. Today there is a turnout on Interstate 80 overlooking the scenic view of the Bear River Valley which descends into the Sacramento Valley. If they had known this, it's likely there would have been fewer casualties in their nightmarish wanderings.

There were no more deaths until January 5, 1847 when unthinkable hardship would once again test the endurance and emotional stability of the group. Young Sarah Fosdick had to contend with the death of her husband, Jay, from exposure and starvation knowing full well that his body was going to be used for food, and if that wasn't enough, Luis and Salvador, who were ahead of the main group, were tracked down, found lying in the snow, and murdered—both shot in the head by William Foster and cannibalized (It was the only instance of deliberate killing for food). He justified his action by stating that they were going to die anyway.

Seemingly endless snow-blinding days and horrible frost-biting nights would pass, but the emigrants eventually floundered down into the lower snow-free region of the Sacramento Valley. After nearly a month of unimaginable suffering encompassing starvation, exposure, exhaustion, and the ruthless edge of madness, their uncertain passage through the snow-covered labyrinth of the Sierra was coming to an end.

Well below the snowline, William Eddy was the first to wander into Johnson's Ranch on January 17. In filthy rags, feet bleeding from frostbite, and his body emaciated by starvation, he approached the cabin of Matthew Dill Ritchie when he saw his daughter. He quietly asked her for bread whereby she immediately burst into tears and rushed for help. She didn't know where Eddy had come from just yet, but his description of the Donner Party's dire condition spread quickly and soon no one could doubt how desperate the emigrants had become. With the arrival of the remaining strung-out survivors straggling in over the next two days, there was an unmistakable summon for help. Their tragic ordeal had finally come to an end but at great cost; only 7 survived: all 5 women, and just 2 of the original 10 men. Their horrific appearance and descriptions of what was actually happening at the camps over the summit was brought into critical focus. An urgency of renewed vigor to help rescue the emigrants now began in earnest and would be spearheaded by James Reed.

****

In July, 2004 an archaeologist working the Alder Creek campsite carefully excavated the ground next to greyish soil where a Donner family firepit once burned day and night. This discovery along with undisputable time period artifacts that date-match the first half of the nineteenth century, supported for the first time the precise location of one of the Donner brothers' camps thought to be lost forever. The archaeologist continues digging and soon uncovers more evidence from the ten-centimeter level. It is the lip of a shattered medicine bottle that was once plugged with a cork and is one of hundreds of fragmented glass, ceramic, lead, and ferrous artifacts that have been untouched for multiple decades. The position of the artifact is recorded and removed, but before tagging and bagging it, the archaeologist holds up the translucent glass fragment to the blue sunlit sky and ponders if it once held something that Tamsen may have used when she attended the gash across George's hand. It's just one piece among multitudes of others, but it contributes to the process of piecing together a story based on the physical remains of a campsite that is part of a complex puzzle.

Archaeology has and always will have the potential to add new information about the Donner Party based on written sources and physical evidence discovered from their campsites. The best hope for any significant finds in the future will likely be in the area of Alder Creek since they have been the least disturbed. Hearsay over many previous years has given credence to a Donner encampment by a large tree, but it was never confirmed archaeologically. However, expanded searches in the wide-open meadow of Alder Creek by various state and university archaeology departments, and volunteers using metal detectors, led to new revelations. Archaeologists became confident enough to narrow down likely spots for long-term encampments. This led to the 2004 excavation and discovery of a longstanding firepit surrounded by a number of period artifacts that confirmed the exact location of one Donner family encampment.

Excavation of Alder Creek campsite July 14, 2004. Photo E. Hart

Compared to the lake camp, George and Jacob's sites are the most convoluted, and which Donner family the hearth belonged to is not yet known. However, there is a hint that it is the encampment of George and Tamsen Donner. Several fragments from a school-use slate board, the equivalent of a laptop for nineteenth century students, were recovered giving one pause to consider a tantalizing association since Tamsen was a school teacher by profession. There is also most certainly a second hearth belonging to the other brother that might contain additional evidence as to whom it may have belonged to, but it is still awaiting discovery.

The grounds of both major campsites occupied by Donner Party emigrants have been altered by multiple use for more than 17 decades. The areas have changed over time due to salvage operations, burial parties, miners, loggers, road development, relic hunters, and natural processes such as the growth of vegetation, flooding, and the acidic soil of the Sierra. All have contributed to this change and work against new discoveries. Even the construction of Interstate 80 in 1960 has more than likely transformed, if not completely ravaged, the last fragile remains of the Graves-Reed cabin. The Breen-Schallenberger-Keseberg cabin/lean-to has also been destroyed. Any remaining artifacts at that location now lie under the sixteen-ton pedestal of the Pioneer Monument that looms 22 feet above every visitor who stands in front of it. It is an almost insurmountable obstacle that will keep archaeologists at bay with the hope of recovering any new information that might survive.

Mother nature has also done her best to reclaim and heal over the tragic scenes played out at the lake camp. For example, Charles McGlashen, the first biographer of the Donner Party, described nature's work in 1880:

> "The big rock against which the Murphy cabin stood is half hidden by willows and fallen tamaracks form[ing] a perfect net-work above the place where the cabin stood...Nature appears to have made every effort to conceal the spot. In addition to the bushes and trees...rootlets extend far down in the soil, and firmly resist either shovel or spade...the waters of Donner Creek still further protects this mournful spot. It is hardly necessary to remark that no relics have ever been found under the site of the Murphy cabin."

Not surprisingly, his assumption about artifacts would turn out to be false over one hundred years later as borne out by a 1984 excavation of the living area below the boulder of the Murphy cabin. Quite a number of artifacts *were* recovered from this superficially disrupted site, and has added a few more scraps of information about its inhabitants and everyday life.[181]

At the Alder Creek camp, the inspection of both written and physical records have been interpreted by anthropologists, osteologists, historians, and writers as to how such artifacts fit into the context of one of the two Donner families. Thus, it reveals more details of their complex story that revolves around remains left from their winter habitation sites and subordinate episodes that followed. There is no doubt that this highly interesting and veritable mixture of analysis and conjecture brings more silent testimony to life. From a wide range of artifacts and the long process of interpretation, another strand in the mosaic of the participants' lives will be better understood long after they were rescued from their make-shift camps during the winter of 1846-47.

---

[181] Hardesty, Donald L., and Michael J. Brodhead. *The Archaeology of the Donner Party*. Reno, NV: University of Nevada Press, 1997.
* Items of interest included broken costume jewelry, broken ceramics, and clay pipe fragments.

Few large artifacts have been found since relic collectors over the decades have taken most of them. However, among the multitude of shattered and corroded artifacts, are thousands of small bone fragments that have been recovered from the Alder Creek and lake camps. Not only did they reveal a surprisingly large variety of animals they ate ranging from the not so surprising cattle, horse, mule, elk, deer, rabbit (the Reeds even ate their only remaining pet dog Cash; the Breen's dog Towser met the same fate), but also lesser known animals such as bear, owl, and rodent-sized creatures that were consumed as well. Perhaps even more surprisingly, none of the fragments have been found to be human with one small exception.[182] This has led some to assert as proof that cannibalism did not take place. Not so. That assumption ignores the accounts of a number of individuals who described what they witnessed and those who wrote down what they saw. With that in mind, the bones themselves have their own unique story to contribute to the Donner Party experience.

When starving survivors determined that deceased victims were to be used as food, they did not, for example, cut off an entire arm and throw it into a black kettle of boiling water watching it bob up and down in ghoulish anticipation of a grim meal. There would be no reason to cook human bones when the removal of soft tissue would provide the most nutrition. Musculature attached to the bones of arms and legs would have been greatly reduced by the time cannibalism became a necessity. This is because as a body starves, it begins to absorb energy from muscles to keep the main organs functioning, so using greatly diminished arm and leg muscles would offer relatively limited sustenance overall.

What was more practicably extracted was soft tissue such as the heart and liver after being laboriously removed from a semi-frozen corpse. This would make sense since starving emigrants would want the largest most nourishing organs to allay their hunger. There would be the presence of butcher cuts on the ribs and sternum as a survivor worked at getting out the internal organs. But the bones that were scarred in that process were *not* cooked and therefore vulnerable to decay. Over the next 170 plus years, organic material from uncooked bones would naturally decompose and be reclaimed into the acidic soil of the Sierra, therefore, eliminating any physical evidence of butchering.

Osteologists, scientists who study bones, have recovered evidence archaeologically from both campsites in the form of observable cutmarks that were all from animals, not humans. This validates that animal bones were broken and repeatedly cooked to extract the last traces of nutritious morrow. The indications of boiling bones can be confirmed through the process of "pot polishing." This occurs during the random movements and collisions of bones against the smooth interior of a kettle: An action that polishes and rounds off edges. During this alteration,

---

[182] Although no human bones have been found at Alder Creek, two *very* small ones have been identified as such at the Murphy cabin site. This may be due to the fragments somehow surviving the rigors of nature, or they are the remnants of a burial and clean-up detail in 1847 by a passing military party not long after the tragedy. The order was given to bury human remains, and gather discarded debris to burn. The Murphy cabin was torched at this time, and there may have been other piles of litter set to fire as well which may explain any future traces of human bone that survive.

bones calcine or oxidize as the organic material within them cooks out. As a result, they become resistant to further deterioration. This treatment of bones by starving emigrants inadvertently gave them a much longer physical preservation period. This is why animal bones have survived to this day and human bones have not. Thus, archaeology and related sciences provide us with additional information about an engaging episode of American history that continues to fascinate us.

12. A Cold Hell of Truth and Tales

By the beginning of February 1847, James Reed, with the help of local officials, private citizens who volunteered, the military, and mountain men all participated in organizing the logistics of a series of rescue parties to save the Donner emigrants. Starting out from Johnson's Ranch which would be the central base of operations, the rescuers were a varied combination of men some with humanitarian intent to selflessly help, and others who sought pay or rewards before they would risk their lives. Regardless of an individual's motives, the first group of rescuers assembled at the Johnson's Ranch staging area where final preparations and departures took shape. It was impossible to bring wagons along because they would sink too deeply in the snow under load, so animals packed with supplies, and cattle to be herded and slaughtered upon reaching the emigrants, were readied for a very dangerous undertaking as snowstorms continued to batter the Sierra with relentless regularity.

After less than a smooth start, the First Relief Party, as it was known, was ready to leave on the morning of February 5. It consisted of 13 men that, surprisingly, included William Eddy. Though still in poor condition from his snowshoe party ordeal, he was determined to reach his wife and two children. Rain began as they progressed toward Bear Valley which made travel increasingly difficult. Animals became mired in mud, and normally easy-to-cross creeks were at flood stage causing several of the rescuer's pack animals to be swept downstream and injured—all before they reached the snowline.

The rescuers would enter the Sierra proper when they arrived at Bear Valley on February 13, but before that objective was reached, Eddy could not, and others would not, go further. Adding to the severity of complications, they faced another logistical problem: the rise in elevation had changed rain into snow that became increasingly deep so that animals were not able to be brought along leaving only one option—travel by foot. After three day's rest at Bear Valley, the seven remaining rescuers departed. Each carried a crude wooden backpack with at least fifty pounds of food and supplies to aid the emigrants. This was no small feat, and the almost superhuman effort that it took cannot be stressed enough, but by the evening of February 18, they had pushed over the summit pass, descended to Truckee Lake, and walked over the frozen body of water to its end where they had been told the lake cabins could be found.[183]

Upon reaching the camp, it appeared vacant, and the only sign of life was the stagnant haze of bluish smoke spreading out from cones of deep drifted snow where the crude shelters were buried. The rescuers began shouting "halloos!" which soon stirred a number of the emigrants into climbing out of their dens and along pathways to the surface. What the rescuers

---

[183] The seven rescuers of the First Relief Party that made it to the lake camp were Daniel Rhodes, John Rhodes, Aquila Glover, R. S. Moultry, Reason Tucker, Edward Coffeemeyer, and Joseph Sels.

saw shocked the senses of some and brought tears to others. The emigrants' situation was far worse than they imagined. Filthy, ragged clothes, boney frames, gaunt cheeks, and the dark stares of the survivors told the story of misery and famine without words. When asked about the snowshoe party, the rescuers were careful not to add more grief to their ordeal by saying that all had made it to safety as they passed out meager amounts of food along with the limited clothing and medicines they brought. A few bodies of the unfortunates who had already perished were seen strewn about half covered with snow. Patrick Breen informed the rescuers that things were even worse at the Alder Creek tents. The next morning, they made the 6-mile trek to visit the Donner camp. As anticipated, they found another horrible situation with property and litter scattered everywhere among several bodies partially exposed for lack of energy to bury them properly.

Like the lake camp, they had resorted to eating whatever they could find including animal hides and repeatedly boiling bones to get out any nutritional value.[184] George Donner was in a terrible condition delirious with infection as a result of his earlier injury that had now advanced up his arm and shoulder. He was somehow hanging on to life in part because he was meticulously cared for by his absolutely amazing and selfless wife Tamsen who refused to leave him.

****

Reason Tucker who led the First Relief Party in February 1847 sheds some light on the quantity of goods the Donner brothers still possessed during their disastrous winter entrapment. He remembered that on his arrival at the Alder Creek camp, that he and others "had cut down a large pine tree, and laid the goods of the Donners on this tree to dry in the sun." A few months later in mid-April, Tucker would return again with a salvage party recalling that "These goods lay there yet, with the exception of those in which Reed's [second rescue] party had taken away."

After handing out what little food they were able to provide, it was decided that four of the Donner children would be brought out. Those left behind would have to gamble on the Second Relief Party to reach them sooner than later. Perhaps surprisingly, at this juncture far into their forced encampment, there had been no resort to cannibalization at either camp, but the idea of it was certainly starting to crop up when Patrick Breen revealed in his diary on February 26 that eating the dead to survive was certainly being considered. He wrote that "Mrs. [Levinah] Murphy said here yesterday that [she] thought she would Commence on Milt. & eat him. I don't [think] that she has done so yet, it is distressing" (Milton Elliott died February 9 of exposure and want. His corpse lay near the Murphy cabin). A similar situation was being considered at Alder Creek. When rescuers arrived there, they were informed that if they could not find lost cattle frozen in deep snow soon, they would begin eating the dead.

---

[184] To be edible, hides first had to have the hair burned off, then cut into pieces, and finally boiled for several hours. This created a kind of glue-like glop, with an unappealing stench and taste to match, providing no nutritional value, but helping ward off the pangs of hunger by filling the stomach with something.

Over the next three days among filth and waste, rescuers assisted the refugees by gathering firewood, cooking, bathing, and tending to the infirm. Having aided the survivors as best they could, on February 21 they started back for Johnson's Ranch with 23 emigrants, 17 of whom were children.[185] It was simply impossible to attempt the removal of everyone due to weakness or illness, and even with the best efforts of the rescuers, two deaths still occurred on the way out. One of the most heart-wrenching losses was the death of Philippine Keseberg's three-year-old daughter Ada who died of exposure. She refused to leave the body behind complicating an already immensely difficult trip out. Only with the most convincing compassion on part of Reason Tucker, he was able to talk her out of giving up her baby and laying it to rest in a shallow grave of snow. The weather held, and five days later on February 26 the First Relief Party with their charges began arriving at Bear Valley where food and supplies awaited.

As to be expected, in a world without electronic devices to help coordinate seamless communication, the transition between the first and second relief parties had to deal with the uncertainty of real-time events and the lack of awareness of who was where doing what. The only thing the First Relief Party could do as they neared the snowline was hope that the Second Relief Party headed by James Reed was moving quickly as possible based solely on what had been planned earlier.[186] Deep snow had caused Reed's party of nine to leave behind their animals and pack in everything on their backs just as the first relief had to do, but in an unusual stroke of luck, Reed encountered the First Relief just below Bear Valley as the first group of survivors were slowly arriving.

There were still a little over thirty emigrants remaining at the lake. This included Reed's family who must have worried him to no end knowing that an unthinkable tragedy might be awaiting him. Moving forward, the Second Relief Party made their way into the heart of the Sierra, and as they worked their way to the summit pass, Reed ran into a small band of straggling emigrants who were escorted by Aquila Glover. To Reed's astonishment he discovered that his wife Margaret, and children, Virginia and James Jr. were in the group. It was a highly emotional encounter that was bittersweet because his two remaining children, Patty and Thomas, were still at the lake. Bolstered by his determination to save his remaining children, Reed hurried on as fast as possible.

It had been eight days in all when the Second Relief Party arrived at the lake cabins on

---

[185] Of the 23 emigrants who started out with the First Relief, two of Reed's youngest children, Patty and Thomas, would turn back as they could not keep up. John Denton and three-year-old Ada Keseberg would die en route. The 19 remaining were Simon and Edward Breen; Elitha, Leanna; their cousin George Donner Jr., and half-brother William Hook; Noah James; Philippine Keseberg; Mary and William Murphy; Naomi Pike; Eleanor, Lovina, and William Graves; Margaret Reed with two of her children Virginia, James Jr., and their servant Eliza Williams; and finally, Doris Wolfinger.

[186] The Second Relief Party consisted of the following men: James Reed, Charles Cady, Charles Stone, Nicholas Clark, Joseph Jondro, Mathew Dofar, John Turner, Hiram Miller, William McCutchen, and Britton Greenwood (son of Caleb).

March first. What they witnessed shocked them to the bottom of their souls. Just one week apart from the first rescue party, the remaining survivors at the lake camp had degraded under the most severe of conditions. In every direction, they were surrounded by the horror and unmistakable evidence of cannibalism—the last-resort of desperation that no one could ignore.

When Reed and others made their way to the Alder Creek camp, things were no different. Bodies that had been mutilated for food were in the open and were strewn among the remaining survivors who were mostly children. Concerned about the approach of deteriorating weather, the Second Relief headed out toward the pass on March third with 17 emigrants who were considered strong enough to make the trek including Reed's two children and seven members of the Breen family.[187]

Two days out with the second group of survivors, which was really more of a strung-out relay of rescuers and emigrants, the group once again had to confront the erratic hold of the Sierra's unpredictable weather. Having crossed the summit pass, they were struck by another blizzard that came barreling over the California mountains. This ultimately left them trapped for three miserable, freezing windblown days and nights. When it passed, the Breens along with three others were too exhausted to go further, so they halted at the edge of a snow-filled valley to wait for the next wave of rescuers to arrive. Reed strongly advised that they push on, but Patrick Breen refused. So continuing without them, Reed and longtime friend Hiram Miller each carried out one of Reed's two children, and were joined by Solomon Hook. In what became known as "Starved Camp," the refugees who remained behind included all seven Breens, three-year-old Isaac Donner, Elizabeth Graves, and her son Franklin Jr.; the latter three died there and were cannibalized.

With the exception of at least two feet of new snow that made travel much slower, things were moving as well as could be expected for the seven men of the Third Relief headed by William Eddy and William Foster. They reached Starved Camp during mid-March where they looked upon the distinctive remains of three bodies who were cannibalized and scattered atop the cone-shaped pit where the survivors huddled in unspeakable misery.[188] Rescuer John Stark stayed behind to provide food and encouragement to get them moving down the mountains and to safety while the remaining rescuers traveled on toward the lake cabins. Upon their arrival, Eddy and Foster discovered the grim news that their sons had died, and Eddy's wife Eleanor had

---

[187] The Second Relief brought out 17 emigrants that included the two remaining Reed children Patty and Thomas; 7 members of the of the Breen family (Edward and Simon Breen had previously left with the First Relief); Betty Donner's 3 children: Mary, Isaac, and their half-brother Solomon Hook; also included were Elizabeth Graves' 4 children: Nancy, Jonathan, Franklin Jr., and her one-year-old daughter Elizabeth.

[188] A fire could be built on top of snow by laying down a base of pine boughs, then making a platform out of larger branches and logs. A fire could then be started with dry wood set upon the simple structure. One drawback, however, was that the heat of the fire slowly consolidated and melted the snow that slowly sank. This sinking firepit is what the survivors at Starved Camp had to deal with. By the time rescuers of the Third Relief were able to help them, they had to climb out of a cone-shaped crater that was at least fifteen feet wide and over twenty feet deep.

perished as well in early February. The next day the rescuers made their way to Alder Creek to bring out survivors, and like a captain of a sinking ship, Tamsen made arrangements for her three children to be taken out, but refused rescue for herself. She would not leave her husband to die alone.

As bad timing would have it, George soon passed away leaving Tamsen completely alone. Before leaving, she respectfully wrapped her husband's body in a sheet, and only then did she make an attempt to rescue herself. But the burdens of her ceaseless energy were coming to an end. Heading out to the lake cabins, she fell through the snow soaking herself in subterranean meltwater, and may have spent the night in the open. Exhausted, she continued to the Murphy cabin where she found Keseberg in horrific squalor. She died either that night or the following day during her effort to reach the summit pass. Her body was never identified.

****

A Fourth Relief was organized, but mainly due to heavy melting snow it was aborted. A month later in mid-April, a final fifth, or salvage party, sometimes referred to as the fourth rescue, was still unable to bring in pack animals, but headed out anyway to recover worthwhile property from the Alder Creek camp. This was carried out with the understanding that they would receive fifty percent of the value of the retrieved goods when sold at auction as compensation for their efforts. The remaining fifty percent was to be used by authorities to benefit the surviving Donner children as every adult in both families had died during their winter encampment.

When the salvagers arrived at the lake cabins, they found, much to their surprise, that Louis Keseberg was still alive—living on human flesh. The rescuers were not kind to this last survivor when it was discovered that he had traveled to the Alder Creek camp to loot Donner property taking silks, jewelry, a set of matching pistols, and $225 in gold. The salvagers were also repelled by Keseberg's answer as to why he didn't eat the meat of an ox exposed by melted snow. One salvager, William Fallon, quoted that his alleged response was "it was too dry. Humans made better eating. The brains made an excellent soup."

Reason Tucker, who had returned a second time with the salvage crew, found "property of every description, books, calicoes, tea, coffee, shoes, percussion caps, household and kitchen furniture scattered in every direction and mostly in the water."[189] They brought out many items from the Donner camp that included yards of fabric such as flannel, velvet, silks, satins, muslins, gingham (think checker board pattern), and wool. There were also pants, shirts, coats, shoes, and boots; two pounds of beads (originally to be traded with Indians), five packs of playing cards, and blankets. Domestic items consisted of cooking pans and tins, a coffee mill, and ceramic plates that were hauled out. Goods soon to be sold at auction also included things such as dozens of combs, a counter pen, a hairbrush, four spelling books (of which there were

---

[189] King, Joseph A. *Winter of Entrapment: A New Look at the Donner Party*. Revised ed. Lafayette, CA: K & K Publications, 1994.

likely more at one time), paints, school supplies, a wax doll, hooks and eyes, rings, a watch key and chain, a shaving glass and case, and a razor. Other tool-oriented items included ropes, files, chisels, augers, a gimlet (tool for drilling small holes), a pry scraper, lead, and a bullet ladle.[190] And this is what we know about. There is also the possibility that some of the salvagers may not have been as honest as expected and failed to report every item removed from the Alder Creek site, thus getting a one hundred percent recovery share. All of the property from the Donner brothers' camp worth recovering was eventually sold on the auction block at Sutter's Fort on June 3, 1847. One individual who participated in the sale purchased a number of items that included thirty-four yards of calico, a cape, a pair of ladies' shoes, and a tea tray (none of which appeared on the previous list with the exception of the calico cloth).

Just how much of the auctioned property ended up being distributed to the Donner children is unclear, but the community of Californians old and new took this responsibility to heart making sure that each child (many of whom had lost toes and finger tips due to frostbite) was provided with an adequate home. John Henry Brown a hotel keeper in San Francisco recalled in his reminiscences *The Early Days of San Francisco* that George Donner Jr. was brought to the city where he gave the ten-year-old "board[,] and lawyer [Lansford] Hastings… gave him…clothes." Friends and strangers alike were more than willing to make him as comfortable as possible. "The boy had many small presents given him in money, which he saved." Others contributed to his fund and a lot in San Francisco was purchased for him that turned out to be valuable.[191]

Hastings furnishing George Donner Jr. with clothing is as close as the record gets in his personal response regarding the Donner Party tragedy. He never publicly or privately spoke of the matter nor assisted in any of the rescue attempts to bring the emigrants to safety. There appears to be no reaction to the incident itself, and he does not seem to harbor any guilt or fault— not that he necessarily should. It is plausible then, that he felt no responsibility in connection with the Donner Party's disaster during their entrapment or its aftermath, nor does anyone else directly related to the event seem to hold him accountable to any large degree.
****

Since no wagons or animals as yet could be taken over the pass because of deep snow, the salvagers had to haul as much property as possible on their backs. Keseberg later recalled that they "started over the mountains, each man carried two bales of goods. They had silks,

---

[190] The 2004 archaeological excavation revealed fragments of slate writing boards previously unrecorded. Tamsen was a teacher planning to open a school in California, so this is consistent with materials she would require.

[191] Brown, John Henry. *The Early Days of San Francisco*. California Centennial Edition Number 20 ed. Oakland, CA: Biobooks, 1949.
* George Jr. and his sister Mary were likely sent to San Francisco due to her need for medical attention. Seven-year-old Mary's frostbite and the subsequent burns on her feet as a result of getting too close to an open fire during rescue required special attention. Both children would later be taken in by James Reed and family.

calicoes, and delaines (high quality wool cloth), along with other articles of great value from the Donner camps. Each man would carry one bundle a little way, lay it down, and come back and get the other bundle. In this way they passed over the snow three times."[192]

Items left at the Alder Creek camp, that were either ruined, broken, or not worth the effort to carry out, littered the open meadow where the Donner's crude shelters stood among the remains of 5 wagons, two substantial fire pits, and a bewildering mess of other articles. Over the ensuing 158 years, time, land reuse, and souvenir hunters would so completely scavenge or alter the area that the exact location of the Alder Creek camps would be lost to folklore. That is until the 2004 archaeological excavation affirmed the site of one hearth clarifying a number of previous misconceptions.

Based on the goods recovered by rescuers and salvagers alike during their various efforts, there is considerable evidence that many unnecessary items were brought to the Alder Creek camp. To be fair, many personal and everyday use items would be deemed as necessary, but property useless for survival is another matter. Material possessions that pointlessly weighed down the wagons of their burdened animals compromised the safety of those dependent upon them. It was a significant risk in an uncertain situation. There was ample opportunity to dump hundreds of pounds of material possessions in a meaningful way before reaching the Sierra, but this would have entailed great monetary loss. The Donners did jettison some property, but for various reasons brought out earlier, they reasoned that keeping much of it was a risk worth taking. The conundrum of what the Donner families decided to keep must have been on par with the hyperbolic saying modern-day rock climbers sometimes face: Lay out everything you want, and then put ninety percent of it back. In essence, do not carry useless weight. Similarly, hard choices made by the Donner brothers, and the consequences of those decisions, contributed to the direct result of their overall situation which cannot hold Hastings accountable for the important advice he offered in his book which was ignored.

****

As the salvagers continued their trek toward the summit pass carrying out the most valuable goods, Keseberg, the last survivor to be brought out, was very weak from his ordeal but managed to make progress. He remembered one day in particular when he was slowly dragging himself up the pass, that he came to a place previously used as a camping-ground. He recalled, "Feeling very tired, I thought it would be a good place to make some coffee. Kindling a fire, I filled my coffee-pot with fresh snow…Happening to cast my eyes carelessly around, I discovered a little piece of calico protruding from the snow…I caught hold of the cloth [and] gave it a strong pull." This revealed the cruelest scene that can be imagined—It was the remains of his three-year-old daughter Ada who had died while being brought out with the First Relief Party; Keseberg had not known of her death until that moment. There is no way to express the

---

[192] McGlashan, C. F. *History of the Donner Party: A Tragedy of the Sierra.* Stanford University Press, 1947. P. 218-219.

nightmarish parental shock that weighed upon him. After all he had been through, his emotional fortitude now teetered on the razor's edge of loss, and his tormented sanity. And it wasn't just Keseberg, every survivor of the Donner Party with any memory of their experience would have to make peace with their own conscience through denial, words, or silence.

13. The California Convention and Beyond

When the War with Mexico ended in February 1848, the Treaty of Guadalupe Hidalgo ceded to the United States a huge territory referred to as the Mexican Cession. The U. S. Government in return agreed to pay out $15 million in cash, and honor claims Mexican citizens held against the United States totaling $3.25 million. California was the prize of course and would be under post-war military rule until a civilian government could be established. Within the same time-frame, like a flash of lightning on a clear night, gold was found by James Marshall who was building a saw mill for John Sutter forty miles east of his fort. His discovery was made literally a week before the war's end and a little more than a month before the United States Senate officially approved the treaty.

By 1849, the rush to California's gold fields was on, and with it, an accelerated need for civil law that the military governance was not especially fond of carrying out. And as the late historian J. S. Holliday noted, California was unique because even though it was federal land, Congress chose not to interfere with the harvesting of gold.[193] There was a significant military presence in California at the time, but it would be sheer foolishness to try and enforce such an order even if Washington, D. C. had chosen to do so. Besides, it would be counter-productive to stop the flow of wealth it would bring to the country. It was truly a free-for-all unmatched to this very day, uninhibited by government interference.

California's military governor Brigadier General Bennett Riley took up the cause to deal with the need for self-governance. Since federal authorities had made no provisions for breaking up the Mexican Cession into territories and establishing civilian control, General Bennett decided to act on his own. This was a bold move because he had no federal authorization to call such a gathering, but something had to be done otherwise lawlessness, an inconsistent judicial system, and vigilante groups would prevail. He called for the people of California to elect delegates from various populated centers of the territory and hold a constitutional convention.

Under Bennett's direction, California would essentially go from a territory to an instant state. To begin the process, forty-eight delegates were chosen from ten city and mining districts, one of whom was Lansford Hastings representing Sacramento. The convention assembled in Monterey in September, and by October 12, 1849 California was well on its way to becoming the nation's newest state upon the consent of Congress. But getting there was not as easy as it appeared.

Neither the Spanish nor the Mexicans had established a precise eastern border for California, so it was an open issue. Beyond the border question, there were other considerations such as where the state capitol should be located, the establishment and limitations of banks, citizenship, suffrage, public education, and the equally pressing matter of slavery which

---

[193] J. S. Holliday speaking engagement at Fallon House Theatre Columbia, California 1992.

emerged as a major concern. With the addition of 525,000 territorial square miles gained in the Mexican Cession, by default the subject of slavery became one of the most important topics in the negotiation of California's eastern boundary.

Among the many delegates in the fall of 1849 who contributed to California's statehood, none was less auspicious than Lansford Hastings who would partake in an exceptional role regarding the formation of the Golden State's political boundaries.[194] There were a number of important reasons for this that revolved around Hastings' wide-ranging geographic knowledge of the region, and his consideration of the Mormons who had already established a thriving community in Utah. Therefore, California's eastern border would be among the most significant debates and deliberations that would be presented during the convention.

It may seem strange that a man who was allegedly so reviled by history should have such a prominent role in the convention, yet Hastings did as he was chosen to chair the Committee on the Boundary. This is simply more evidence that he was seen in a much different light than the self-centered scoundrel he has been portrayed. He was viewed by many as a capable attorney and a seasoned western traveler who was not afraid to explore or lead. His voice was essential at the convention as he brought to the table maps and proposals that would

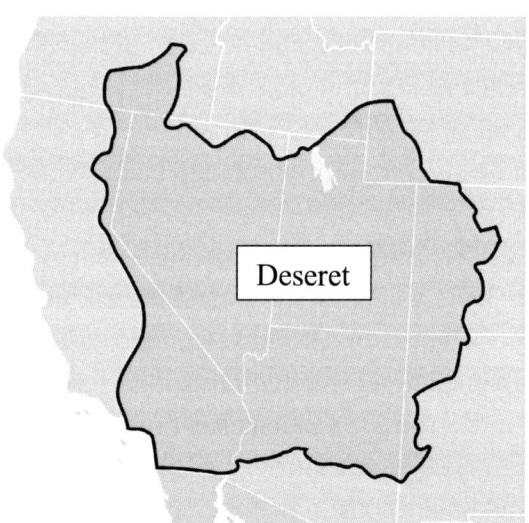

help bring into focus what he thought California's border might or should encompass.

Being familiar with the geography of Oregon, California, and the Great Basin, he offered his experience suggesting that the eastern boundary extend to the 116th line of longitude which would include known and possible future resources. It had the potential, however, to create conflict with the Mormons by not including them since they had designs on becoming a state known as Deseret during the same period.[195] Hastings believed that if California's boundary went too far east, it would not only be unfair to the Mormons who already inhabited Utah Territory with more than 20,000 people, but would also provoke Southern slaveholders into making claims that would extend the practice of slavery further west.

During negotiations, many boundary recommendations were made. One included a wild proposal to make California a massive state that reached all the way to the Rocky Mountains.[196]

---

[194] Goodwin, Cardinal. "The Question of the Eastern Boundary of California in the Convention of 1849." *The Southwestern Historical Quarterly*, No. 4, XVI (January 1913): 227-58.

[195] Deseret was a state proposed by the Mormons in 1849. It included nearly all of modern Utah and Nevada, most of Arizona, parts of five future states, and about one-third of California providing access to the Pacific Ocean. It was rejected by Congress. A greatly downsized Utah Territory would become the 45th state much later in 1896.

Not only would the Mormons, who were already established at Salt Lake City, be ignored if California claimed such a huge portion of territory, but the state would simply be ungovernable. One of the big reasons for the extreme border was to keep slavery from expanding. But a slavery-free California would be so large that it would eventually have to be broken down into smaller parts opening the potential for new slave states to crop up. Hastings reacted to the issue of an extreme eastern boundary by taking into consideration the exclusion of the Mormons and arguing in the convention that "You have no right to include all that territory. It contains a vast population [of Mormons] as much entitled to respect…" and would be… "fifteen hundred miles remote…out of reach of your laws and authority, and impossible for them to be represented in your Legislature."[197] Additionally, if California's eastern border was too expansive, Congress would give pause in allowing California to become a state as the slavery question continued to divide the country, and it was not going away.[198]

Pro-slavery factions wanted the territory of the Mexican Cession open to the practice in order to be able to exploit the doctrine of popular sovereignty. This allowed the people who moved into a territory to decide if it was to be free or slave when applying for statehood. Another factor that had to be considered was that if California's eastern boundary extended too far, Southern Congress members would never agree to statehood.

Both the California Convention delegates and the far-away Mormons at Salt Lake City had to come to grips by giving up massive areas of the Great Basin and reducing their claims in order to allow their proposed territories to be governable. California was massive enough to begin with, but Congress was willing to overlook that since they believed that a large section of its interior was similar to the Great Basin and therefore useless. Along the eastern base of the Sierra Nevada, the Mormons established a settlement named Genoa to lay claim to territory they wanted to include in Deseret, but that would place them in the same predicament of not being able to effectively govern such an expansive area.

It was Hastings who offered a more workable plan modified from his first version. This time the line of longitude would be adjusted to the 118th degree. Again, this would harness known and possible future resources while cutting out the mostly barren land of the Great Basin that was considered no great loss or contribution to the spread of slavery. One major issue still existed however, and that was the natural barrier of the Sierra Nevada. Hastings made it clear that any settlements on the eastern base of those mountains would effectively be cut off from the interior of California and the West Coast for about half of the year because of snow, therefore, being excluded from practical governance. Besides, at the time, the Great Basin had not yielded

---

[196] Johnson, David Alan. *Founding the Far West: California, Oregon, and Nevada, 1840-1890.* Berkeley, CA: University of California Press, 1992.

[197] Hansen, Woodrow James. *The Search for Authority in California.* California Heritage No. 47. Oakland, CA: Biobooks, 1960.

[198] In addition, miners, or those who understood mining, did not want slave labor to undercut the work of individuals.

any significant mineral deposits, so its inclusion was not worth the problems it could cause.[199] This understanding would lead Hastings into suggesting a plan that would eventually be adopted.

Elisha Crosby, an attorney and convention delegate from Sacramento had nothing but praise for Hastings concerning the boundary issue which was to run down the crest of the Sierra giving up the eastern portion of the mountains into what would become Nevada Territory. He stated that "Mr. Hastings is entitled more than any other man to the credit of fixing that line. He had more to do with it by presenting arguments & working for it than anyone else."[200]

In the end after much discussion, the logical boundary was to have California's northern border start from the 42nd parallel that ran along the base of Oregon Territory—a line that had been negotiated between the U. S. and Spain in 1819. From that northern starting point, the 120th degree of longitude would mark California's eastern boundary. Following the spine of the Sierra to Lake Tahoe, the border would then angle down to the 35th parallel to meet the Colorado River which would terminate at the United States-Mexican border. The western boundary would be the Pacific Coast. This plan would alleviate a variety of issues ranging from representation of all districts throughout the year, and potential disagreement with the Mormons. Most importantly, it made Congressional approval of California as a free state palatable through the Compromise of 1850, and left the issue of slavery and the remaining territories placed directly upon the Federal Government. Thus, California was brought into the fold as the 31st star in the Union on September 9, 1850.

****

As before the convention, Hastings did not retire his skills in law, nor his involvement in politics through appointed or elected positions. He frequently advertised his legal services in two prominent newspapers: *The Californian* and *California Star*. In addition to his professional expertise, he had a wide-range of personal interests and business dealings.[201] In 1845-48 he partnered with John Sutter by scouting a site for a grist mill. He was also invested with Sutter in

---

[199] The silver mines of the Comstock Lode were not discovered until 1859. Had they been found earlier, there would likely have been much more discussion and modification of California's eastern border regardless of the obstacles. Technology such as the telegraph would have provided a means to connect both sides of the Sierra for governance purposes.

[200] Crosby, Elisha Oscar. *Memoirs of Elisha Oscar Crosby: Reminiscences of California and Guatemala 1849-1864.* Los Angeles: The Ward Ritchie Press, 1945.

[201] To earn a living in California before, during and after the Mexican War, Hastings advertised his law practice in the *Californian and California Star* newspapers. Interestingly, there was an announcement in the *Californian* from the current military governor, Bennett Riley, conveying that "Hastings is to visit all of the principal cities and settlements of the northern department of California, to take enlistments of patriotic citizens in a battalion of volunteers, for service…." In the March 15, 1848 edition Hastings advertises "Attorney Counsellor at Law and Solicitor in Chancery, San Francisco, Upper California." Continuing in some detail he states that he "will now devote his entire attention to his profession; he will attend to the collection of debts, and to all other business connected with his profession in any portion of the Territory…"

lots he surveyed for him at the aptly named Sutterville near the Sacramento River. At the same time, Hastings built a house on a proposed land grant named Montezuma on the upper California Delta where he planned to survey lots for a Mormon migration that never came.[202] Hastings even joined in a cattle contract with no other than James Reed who apparently held no ill feelings toward Hastings in the aftermath of the Donner Party incident.[203] During the rush for gold, he and Sutter paired together once again setting up a short-lived store in Coloma. That same year, Hastings was elected school trustee in San Francisco, and was appointed judge of the northern district.[204]

Hastings, whose income was based largely on his professional fees, married his second wife, Charlotte Toler, in July 1848. Having failed in just about every venture he was involved with, he decided to move his family to Arizona City, present-day Yuma, in early 1858.[205] Always looking to make things happen instead of waiting for something, he asked the territorial governor to be appointed notary public and was granted the position. He also served as postmaster general there as well. The next several years were more or less unremarkable, the exceptions being the death of his wife in 1861, and Hastings' belief that the Colorado River in Arizona Territory had the potential to become the next important trading center in the west.

To promote this idea, he wrote to Brigham Young, leader of the Mormon stronghold at Salt Lake City. Stating that his goal was to link commerce with them via the Colorado, he touted the river and its tributaries as "destined to become the Mississippi of the Pacific" by which trade at the mouth of the river would connect goods from New York and San Francisco alike. He admired the work ethic of the Mormons and desired to be connected with trading opportunities by which he might benefit himself. However, his enthusiastic plan with the Latter-day Saints never materialized in large part because no one had ever traveled the entire length of the Colorado to see if it was, in fact, possible to navigate. With the outbreak of Civil War, it would not be explored entirely until 1869 when the expedition of John Wesley Powell, a one-armed Civil War veteran tied to a chair in a wooden boat, whisking down rapids two stories high, proved that it could be done. But in doing so, he confirmed that the wildness of the Colorado River would never allow it to be anything close to a "Mississippi of the Pacific."

****

---

[202] Hastings would not become a Mexican citizen, so it was never granted.

[203] CALIFORNIA STATE LIBRARY
Buchanan, John C. "Letter to James F. Reed." May 2, 1847. MSS Box 345.

[204] Bancroft, Hubert Howe. *California Pioneer Register & Index, 1542-1848*. Baltimore, MD: Regional Publishing Company, 1964.

[205] Andrews, Thomas F. *THE CONTROVERSIAL CAREER OF LANSFORD WARREN HASTINGS: PIONEER CALIFORNIA PROMOTER AND EMIGRANT GUIDE*. PhD diss., University of Southern California, 1970. Los Angeles, CA: Thomas F. Andrews, 1970. 1-286.

During 1860 the states' rights issue had become increasingly fueled and convoluted, in part, by a politically strong influential minority of southern slaveholders in Congress who cloaked their economic justification to own another human in a morally abhorrent manner. The 1860 census, based on 36 states at the time, revealed that there were fifteen slaveholding states and 8 percent of the population possessing slaves.[206] The point is that states' rights and the limits of federal authority over the states was controversial at best regardless if one was a Northern abolitionist in support of it or a slaveholding Southerner. But with the election of Abraham Lincoln, the South felt that he would force the matter to a head against the South's better judgment. As a result, South Carolina became the first of 11 states to secede from the Union setting the stage for the Civil War.

The controversy of states' rights was a divisive issue that genuinely concerned many Americans at the time who worried about too much federal power over the states. The theory was that the states approved the U. S. Constitution and the Federal Government; therefore, states could override federal law considered unconstitutional, or even contemplate secession from the Union. This being the case, it was not the issue of slavery that led Hastings to sympathize with the South, but federal authority. Hastings' personal convictions certainly had less to do with slavery, and more to do about the controversial but legitimate view of states' rights.

The issue of states' rights first reared its head with the Kentucky and Virginia Resolutions of 1798-99. This was a response to the Alien and Sedition Acts which gave then president John Adams power to deport or arrest anyone thought to be a threat to America. This was viewed by many as the Federal Government exceeding its power over the states that might disagree with such a controversial policy, and was a blatant disregard of an individual's civil liberties under the Constitution. Therefore, it was argued by some that states had the right and duty to declare unconstitutional and reject any acts of Congress that were not authorized in the Constitution—thus, a states' rights issue. It was put to rest without further controversy at the time with the election of Thomas Jefferson who did not allow the Alien and Sedition Acts to renew, but the matter would return for another round with more intensity 35 years later.

This highly combative challenge to federal power appeared again when the state of South Carolina threatened secession over the perception of unfair import taxes on foreign goods. The Nullification Crisis of 1832 brought into focus a direct confrontation with federal authority and the issue of states' rights. It came about as a series of Congressional tariffs passed to increase the price of imported goods which would protect the Northern manufacturing economy from foreign competition. It may have seemed like a good idea at first, but the added taxes did not benefit the Southern agrarian economy as they were dependent on European trade for their needs. As a result, the price of foreign goods cost more with no advantage to the South. South Carolina declared the tariffs null and void and, as a state, challenged the legality of the Federal Government to pass such laws that hurt them economically. Again, many viewed this as a

---

[206] "The Civil War Home Page." Results from the 1860 Census. 2020. Accessed December 03, 2018. http://www.civil-war.net/.

states' rights question, and it was such a heated topic that South Carolina threatened to secede from the Union. President Andrew Jackson countered by threatening to send in thousands of troops to enforce the tariff if order was not restored. Eventually cooler heads prevailed, and a compromise was reached ending the crisis for the moment but not the controversy. This hard line resulted in Jackson's Vice President, John C. Calhoun, resigning from office in order to run for a more influential Senate seat representing South Carolina.

As an Ohioan, Hastings grew up in a state cut from the Northwest Territory that never allowed slavery, nor did he ever own another human being at any point in his life. There is little question that Hastings possessed the prejudices of his day, but his sympathetic association with the South was more likely connected with his belief that the Federal Government did not have the right to usurp power over the states rather than personally supporting the "peculiar institution"—slavery. Hastings' position on the issue is only speculation, and to date there is nothing to confirm or deny it one way or the other.

It is a short leap of imagination, however, to deduce why Hastings may have taken a strong position regarding the states' rights issue. Even though slaveholders used states' rights to justify any attempt of the Federal Government to end slavery or its extension, Hastings did seem to favor a weaker Federal Government over a state's autonomy to reject a federal law deemed unconstitutional. This might suggest why Hastings took on a militaristic initiative to bring Arizona Territory into play for the South during the Civil War. He may well have agreed with Thomas Jefferson's idea that "a little rebellion now and then is a good thing, and as necessary in the political world as storms in the physical."

By 1863 as the Union and Confederate forces of the country entered the second year of Civil War, Hastings made plans to help bring Arizona into the Southern sphere. His support very likely had more to do with the belief that the Federal Government had overreached its constitutional authority than anything else. This may have had a major influence on Hastings' personal desire to support Southern disunion and take action on behalf of the South.

By keeping a line of access open from Arizona Territory into California, its resources would be threatened in its role to support a strong central government. Hastings understood that California was a monetary slot machine for the North as the state shipped tons of gold and copper east in order to fuel the Federal Government's war effort and establish its superiority over the states. Although Hastings was rebuffed by Southern leaders who did not think his plan was feasible, it fits in with Hastings' aggressive personality to act rather than take a passive role and do nothing regardless of the odds.

Outlasting the Union Government's will to fight was the only feasible option for a much less powerful Confederacy to "win" the Civil War. The South hoped that the North would relent and end the conflict leaving the Confederate states to do as they pleased. This was not going to happen under President Lincoln. And when the war came to an end in 1865 after four long years, the superiority of federal power over the states was established once and for all, laying to rest the issue of states' rights forever. For those of the post-war Confederate states who may have felt disenfranchised, it may come as no surprise that Lansford Warren Hastings had a plan which was to provide a refuge for the defeated ex-patriots. And that meant leaving the country for a new beginning in South America.

14. The Making of a Scapegoat

It's very easy to neatly enshrine Lansford Hastings in the dishonest light of presentism.[207] He has been made to be a villain in a relentless (and inaccurate) campaign centering on his persuasive powers to entice the Donner Party into following him on his promoted cutoff without the slightest concern about the well-being of anyone but himself.

Most adjectives used to describe Hastings and his cutoff have forwarded unflattering connotations ranging from scoundrel to psychotic. Perhaps it was those perceived qualities that tempted author George Stewart to corral Lansford Hastings into a villainous role in the story plot of his masterfully written and hugely popular *Ordeal by Hunger* (1936). A classic of western literature in its own right, Stewart may not have realized at the time, but he would be instrumental in creating one of the most powerful linchpins in print that solidified Hastings' persona. He was transformed into a ruthless, self-serving, ambitious antagonist who would stop at nothing to achieve his presumed narcissistic ends in the conquest of California—others be damned.

Hastings has been viewed as a Judas among the heroes of western migration, but like the real Judas, a new understanding has emerged reassessing his role in history as a messenger and not a betrayer of Christ. We now know Judas to be someone entirely different in the context of his time.[208] There is a similar comparison with Hastings. Stewart made his notions about him alongside the unfavorable implication of an unrevised Judas of old who was thought to possess equal mendacity. It makes good reading, but as a result of Stewart's presumptuous assessment of Hastings, his literary work has, more than anyone else, entrenched the myth of Hastings' character into a disreputable archetype that simply isn't true but is repeatedly cited, rarely questioned, and reproduced with factory-like precision.

The circumstances revolving around the changing environment and choices that Hastings as well as the Donner Party sifted through were many. Making decisions on the fly was common and often necessary, and no one was swindled into a belief that Hastings' route, the one they assented to follow as a group, was the cornerstone of their success in order to make up time lost. Nor were they completely oblivious of the potential difficulties that awaited them. With convincing pressure from James Reed, the Donner Party accepted full responsibility for the undertaking of crossing the Great Basin using the new cutoff. There were a number of

---

[207] Presentism is the application of current ideals and moral standards used to interpret historical figures and their actions in the past. Attitudes and cultural values often change over time, and presentism creates a distorted understanding of the subject matter making it more difficult if not impossible to interpret history fairly. An example would be removing the statue of a Civil War general because he supported the South. Or perhaps this example: Lansford Hastings should have advised James Reed not to attempt his new cutoff if he was an honest man.

[208] Lovgren, Stefan. "Lost Gospel of Judas Revealed." Science. April 05, 2006. Accessed May 26, 2021. https://www.nationalgeographic.com/science/article/lost-gospel-judas-revealed-jesus-archaeology.

reasons to believe that it had worthwhile advantages as they worked their way toward California, and in taking that chance, they knew there was considerable risk. Hastings made it clear in his guide that "Very few cowards ever venture voluntarily, to meet all those imaginary and real dangers...in crossing the Rocky Mountains." He suggests that it takes great energy and bravery to emigrate, and he never tries to sugarcoat those facts.

As the collisions of men and their actions in the process of making history can later attest to, Hastings' chance meeting with Fremont led to the plausibility of the southern desert route becoming a reality. Only then did Hastings ponder the prospect of a wagon trail and not only sought to exploit its rough-edged possibility by quickly exploring and promoting it, but offering to lead emigrants of the 1846 migration west for the first time with wagons. Armed with unbridled exuberance and limited, but workable, geographic knowledge, never does he advise that this new cutoff is a "shortcut" in any definitive way, nor did he make any recommendations that emigrants rely on it as such. It was just simply more direct.[209] He logically thought it was a realistic cutting-edge trail alternative that he pieced together with limited but expanding information, and his gut instincts to make it happen. It did not take a genius to infer that a route south of the Great Salt Lake would be perceivably less lengthy than the "regular" road via Fort Hall. It just wasn't determined to be how much—perhaps up to 300 miles, and would the cost in time still result in advantage?

****

In a sense, Hastings was ahead of his time. It is true that the most direct route between points A and B is often the shortest way to get somewhere. Unfortunately, obstacles such as mountain ranges, fresh water and grass sources, sand, mud, heavy wagons, less than complete geographical knowledge were all conspirators. They were linked together in a dance that perilously tried to force geography into submission and challenged every emigrant wagon train led by Hastings on his cutoff in 1846. And then there was the latent Donner Party, whose journey was complicated with the added factor of lost time to stem the far-reaching distance to the Sierra before the approach of adverse weather stopped them cold. Therefore, time and distance were the two variables of risk that no one could extract with certainty, yet were critically important to the success or failure of their endeavor. This is why Hastings encouraged emigrants to reach the Sierra by October first in his guide.

Attempting to find a more direct route was nothing unusual during this period of westward expansion. New routes may have been potentially challenging, but often the preferred choice if it led to an advantage of the intended goal. For example, the Stephens Party of 1844-45 attempted to strike a direct but difficult path up the Truckee River and across the summit of the Sierra. They knew that two earlier groups in 1841 and 1843 had taken longer routes south along the eastern edge of California, but failed to successfully bring wagons across the mountain barrier into the Great Central Valley. Therefore, they opted to gamble on a new, difficult route that in the end was successful by locating a pass to admit wagons over the summit of the Sierra.

---

[209] Until the cutoff was actually tried with wagons, Hastings' "most direct" alternative turned out to be less mileage overall but with a cost of more time which negated its usefulness.

But with the demise of the Donner Party who took the same route the following year, it became a questionable trail that lost momentum. It was not the difficulty of the Truckee passage that was the problem, but the fear of what happened to the Donner Party because of their late season crossing. As a result, in 1848, directly due in large part to the residual effect of the Donner Party disaster, the Mormon-Carson Route was established south of Lake Tahoe. It became the most traveled road across the Sierra for many years even though it was longer and more difficult than the Truckee route because of a double summit crossing. It was also not stigmatized by the Donner Party's misfortune.

In 1860, surveyor Theodore Judah, an engineer looking for a potential route for the Transcontinental Railroad, located a suitable line across the Sierra into the Great Basin. He found that the Truckee River Route was the most feasible not only because it was the most direct route into California, but it would also be the least expensive since only one summit pass had to be negotiated. There are reasons for direct pathways, and Hastings was not unreasonable in encouraging it through the personal promotion of his "most direct" cutoff south of the Great Salt Lake. Yet he is often criticized for his calculated daring.

Author Ethan Rarick proposes that the error in Hastings Cutoff is that the shortest route is not always the best:

> "Ironically, it was the presumed advantage of Hastings' route that was in fact its central flaw. Like a modern engineer building a freeway, Hastings laid out his course with a straight-edge, heedless of the constraints of mountain or desert...military units might conquer whatever barrier lay before them, but family wagons and livestock needed to treat the most difficult topography with grudging respect, circumventing obstructions rather than assaulting them. Travel by compass bearing alone was an arrogant fantasy."[210]

What Rarick concludes is generally true about wagons and livestock. However, travelers using pack animals on Hastings Cutoff did so without too much drama, and their crossing was a very different story much to their advantage because they could move fast. And even though travel by wagon was indisputably difficult, Hastings described the route as "more direct" not a straight line. If he did, then it would have been an "arrogant fantasy." Hastings was able to course out with confidence a new wagon route based on reasonable information and personal reconnaissance. He also traversed a majority of his proposed cutoff before leading over 70 wagons and hundreds of emigrants across it without the loss of a single human life. It was the Donner Party's late arrival upon the scene that was the actual fatal flaw of the entire story for which Hastings has become the scapegoat.

Emigrant John R. McBride had a different take on the promoter that veers far from the patented criticism of him. He was heading to Oregon in 1846 and related his encounter with Hastings providing a contradictory viewpoint of others who would in later years bill Hastings as a historical pariah:

---

[210] Rarick, Ethan. *Desperate Passage: The Donner Party's Perilous Journey West*. Oxford: Oxford University Press, 2009.78-79. Print.

"Near the end of the Sweetwater we came upon the camp of three men; the leader was Lansford W. Hastings, his comrade was a man by the name of Hudspeth and a California vaquero (herder). Hasting's [*sic*] name was familiar to us from his journal of the journey in 1842, which had been published in Cincinnati, I think and was in the hands of our party. It had been used as a guide book, and seeing the author of it was like meeting a friend... He painted the attractions of California in glowing colors; and as he was a man of plausible manners and fine address, he made some impression, and finally a portion of our train changed their destination further on."[211]

McBride also reminisced years later that "...we met another party of mountaineers on their way to St. Louis. One of the number was...a brother of William L. Sublette, one of the most noted of the leaders of the western trappers and fur hunters. He was recently from California, and was quite outspoken in his criticism of Hasting's scheme of a new route to California. He said it was an impracticable route for teams, and if they attempted it, would lead to disaster. His predictions, however, were erroneous; for Hastings, having induced some 60 plus wagons to follow his leadership, piloted them safely through his proposed route to California."[212]

It is interesting to note that McBride is silent about Hastings long after the Donner Party disaster. This is an important distinction as McBride reserved any hint of moral judgment regarding Hastings unlike many others. It is chiefly later nineteenth and twentieth century writers and historians who have attempted to integrate a moral aspect into Hastings' actions that hint at or caused the Donner Party's downfall. This may have come from the fact that forty-five of the eighty-seven members of the company were children under the age of eighteen. Very few of the Donner Party members themselves were critical of Hastings immediately after their ordeal, if at all, and if they were, it was decades after their suffering and often from questionable sources.

Nevertheless, the finger pointing began early when J. Quinn Thornton, an 1846 emigrant heading to Oregon, who had at one point travelled with the Donner Party, published in 1849 *Oregon and California in 1848*. Its construction is a mishmash of facts, half-truths, alleged sources, errors, and outright suspect comments stated about Hastings.

The negative remarks in reference to Hastings may have reflected Thornton's hatred of Jesse Applegate a promoter of a new route to Oregon who led emigrants on a disastrous route that cost those who followed him nearly all of their possessions as well as threatening their lives.[213] Thornton, who fell in with Applegate, experienced the firsthand trauma of being egregiously misled and was undoubtedly bitter. Thornton may have had the Donner Party's

---

[211] McBride, John R. "Pioneer Days in the Mountains." *Tullidges Quarterly Magazine*. July 1884, 311-320.

[212] McBride, John R., reminiscent account, *Capital Journal* (Salem, OR, February 4 to March 23, 1926).

[213] Johnson, Kristin. Unfortunate Emigrants Narratives of the Donner Party. First ed. Logan, Utah: Utah State UP, 1996.

interests in mind when he learned of their suffering. He attempted to sooth their cannibalistic pocked ordeal by placing blame for their misfortune on the western promoter himself. Hastings, who seemed a justifiable scapegoat in Thornton's mind, failed to bring into focus the Donner Party's own personal responsibility based on decisions *they* made.

Thornton's record of lashing out at Hastings began as early as June 16, 1846 when he sneeringly commented that "Lansford W. Hastings, who, if an opinion may be formed of him from the many untruths contained in his *Emigrants' Guide To Oregon and California* is the Baron Munchausen of travelers in these countries...."[214] To sway matters further against Hastings over time, Thornton's work, with the exception of Charles McGlashen's *History of the Donner Party* were the only comprehensive accounts of their calamity for almost one hundred years. There is no question that Hastings painted California oft times in exaggerated terms, but that does not take away from the fact that his book was an excellent guide informing emigrant's on how to prepare for an extended wagon journey. Thornton conveniently overlooks that.

Unknown at the time, Hastings and his soon-to-be infamous cutoff would become inseparably linked with the Donner Party and label Hastings as a dealer of incompetence. This would come mainly from a host of sources shortly after their tragedy but would spill over into the next century misleading readers about Hastings even more. This is in large part because historians and writers such as Bernard DeVoto, Charles Kelly, Ralph Moody, and many others have greatly perpetuated the Hastings stereotype. They have influenced future authors as well as historians who have selectively interpreted, accepted, or parroted a highly charged defacement of Hastings. They have characterized him as an unscrupulous, self-centered scourge with no moral compass—a dealer of doom to unwitting innocent people. This set the stage for continuing criticism and misunderstanding of Hastings in the most damning way without objective consideration of what actually took place in his association with the Donner Party.

George McKinstry, who traveled Hastings Cutoff with Bryant's mule train, offered his opinion that suggested the Donner Party's blunders, not Hastings', caused their own difficulties. He claimed that "The men of the Donner Party may not have worked as energetically as they would have, if gifted with the foresight, but they started on "Reed's route" [The route Hastings suggested when Reed caught up to him]…and emerged into Salt Lake Valley on August 22…. Reed was always very sensitive to charges that the plight of the Donner Party resulted from his influence to cut this new road across the [Wasatch] mountains, and he may have displayed a thin skin."[215]

By the first half of the 1900s, Hastings' negative image had become a singular

---

[214] The reference to the fictional Baron Munchausen and his fantastical travels is a literary metaphor linking Hastings as a teller of preposterous stories—a liar.

[215] Morgan, Dale L. *Overland in 1846: Diaries and Letters of the California-Oregon Trail. Vol. 2.* Lincoln, Neb.: University of Nebraska Press, 1993. (Page 794n 188).

stereotype that would endure.[216] In the past and present judgment of others, he is portrayed as a selfish blameworthy antagonist who spearheaded the demise of the Donner Party with convoluted influence and intent. That makes a great story line, but is hardly based in fact. In reality, Hastings had an almost spectral connection with the Donner Party yet the story has reverberated into an almost obsessive focal point that has Hastings leading them on like lemmings over a cliff.

The haste to portray Hastings as a scapegoat has had a long and varied history over the years. The following selections from a variety of past and recent publications contain some of the standard and more creative embellishments to describe him. Since Hastings is the scapegoat of choice, it will be quite a challenge to resurrect a fair assessment of him based on multiple decades of critical branding:

Jesse Quinn Thornton (1849) *Oregon and California in 1848*
"Mrs. George Donner was gloomy, sad, and dispirited." He also states surprise that "her husband and others could think for a moment of leaving the old road, and confide in the statement of a man of whom they knew nothing, but who was probably some selfish adventurer."[217] Thornton's questionable tirade goes on: "Some poured bitter imprecations upon the head of L. W. Hastings, for having deceived them as to the road upon which he had conducted them." Hastings neither conducted nor deceived anyone. He was nearly two weeks ahead with the emigrants he was leading when Reed caught up to him. Yet he fails to mention that Hastings went out of his way to help Reed, nor later does he hint of a backlash for making poor choices by chancing Hastings' October first warning to attempt crossing the Sierra.

John Bidwell (1877 Bancroft research interviewer) *Century Magazine*
He suggests Hastings came to California seemingly with one purpose in mind—"wresting California from Mexico, and establishing an independent republic." He stated that Hastings was "ambitious himself to be its President." He returned to the states in 1844 via Mexico to reach Texas and confer with the Pres[ident] in that Republic in regard to his plans." There is no evidence that Hastings ever met with Texan President Sam Houston. Four years later, however, in a series of magazine articles, Bidwell recalled that the evidence he possessed about Hastings was based on hearsay, not fact. He justified his confession by stating that "He [Hastings] disclosed his plan to a man who revealed it to me."[218] Nevertheless, the damage was done and the root of the Hastings myth persists to this day in a wide variety of negative interpretations.

---

[216] Andrews, Thomas F. "The Ambitions of Lansford W. Hastings: A Study in Western Myth-Making." *The Pacific Historical Review* 39 no. 4 (1970): 473-491.

[217] Johnson, *Unfortunate Emigrants*, page 22, notes that "This oft-cited presentment of Tamsen Donner's may owe something to hindsight on Thornton's part."

[218] "California, 1841-48," [dictation for H. H. Bancroft, 1877], 110-111, MS, Bancroft Library, University of California, Berkeley.

Arthur North (1915) *The Cut-off* (Sunset Magazine)
"Tamsen speaking with her small compelling face flushed with a delicate pink glow. I matter not. Pray for the little children. Oh, who is this Lansford Hastings that he should lead us all awry? A wandering lawyer, a briefless boy in his twenties, claiming to be friend of General Sam Houston...." Since Hastings never met Houston, that certainly discredits North's mellow-dramatic rejoinder from Tamsen Donner. Bidwell's influence and the beginning of a morally bankrupt Hastings begins to creep into the story.

Charles Kelly (1930) *Salt Desert Trails*
"As a reward for his leadership, Hastings hoped to be elected president of California." The persistence of Bidwell's damage placed upon Hastings' character is obvious and extensive.

George R. Stewart (1937) *Ordeal by Hunger*
"What made Hastings so blind to the difficulties [of his route]? Before the eye of his imagination hovered the brilliant figure of Sam Houston [president of Texas fame]. Hastings wanted to play Houston for California." Bidwell's influence repeatedly returns unchallenged. Stewart also claims the cutoff was "idiotically foolish" and uses Hastings as a literary tool, the antagonist of the Donner Party, thus establishing his role for decades to come.

Bernard DeVoto (1943) *The Year of Decision 1846*
Portraying Hastings as "recklessly ambitious," he also suggests that "If the young man, stuffed with vision, ignorance, and the will to lie for empire's sake has had any romantic appeal so far, he now loses it." It is interesting that DeVoto never took the time to objectively evaluate Hastings' motives and actions.

Irene D. Paden (1949) *Prairie Schooner Detours*
"Posterity had been served, but at the expense of many lives later sacrificed in the Sierra snows because of time lost now. And again, it was Lansford Hastings' propensity to decide the destiny of others that was a determining factor." She fails to consider that James Reed was the actual salesman that put the Donner Party on an irreversible path leading to their doom.

Walter M. Stookey (1950) *Fatal Decision*
"Hastings, the would-be politician and dictator." This is one of the more creative claims against Hastings that perpetuates the repetitive echoing of Bidwell's false narrative, and extends Hastings' desire not to become simply president of California but dictator!

David Lavender (1963) *Westward Visions*
"Lansford Hastings, whose almost psychotic need to control others would contribute, in 1846, to the ghastly Donner tragedy in the Sierra mountains." This statement *almost* takes Hastings' character to a deeper low that apparently justifies his unhinged psychosis to control others.

Ralph Moody (1963) *The Old Trails West*

"The Donner Party tragedy, the most famous in American trail history, was brought about largely by the chicanery of Lansford Hastings. [He was] ambitious, dishonest and a clever propagandist." On the other hand, he defined his character by leading what he preached.

Ric Burns (1992 PBS video) *The Donner Party*

"Some cursed Hastings for the false statements in his open letter and for his broken pledge at Fort Bridger." Heavily relying on Thornton's secondary source *Oregon and California in 1848*, the "broken pledge" refers to the ridiculous assumption that Hastings should have waited indefinitely for any straggling wagon train, before leaving Fort Bridger. Author Harold Schindler makes the erroneous claim that [Hastings Cutoff] "killed people." The video narrative also fails to recognize that Fort Bridger was directly connected by a trail to Fort Hall which allowed anyone with any doubts about Hastings Cutoff to easily bypass it. Another quote from Thornton later in the video alleges that "More than one vowed vengeance upon Hastings, for having decoyed them into his cutoff." Decoyed? This seems a bit incredulous while huddled together flirting with death in a snowstorm, but then the questionable source of the quote once again comes from Thornton who has helped promulgate a false image of Hastings as a scapegoat approaching two centuries later.[219]

Daniel Brown (2009) *The Indifferent Stars Above*

"For many of them, there was now no doubt that Lansford Hastings could not be trusted." Yet they had full confidence in James Reed who had just spoken with Hastings a few days earlier! It was Reed who was instrumental in convincing the Donner Party to take the new untested segment of trail across the Wasatch, not Hastings, and they did so unanimously.

YouTube video (2015) https://youtu.be/piE1FoLxO30

Just past the one-minute mark, a university intern "retracing the fateful steps" of Hastings Cutoff ponders that he was "surprised Hastings didn't get murdered." This speaks for itself with the illogical notion of an emigrant murdering Hastings solely on the premise that the cutoff was difficult, but far from impossible.

There is no argument that Hastings was an accomplice with others to potentially influence and win over California from a faltering Mexican Government prone to multiple regime changes. He clearly did his part to accelerate American emigration to California, but there is simply no evidence that he was the "head" of any hatching plot to lead emigrants to take California with him as "president" as suggested by some. But these little questioned *facts* about him are overwhelmingly ignored—Thus, a convenient scapegoat.

---

[219] The author of this book learned during a discussion with contemporary historian, Albert Hurtado, by asking how could such controversial statements be accepted with little or no questioning? His response, "That's all we have."

Considering Hastings' pessimistic view of a weak and ineffective Mexican Government, there is little question that he desired American domination of California's future. He felt it was imminent and promoted it as such in a quotation from his guide book:

> "…contemplate the time, as fast approaching, when the supreme darkness of ignorance, superstition, and despotism, which now, so entirely pervade many portions of those remote regions, will have fled forever, before the march of civilization, and the blazing light, of civil and religious liberty; when genuine *republicanism*, and unsophisticated *democracy*, shall be reared up, and tower aloft, even upon the now wild shores, of the great Pacific…and an all-wise, and over-ruling Providence."

Hastings' italicized words may have been referring to the suspension of Mexico's constitution by its president-dictator, Santa Anna, and of course Texas's struggle for independence in 1836. The former passage reflects his passion and justification for American institutions and the innuendo of Mexico's pseudo-democracy. Again, the superiority of American institutions and "Providence" were certainly driven by the concept of Manifest Destiny in the eyes of Hastings and a multitude of other Americans during this time. Hastings clearly was not paving the way for his own immortality at the expense of others, but was promoting what he thought best for his countrymen within the ideals of Manifest Destiny.

15. An Unsettled Man and the Haste to Blame

A controversial man by any stretch, Hastings also possessed many qualities to admire, yet a coarse image of him is often front and center. Gazing upon the only known photo of him, there lies some insight as to who he was and how he has been interpreted. Based on his image, and the overwhelming onslaught of repeated and unfair treatment of his character and motivations, some may find it easy to harbor a preconceived notion that suggests a scoundrel. His receding hairline, wide forehead, and stocky demeanor may be associated as the likeness of a deceiver or a charlatan whose roots of defamation have followed him to this very day. On the other hand, he may be viewed by others as a determined man through his set jawline and the piercing look of his deep-set eyes. Perhaps those same features can lead one to an irresistible inference of foresightedness, experience, and leadership that casts aside unjustified innuendo and the singularity of convenient blame for the misfortune of others.

Lansford Warren Hastings

In the end, however, there is plenty of blame to go around for the Donner Party disaster. One could argue that the chain-reaction of blame started with John C. Fremont and his exploring expedition by expanding our geographical understanding of the Great Basin. Certainly, blame can be attached to Lansford Hastings who dared to push the limits of the new road he promoted on the tail of Fremont. Jim Bridger and Louis Vasquez must also share in it since they enticed emigrants to take Hastings Cutoff in order to increase business at their isolated outpost. James Reed surely must be to blame for his overconfidence in convincing the Donner Party that they could overcome any obstacle in their way. Blame might also spill over into the accusatory remarks of John Bidwell for causing an unchecked criticism of Hastings' character and intent. Or, conceivably, it could be that no one is really to blame at all. Everyone was simply caught up with the same hopes, actions, gains, uncertainties, misunderstandings, mistakes, and failures that were simply part of the ongoing drama of western expansion while facing the consequences of the interactions all shared.
****

James Reed will always remain the bane of the anti-Hastings crowd because he never criticized Hastings. In fact, the two men were very much alike when it came to leadership and personal responsibility. It is also interesting that the man who was perceived to put Reed's family at extreme risk, ended up doing business with him. Their venture as partners investing in a cattle deal attests to the assumption that Hastings was not held responsible by Reed. After all he and his family had been through, he still did not blame Hastings for his misfortune. The fact of the matter is that Reed and Hastings were typical of their day in representing the ideals of Manifest Destiny and accepting the dangers that were sometimes part of it. Reed himself might argue that it was not Hastings to blame, but every adult in the Donner Party itself who moved forward in taking the new cutoff regardless of how influential he was. Reed even stated long after his banishment for killing Snyder that "I would have had the whole of them over the mountains before the snow would have caught them; and those who got through have admitted this to be true." And he was probably right.[220]

****

After his active participation and failed attempt to assist the South during the Civil War, Hastings wrote his second guidebook, *The Emigrants' Guide to Brazil,* published in Mobile, Alabama, 1867. This final chapter in his life certainly helped damn him in the eyes of history, but it was designed to attract expatriated Southerners and establish a post-war colony in South America. Perhaps a new constitution would have resulted from this new colony with an emphasis on the power of the states over federal authority, but we will never know as the settlement Hastings promoted would end in failure like so many other endeavors he sought without success.

In 1870 while Hastings was en route to Brazil for a second time with a ship full of colonists, he died at the age of 51(possibly from yellow fever or malaria) and was buried at sea. A seemingly boundless ocean may have been the most appropriate resting place for a man who viewed the world, like him or not, from his own restless, unbridled horizons. His life represents the antithesis of those who have concluded the opposite.

****

Unlike multiple decades ago, the Pioneer Monument in Donner Memorial State Park, Truckee, California is no longer surrounded by the randomness of a pine speckled forest floor. Instead of the statue blending in with nature reaching out with sudden surprise, one now approaches the towering monument by way of a long concrete corridor that is perfectly manicured and completely detached from what once was. With an almost religious-like reverence, the avenue directs the humbled visitor towards the bronze cluster of a man, woman, and their children moving forward from the top of a base twenty-two feet tall. It is as if one has been allowed to approach the shrine of Greek gods on a frontier level as they look forward to the unknown of the world beyond. Even if oblivious as to what actually happened on the very spot where the monument stands, one can still feel the intensity of the powerful symbolism it represents. Does it evoke thoughts of how far we have come, or is it how far have we yet to go bridled only by the risks we fail to take?

---

[220] Letter from James Frazier Reed to Gersham Keyes, 2 July 1847, in Morgan, *First Overland*, p. 304.

The approach to the Pioneer Monument at Donner Memorial State Park.

****

     The Donner Visitor Center is closing for the day as darkness approaches, but instead of heading to the parking lot, the temptation to walk along the short path covered by a few inches of snow to where the Murphy cabin once stood becomes irresistible. A crystal-clear winter sky is overhead, and the first stars begin to make their appearance. Standing by the indifferent boulder that once helped protect fearful emigrants, the seemingly unreachable loneliness of centuries past begins to creep in. Yet one feels the closeness of civilization by the incessant hum of traffic from cars and trucks hurling along Interstate 80 in the background. And from the south, the straining drone of a diesel train thrusting its engines from some hidden mountain canyon in the far-off distance signals progress. But then stillness and silence surround you for a few moments, and in the mind of your imagination, standing on the same ground of those who came before, you begin to feel and understand the rare historical epiphany that binds us together as Americans.

The Donner Party's struggle highlights the complex layers of human endeavor ranging from relative success to a speculative move for a better life. It includes the trailside burial and lonely farewell of a loved one which led to an unassuming change of plans. There is also the extended kindness for an ailing traveler, and the awe of foreboding geography. The narrow escape from impending failure and material loss, to intensified frustration leading to the abruptness of self-defense and death. It also embraces the hard-nosed abandonment of another human being and the anguish of a fatal accident. Finally, their winter entrapment brought out the full gamut of compassion, collective and individual determination, cold indifference, and heroics. Most anyone can relate to their travails of innocence and experience. It's all there.

As for Hastings, we may confuse charisma with competence, rhetoric with results, celebrity with genuine achievement. We can find a convenient scapegoat for tragedy, let a variety of motives and decisions escape responsibility, and imagine that the worst evils are always caused by others, rather than by the personal choices that transpire from a perceived reality.

Lansford Hastings is a man who has been wrongly portrayed by the imagery of assumption and bias. He was not an ineffective, evasive, serial blunderer, nor was he a fiend clasping his hands at the misfortune of others. He is a man who has been demonized without the consideration of his wider actions in the context of the historical period he represents. He is the personification of Manifest Destiny and imperfect just like everyone else. Yet, he stands out as an individual who should, in many ways, be respected.

Perhaps then, the register of everyday people in this book will emerge as those who are not so extraordinarily different from us. This allows us to reflect, recognize, or perhaps relearn, that by simply being secure in the determination of our choices, and not fixing accountability elsewhere at the first sign of struggle, we may rediscover how resolute a people we once were, and still can be today across the abstract bridge of time. And as historian Thomas Andrews has brought to our attention, "Sitting in judgment of Hastings has led to the loss of the primary goal of the historian—understanding."

Appendix: Donner Party Encampments

*There was quite a bit of movement among emigrants from one shelter or camp to another over time. This back-and-forth migration was especially true among the single men without families or food as conditions deteriorated. Age in parenthesis. D = Died and S = Survived in superscript. Total of 81 individuals.

Lake Encampments: [59 people]

Breen-Schallenberger Cabin
Patrick Breen (51),[S] husband of Margaret (40) [S]
    Children: John (14), [S] Edward (13) [S]
    Patrick Jr. (9), [S] Simon (8) [S]
    James (5), [S] Peter (3) [S]
    Isabella (1) [S]
Patrick Dolan/Independent (35) [D]

Lean-to against Breen-Shallenberger Cabin
Louis Keseberg (32)[S] husband of Philippine (23) [S]
    Children: Ada (3), [D] Louis Jr. (5 months) [D]
Augustus Spitzer/Hired (30) [D]
Charles Burger/Hired (30) [D]

Murphy Cabin
Levinah Murphy/Widowed (36) [D]
    Children: John Landrum (16) [D]
    Mary (14), [S] Lemuel (13) [D]
    William (10), [S] Simon (8) [S]
William Foster (31), [D] Husband of Sarah (20) [S]
    Child: Jeremiah (2) [D]
Harriet Pike/Widowed (18) [S]
    Children: Naomi (2),[S] Catherine (1) [D]
William Eddy (28), Husband of Eleanor (25) [D]
    Children: James (3),[D] Margaret (1) [D]

Double Cabin: Graves Side
Franklin Graves (57),[D] Husband of Elizabeth (46) [D]
    Children: Mary Ann (20),[S] William (17),[S] Eleanor (14),[S]
    Lovina (12),[S] Nancy (8),[S] Jonathan (7),[S] Franklin Jr. (5) [D]
    Elizabeth (1) [S]
Amanda McCutchen (23) [S]
    Child: Harriet (1) [D]
Jay Fosdick (23) [D] Husband of Sarah (21) [S]

Double Cabin: Reed Side
Margaret Reed (32)[S]
    Children: Virginia (13),[S] Martha (Patty) (8),[S]
    James Jr. (5),[S] Thomas (3)[S]
Baylis Williams (25),[D] sister Eliza/Both Hired (31)[S]
Charles Stanton/Independent (35)[D]
Luis and Salvador/Assisted Stanton (Ages unknown)[D]
John Denton (28)[D]
Milton Elliott/Hired (28)[D]
Antonio/Hired (Age unknown)[D]

Alder Creek Encampments: [22 people]
Brush Shelter 1:
George Donner (62),[D] Husband of Tamsen (45)[D]
    Children: Elitha (14),[S] Leanna (11)[S]
    Francis (6),[S] Georgia (4),[S] Eliza (3)[S]

Brush Shelter 2:
Jacob Donner (56),[D] Husband of Elizabeth (Betty) (38)[D]
    Children: George Jr. (10),[S] Mary (7),[S]
    Isaac (5),[D] Samuel (4),[D] Lewis (3)[D]
    Stepsons: Solomon Hook (14)[S]
    William Hook (12)[D]
Doris Wolfinger/Widowed (20)
Joseph Reinhardt /Hired (30)[D]
Samuel Shoemaker/Hired (25)[D]

In Unknown Shelters:
*Hired hands likely at Alder Creek:
James Smith (25)[D]
Jean Baptiste Trudeau (16)[S]
Noah James (16)[S]

Died Before Reaching the Sierra:
Sarah Keyes (70)
Luke Halloran (25)
John Snyder (25)
Mr. Hardcoop (60)
Mr. Wolfinger (Age unknown)
William Pike (32)

Arrived in California Before Entrapment:
Charles Stanton (35)[D] *Returned to help emigrants
William McCutchen (30)
James Reed (45)
Walter Herron (27)

Index

A

Adobe Rock, 60
Alcove Springs, 30
Alder Creek, xii, 17, 18, 68, 73, 92, 93, 95, 97, 99, 100, 102, 106, 107, 108, 111, 113, 114, 115, 116, 140
Alien and Sedition Acts, 123
American River, 26, 29, 79, 105
Andrews, Thomas, 138
archaeology, 18, 68, 106, 107
Arizona, 6, 86, 119, 122, 124

B

Bartleson-Bidwell Party, 23
Bidwell, John, 22, 76, 79, 80, 131, 135
Big Blue River, 30
Boggs, William M., 31, 40
Bonney, Wales, xi, 43, 44, 48, 49
Breen, Patrick, 111, 113, 139
Bridger, Jim, 41, 53, 89, 135
British, 3, 4, 5, 7, 10, 21, 23, 49
Brown, Daniel, 133
Bryant, Edwin, xi, 30, 31, 40, 45, 58, 59
Burns, Ric, 133

C

cabins, 100, 101
California Convention, 118, 120
California Trail, iii, iv, v, ix, x, 11, 28, 46, 49, 51, 57, 60, 70, 71, 104
Californios, 7, 8, 30, 45, 76, 79, 81, 84, 85, 88, 103
cannibalism, vi, 35, 105, 108, 113
Cedar Mountains, 50, 53, 54, 57, 64, 65
Chiles-Walker Party, 24
Chimney Rock, 37
Civil War, 122, 123, 124, 126, 136
Clay, Henry, 8
Clyman, James, 40, 41, 51, 52, 53, 81, 83
Cold Stream Canyon, 33, 93, 94
Colorado River, 121, 122
Columbia River, 3, 33
Confederate, 124
Courthouse Rock, 37

D

Denton, John, 17, 112, 140
Deseret, 119
DeVoto, Bernard, iv, 75, 84, 130, 132
Dog Valley, 33, 82
Donner Lake, 82, 94
Donner Memorial State Park, 136

Donner Party, i, iii, iv, v, vi, vii, viii, ix, x, xi, xii, xiii, 11, 14, 16, 18, 19, 20, 23, 25, 26, 27, 30, 31, 33, 35, 36, 38, 42, 48, 49, 50, 52, 54, 56, 57, 58, 59, 60, 61, 62, 63, 64, 65, 66, 67, 69, 70, 71, 72, 73, 74, 79, 82, 89, 90, 91, 92, 93, 94, 95, 97, 99, 100, 101, 102, 104, 105, 106, 107, 108, 114, 115, 116, 117, 122, 126, 127, 128, 129, 130, 131, 132, 133, 135, 136, 138, 139
Donner Pass, 82
Donner Tamsen, 17, 27, 62, 73, 106, 131, 132
Donner, George, vii, 16, 17, 18, 19, 31, 49, 57, 63, 67, 68, 69, 95, 111, 112, 115, 131, 140
Donner, Jacob, 49, 69, 104, 140
double cabin, 101

E

Eddy, William, 67, 72, 104, 105, 110, 113, 139
Emigrants' Guide to Brazil, 136
Emigrants' Guide to Oregon and California, iv, vi, 14
Emigrants' Trail, x, 21, 35
England, 3, 5, 6, 7, 8, 11, 83, 103, 121
exceptionalism, xi
expansionist, vi, ix, 1, 2, 5, 9, 45, 83

F

family wagon, 15, 16, 61, 67, 68, 71, 72
Fitzpatrick, Thomas "Broken Hand", 22
Forlorn Hope. *See* snowshoe party
Fort Bernard, 40
Fort Boise, 33
Fort Bridger, iii, v, vi, x, xi, xiii, 20, 24, 30, 31, 32, 40, 43, 44, 45, 46, 47, 48, 49, 50, 51, 52, 53, 54, 56, 57, 58, 59, 60, 62, 64, 70, 73, 83, 89, 133
Fort Hall, v, x, 21, 22, 23, 24, 30, 31, 33, 38, 39, 41, 42, 43, 44, 46, 47, 48, 49, 52, 53, 56, 57, 58, 59, 60, 70, 78, 80, 83, 127, 133
Fort Laramie, 21, 31, 40, 41, 43, 48, 52
Fort William, 21, 24
Forty Mile Desert, 23, 73, 91
Fosdick, Sarah, 105
France, 3, 6, 85
Free Soil Party, 9
Fremont, iv, vi, vii, x, 14, 22, 30, 31, 35, 36, 37, 38, 39, 40, 42, 43, 44, 46, 47, 48, 51, 52, 57, 70, 76, 78, 80, 81, 82, 83, 89, 103, 127, 135
Fremont's Fourth Expedition, 35
Fremont's Third Expedition, vi, 38, 43, 46, 51

G

Gold Rush, ix, 2, 12, 45, 54, 76, 84, 88
Gray, Robert, 3
Grayback Mountain, 52, 53, 63, 65

Great Basin, iii, iv, v, x, 39, 43, 46, 47, 56, 61, 62, 64, 72, 73, 74, 78, 83, 92, 119, 120, 126, 128, 135
Great Central Valley, 23
Great Salt Lake, iii, iv, vi, x, 11, 22, 23, 28, 32, 38, 41, 42, 43, 48, 58, 60, 61, 65, 66, 68, 77, 80, 81, 82, 84, 89, 127, 128
Greenwood, Caleb, 24, 25, 26, 33, 81

H

handcart experiment, 34
Harlan, iii, vii, 40, 45, 59, 64, 65, 67, 92, 103
Harlan and Young, iii, 40, 45, 59
Hastings Cutoff, v, xi, 16, 23, 28, 31, 32, 33, 36, 40, 41, 42, 43, 48, 49, 53, 54, 55, 56, 57, 58, 59, 61, 68, 69, 70, 72, 89, 90, 97, 128, 130, 133, 135
Hastings death of, 136
Hastings, Lansford, iii, vi, vii, viii, x, xi, xii, xiii, 11, 29, 30, 37, 38, 43, 51, 56, 70, 74, 75, 77, 80, 82, 99, 103, 118, 119, 124, 126, 132, 133, 135, 138
Herron, Walter, 16, 72, 93, 99, 140
Holliday, J. S., xi, 2, 118
Hope Wells, 50, 52, 53, 54, 55, 62, 63, 64, 65, 66
Hudspeth, James, iii, 40, 43, 48, 50, 53, 57, 59, 62, 81, 89
Humboldt River, iv, v, ix, 23, 24, 44, 46, 51, 57, 69, 70, 71, 72, 82, 92, 99
Humboldt Sink, 24, 72, 73, 91

I

Independence Rock, 48, 76

J

Jackson, Andrew, 5, 84, 124
James, Noah, 17, 104, 112, 140
Jefferson, Thomas, 3, 4, 123, 124
Jefferson, Thomas Hemings, 53, 54, 56, 66
Johnson Ranch, 110
Judah, Theodore, 128

K

Kelly, Charles, 132
Keseberg, 49, 63, 67, 68, 73, 91, 100, 101, 107, 112, 114, 115, 116, 139
Keseberg lean-to, 101
Keyes, Robert Cadden, 29
Keyes, Sarah, 15, 30, 31, 37, 73, 140

L

lake camp, 93, 97, 99, 100, 104, 105, 106, 107, 110, 111, 113
Larkin, Thomas, vii, 2, 39, 45, 76
Lavender, David, 132
Lewis and Clark, 3, 4, 21
Lienhard, Heinrich, 54, 65, 70
Lincoln, Abraham, 41, 123
Louisiana Territory, 3

Luis and Salvador, 92, 93, 104, 105, 140

M

Mackenzie, Alexander, 3
Manifest Destiny, viii, ix, xii, xiii, 1, 2, 4, 5, 7, 8, 9, 10, 11, 12, 20, 38, 44, 65, 74, 75, 77, 79, 80, 83, 88, 98, 134, 136, 138
Marsh, John, 76
Marshall, James, 11, 29, 76, 118
Maxey, James, 15
McBride, John R., 12, 44, 128
McCullough, David, 27
McCutchen, William, 67, 92, 93, 112, 140
McGlashen, Charles, 107, 130
Meek, Stephen, 33
Mexican Cession, 6, 86, 118, 119, 120
Mexican War, 11, 121
Mexico, vii, xi, 2, 5, 7, 8, 10, 42, 46, 75, 77, 79, 81, 83, 84, 85, 86, 87, 88, 89, 99, 103, 118, 131, 134
Miller, Hiram, 17, 112, 113
Monroe Doctrine, 6
Moody, Ralph, 133
Morgan, Dale, vi, 51, 75
Mormon-Carson Route, 128
Mormons, 11, 35, 77, 119, 120, 121, 122
Murphy cabin, 100, 101, 107, 108, 111, 114, 137

N

Native Americans, 1, 4, 5, 8, 21, 40, 71, 76, 84, 86, 87, 88
Nile's National Register, 39
North, Arthur, 132
Nullification Crisis of 1832, 123

O

O'Sullivan, John, 10
Oregon Country, vii, 3, 7, 9, 10, 11, 22, 33, 76, 83, 87, 103
Oregon Spectator, 30
Oregon Trail, iii, 7, 11, 15, 33, 52, 57, 77, 130
orographic uplift, 94
Overland Pass, iv, 70
overloaded wagons, viii, 20, 67

P

Paden, Irene, x, 132
Pike, William, iii, 60, 73, 91, 93, 140
Pilot Peak, 51, 52, 53, 54, 55, 64, 82
Pilot Spring, 50, 53, 54, 55, 56, 57, 62, 63, 64, 65, 66, 67, 69
Pioneer Monument, 101, 107, 136
pioneer palace car, 15, 16
Platte River, 17, 18, 21, 22, 24, 30, 35, 37
Polk, James K., 9, 84
Prairie Schooner Detours, x, 132
presentism, 126

R

Redlum Spring, 50, 52, 53, 54, 55, 56, 57, 63, 83
Reed, James, iii, 14, 15, 16, 29, 30, 31, 40, 41, 42, 46, 49, 52, 58, 60, 62, 63, 66, 68, 71, 73, 92, 93, 97, 99, 103, 106, 110, 112, 115, 122, 126, 132, 133, 135, 140
Reed, Margaret, 112, 140
Reed, Virginia, 16, 52
Reed-Hastings cattle contract, 122
Reinhardt, Joseph, 17, 73, 104, 140
rescue parties, 110
Rocky Mountains, 21, 35, 37, 48, 119, 127
Roller Pass, 93, 94
Ruby Mountains, v, vi, 36, 48, 51, 69, 82
rugged individualism, 5, 13

S

Sacramento Valley, viii, xii, 11, 26, 30, 57, 78, 79, 92, 105
Salt Desert, iv, v, 22, 43, 51, 52, 53, 54, 56, 57, 61, 62, 63, 64, 65, 66, 67, 69, 70, 82, 103, 132
Salt Lake City, 16, 34, 35, 75, 120, 122
salvage parties, 18, 114
San Francisco, 3, 7, 11, 12, 76, 79, 87, 88, 115, 121, 122
San Joaquin Valley, 23
Sangamo Journal, 16, 27, 49
Santa Anna, 8, 85, 134
Schallenberger, Moses, 25, 100
Scotts Bluff, 37
Secret Pass, iv, v, 46, 47, 48, 51, 57, 69, 70, 82
Shoemaker, Sam, 17
Sierra Nevada, vi, 25, 28, 29, 33, 36, 57, 61, 71, 74, 81, 92, 95, 120
slavery, 1, 8, 9, 118, 119, 120, 121, 123, 124
Smith, Jedediah, 21, 22
snowshoe party, 104, 110, 111
Snyder, John, 61, 71, 72, 73, 92, 99, 140
South America, 84, 125, 136
South Pass, 21, 24, 31, 40, 43, 44, 48, 53, 83
Spain, 2, 3, 5, 84
Spanish mission period, 84
Spitzer, Augustus, 17, 73, 139
Springfield, Illinois, vii, 14, 16, 27, 30
Stanislaus River, 23
Stanton, Charles, iii, 60, 67, 92, 93, 104, 140
states' rights, 1, 123, 124
Stephens (Donner) Pass, 78, 93
Stephens-Townsend-Murphy Party, 24
Stewart, George, 75, 126, 132
Stookey, Walter, 132

Sutter, John, 29, 78, 79, 99, 118, 121
Sutter's Fort, vi, x, 18, 27, 38, 44, 51, 65, 67, 69, 72, 76, 78, 80, 89, 92, 93, 95, 99, 102, 104, 115
Sutterville, 79, 122

T

Texas, xi, 6, 7, 8, 9, 10, 84, 85, 86, 88, 103, 131, 134
Thornton, J. Quinn, 31, 57, 129, 131
Tocqueville, Alexis de, 9
Transcontinental Railroad, 84, 128
Truckee Lake, 25, 26, 82, 97, 99, 110
Truckee Meadows, 73, 74, 82, 91, 95, 99
Truckee River, 25, 26, 33, 57, 73, 82, 92, 127
Truckee River Route, 33, 57, 78, 128

U

Union, 9, 76, 121, 123, 124
United States, i, vi, vii, 1, 2, 3, 4, 5, 6, 7, 8, 9, 10, 11, 12, 14, 21, 29, 39, 54, 78, 83, 84, 85, 86, 88, 89, 103, 118, 121
United States Magazine and Democratic Review, 10
Upper California, vi, vii, 2, 7, 14, 39, 60, 75, 84, 87, 121

V

Vancouver, George, 3
Vasquez, Louis, 53, 89, 135

W

Walker, Joseph Reddeford, 23
War of 1812, 5
War with Mexico, 10, 45, 85, 103
Wasatch Mountains, iii, 48, 53, 83
Washington, D. C., 7, 8, 39, 83, 87, 118
Weber canyons, iii, iv, 59
Weber River, iii, 59
What I Saw in California, 45
Willie and Martin Handcart Companies, 34
Wolfinger, Doris, 73, 92, 96, 112, 140
Wolfinger, Mr., 73, 93, 140

Y

Yerba Buena, 11
Young, Brigham, 34, 77, 122
YouTube, 133
Yuba River, 26